New Families
New Finances

Wiley Personal Finance Solutions

New Families, New Finances: Money Skills for Today's Nontraditional Families
by Emily W. Card and Christie Watts Kelly

Suddenly Single: Money Skills for Divorcées and Widows
by Kerry Hannon

NEW FAMILIES NEW FINANCES

Money Skills for Today's Nontraditional Families

**EMILY W. CARD
CHRISTIE WATTS KELLY**

JOHN WILEY & SONS, INC.
New York • Chichester • Weinheim • Brisbane • Singapore • Toronto

This book is printed on acid-free paper. ∞

Copyright © 1998 by The Virtual Corporation, Inc. All rights reserved.
Published by John Wiley & Sons, Inc.

Published simultaneously in Canada.

No part of this publication may be reproduced, stored in a retrieval system or transmitted in any form or by any means, electronic, mechanical, photocopying, recording, scanning or otherwise, except as permitted under Sections 107 or 108 of the 1976 United States Copyright Act, without either the prior written permission of the Publisher, or authorization through payment of the appropriate per-copy fee to the Copyright Clearance Center, 222 Rosewood Drive, Danvers, MA 01923, (978) 750-8400, fax (978) 750-4744. Requests to the Publisher for permission should be addressed to the Permissions Department, John Wiley & Sons, Inc., 605 Third Avenue, New York, NY 10158-0012, (212) 850-6011, fax (212) 850-6008, E-Mail: PERMREQ @ WILEY.COM.

This publication is designed to provide accurate and authoritative information in regard to the subject matter covered. It is sold with the understanding that the publisher is not engaged in rendering legal, accounting, or other professional services. If legal advice or other expert assistance is required, the services of a competent professional person should be sought.

Designations used by companies to distinguish their products are often claimed by trademarks. In all instances where the author or publisher is aware of a claim, the product names appear in Initial Capital letters. Readers, however, should contact the appropriate companies for more complete information regarding trademarks and registration.

Library of Congress Cataloging-in-Publication Data:

Card, Emily.
   New families, new finances : money skills for today's
nontraditional families / by Emily W. Card and Christie Watts Kelly.
     p. cm.—(Wiley personal finance solutions)
   Includes bibliographical references and index.
   ISBN 0-471-19612-6 (pbk. : alk. paper)
   1. Finance, Personal. I. Kelly, Christie Watts. II. Title.
III. Series.
HG179.C329   1998
332.024—dc21   97-37906

Printed in the United States of America.

10 9 8 7 6 5 4 3 2 1

To the Watts, Dempsey, Carmichael, Kinard, Durant, Williams, Arnold, Seaboldt, Brosveen, Lindsay, Card, Cobble, Maxwell, Bell, Lingerfelt, Kelly, Goad, Mayo, Taylor, and Davis families.

CONTENTS

Acknowledgments	xi
Introduction	xiii

PART ONE UNDERSTANDING YOUR FAMILY

CHAPTER ONE   COMMON GROUND — 3
   Variables That Affect Family Finances — 4
   Universal Issues for Nontraditional Families — 5

CHAPTER TWO   ROLL CALL — 11
   Roundup of Nontraditional Families — 11
   Putting It All Together: Then and Now — 22

CHAPTER THREE   FINANCIAL GOALS AND STRATEGIES — 27
   Setting Financial Goals — 28
   Working the Magic — 30
   Means to the Ends: Techniques — 31

PART TWO PROTECTING YOUR FAMILY

CHAPTER FOUR   SPENDING WISELY — 39
   Budgeting: Today's Steps toward Tomorrow's Goals — 39
   The Flip Side of Budgeting: Be an Active Consumer — 50
   Buying or Renting — 55
   Legal Lessons: Using Federal Credit Laws — 64

CHAPTER FIVE TAX STRATEGIES — 69
- The Five Tax Basics — 70
- Comparing Taxes — 80
- Your Annual Financial Checkup — 85
- Legal Lessons: Tax Policy — 86

CHAPTER SIX FAMILY FINANCIAL EMERGENCIES — 95
- Credit Crisis — 97
- When a Crisis Deepens — 100
- After the Crisis Is Over: Restoring Your Credit — 103
- Legal Lessons: Federal Credit Protection — 105

CHAPTER SEVEN BOUNDARIES: YOURS, MINE, AND OURS — 111
- Yours, Mine, and Ours: Theory and Practice — 111
- Making It Work: Balancing Income, Career Advancement, Children — 119
- Yours, Mine, Ours, and *Theirs:* Dealing with the Kids' "Other" Parents — 123
- Legal Lessons: Domestic and Marital Property Rights — 128

CHAPTER EIGHT IT'S NEVER TOO EARLY — 137
- Healthy Money Attitudes — 137
- Teaching Children about Money: Theory and Practice — 138
- Getting the Kids on Your Side — 143

PART THREE ENRICHING YOUR FAMILY

CHAPTER NINE INVESTMENTS FOR CHANGING TIMES — 149
- How Much Money Should You Put Where? — 149
- Which Investments Are Right for You? — 155
- Making a Difference with Socially Responsible Investing — 166
- Why Should You Use a Professional Advisor? — 167

CHAPTER TEN SELECTING AND PAYING FOR EDUCATION — 173
- The Child Care Challenge — 173
- Ensuring a Bright Future — 178

College: Getting the Most for Your Money	179
When More than One of You Are in School	193

CHAPTER ELEVEN   RESCUING YOUR RETIREMENT   197

Overcoming Your Retirement Hurdles	198
Legal Lessons: Borrowing from Your 401(k)	212

CHAPTER TWELVE   INSURANCE TRADE-OFFS   215

Start with What You Have	215
Build Your Family's Foundation	217
Insure Your Property	225
Make the Most of Your Coverage	227
Legal Lessons: Legal Health Insurance Protections	230

CHAPTER THIRTEEN   AFTER YOU'RE GONE   235

State and Federal Laws That Affect You	235
Your Estate Planning Toolbox	237
The Importance of Advisors	248
Legal Lessons: Where to Keep Estate Planning Documents	249

CONCLUSION   253

Cleaning Up Your Financial Act	253
Making a Difference for Other Families	254
Contacting Government Officials	254

APPENDIX A   AGENCIES ENFORCING CREDIT LEGISLATION   255

APPENDIX B   VENTURE INVESTMENT ORGANIZATIONS   255

APPENDIX C   CHILD CARE RESOURCES   255

APPENDIX D   HELPFUL ORGANIZATIONS   255

BIBLIOGRAPHY   271

INDEX   275

ACKNOWLEDGMENTS

Our editor, Debra Wishik Englander at John Wiley & Sons, provided just the right creative tension to keep us on track without distracting us. Carrie Trowbridge, researcher, showed us new ways to deal with new facts. Agent Denise Marcil saw us through book number two together. Attorneys R. Miles Mason of Memphis, Tennessee, Laurice E. Smith of Memphis, Tennessee, and Susan Weiss of Santa Monica, California, clarified family law issues. Attorneys James Lee Phelan of Memphis, Tennessee, and Robert D. Mayer of Los Angeles, California, offered additional legal insights. Certified public accountant Dana Johnson of Santa Monica, California, sat through countless interviews and guided us to helpful research issues. Many government officials provided data, but we'd like to give special thanks to IRS spokesperson Don Roberts for walking us through the new tax law.

We couldn't have done it without the peace of mind provided by those who care for our children. Many thanks to New Roads School, Santa Monica, California; David Bryan, for continuing educational innovation; and Adam Philipson, a true friend. Thanks also to Christ United Methodist Child Development Center and St. Luke's Day School of Memphis, Tennessee, for providing excellent care.

Our families were patient and understanding. When they weren't, we screamed our heads off and kept on writing.

INTRODUCTION

Although only 7% of all families fall into the traditional category—a working father, homemaker mother, and two-plus children—most financial planning assumes this family structure as the starting point for advice. Our book is for the other 93%, today's families.

If your family falls into the 93%, you've found your financial niche. We start with the assumption that you've spent your life being programmed to think of the traditional family as normal, while your day-to-day decisions must be made in a different—but very valid—context. Thus, your perceptions of what you *ought* to do face constant challenges, as you do what you are *capable* of doing.

We have nothing against traditional families—in fact, most of us grew up in them. But if your family falls into the traditional model, this book is not for you. Most of the field of financial planning covers your needs, and the tax and legal system assumes you're the norm.

Our goals for you—members of the 93%—and for this book are twofold:

- To change the way you view your family finances to fit your actual circumstances
- To provide the specific strategies your family needs to maximize its own unique financial opportunities and challenges

Today's families experience financial stresses unique in modern industrial society, although most of us enjoy lifestyles only dreamed of in the past. Our elevated expectations represent remnants of the unparalleled arc of prosperity stretching from the end of World War II to the early 1970s. For the two brief decades from 1945 to 1965, the depression was behind us and the women's movement was just being born. These 20 years were responsible for two factors important to family life: This was the era of the traditional family and baby boomers were born during this span. An entire generation's perceptions of future family life were formed on a false hypothesis—that family life as it emerged after World War II would continue into the foreseeable future.

The rosy picture of family perfection—with the now-caricatured manicured suburban lawns and aproned Mom waiting for Dad to return at five for family dinner—never captured the popular imagination before the war, and for good economic and demographic reason. During the depression, families were lucky if anyone had work. In the 1920s, America had just tipped from a rural to an urban society, the middle class was relatively small, and women were exploring all kinds of options.

But the women's movement didn't cause the current crisis within families. Ironically, analysts today who blame family stress on the rise of the women's movement have it backward. Economic pressures of the mid-1960s to the early 1970s set the stage for the rapid expansion of women's roles, an expansion that, despite the actions of leaders calling for gender equality, could never have occurred so quickly without the triple macroeconomic pressures of the Vietnam War, the war on poverty, and the oil embargo of 1973 and subsequent worldwide rise in oil prices.

Looking back, economists now realize that real family incomes have remained just about level since late 1973. As the steadily rising inflation of the 1970s and the ballooning federal budget deficits of the 1980s ate into economic productivity, families needed to work harder to stay even.

In fact, many women realized that productive work would change their own lives and that of their children. Most studies today agree that after the first year or two of childhood, both children and mothers are better off when the mother works at least part-time.

But what started as an idea of full economic equality soon became an absolute economic necessity. The number of women who worked because they had to rose from 20% in 1970 to 80% in 1997.

Coupled with economic and social pressures that brought mothers into the workforce in ever increasing numbers, the growth of a new social openness led to other changes in family structures. The divorce rate rose, more women (and men) became never married single parents, and, with remarriages, the blended family joined the American landscape.

As norms of equality spread to wider circles, sexual preference joined the list of civil rights. As an increasing number of gay and lesbian couples became parents, school rosters in urban areas began to reflect families with two dads or two moms.

Other changes also ate away at the traditional model. Cross-ethnic adoptions began to bring multiculturalism into the home. Increasingly, awareness of the rights of disabled persons facilitated family life for individuals who a generation ago would have been condemned to narrower lifestyles.

Sometimes men take on the role of homemaking and women breadwinning. In fact, in 1995, 22% of women outearned their husbands.

Even the age barriers to parenthood seemingly have fallen, with parents who look like grandparents and teens with children alike in school and day care.

With all these new models to choose from, we find ourselves without financial road maps. From our legal system to our tax system, the underlying assumption involves a single earner coupled with a built-in support person devoted to servicing the full-time worker. Corporations pay lip service to family life, but employers expect long hours from employees. Husbands support their wives' careers—up to a point, and that point often involves the moment when dinner should arrive on the table.

With all these built-in centripetal forces, the miracle is that families who don't fit the old mold manage to survive at all. Yet survive and thrive we do. In fact, the dinosaur is the family in which the husband works and the wife runs the household.

Many social, political, and legal changes are necessary to reflect family realities. But families can't afford to wait for public policy to catch up with current demographics. We need strategies and tactics to manage our money and our time, for, of course, the two are inextricably intertwined in the family scenario that faces us today.

All too often, though, when we feel pressure, our immediate response is "Where did I go wrong?" rather than "Where did the system go wrong?" While we wait for the institutions to make the necessary far-reaching adjustments, we must find *coping* mechanisms that we can turn into *sustaining* tools.

THE 93% SOLUTION AND THE FIVE KEYS TO FINANCIAL SUCCESS

We're not on our own—but most of us don't know it.

While nontraditional families—the 93%—face psychological stresses arising from their failure to fit an outmoded model, time and money stresses can be addressed by using the five keys to financial success.

FIVE KEYS TO FINANCIAL SUCCESS

Key 1: Accept that we can't blame most troubles on money. Many other problems masquerade as financial. When we examine our finances more closely, we find psychological barriers coupled with engrained habits preventing financial security.

Key 2: Realize that we are not alone. We're not on our own—but most of us don't know it. We must take time to build and sustain networks so that we can find daily support from others in our position.

Key 3: Recognize that we've been thrust into roles for which most of us aren't fully prepared. For women, seeing ourselves as responsible for the economic well-being of our children proves particularly stressful. For men, taking time to partner with household maintenance—that includes cooking and cleaning as well as yard mowing and household repairs—seems a stretch in the competitive, long days necessary to keep a job.

Key 4: Believe that a path to financial security exists for the new family. Your challenge lies in discovering the unique mixture of earning, spending, and saving that works for your singular family.

Key 5: No family ever attains 100% financial perfection. When you have your finances in order, you're dead. So settle for getting what you can done and learn to enjoy life.

Part One

UNDERSTANDING YOUR FAMILY

CHAPTER ONE

Common Ground

Today's families find themselves on the financial, emotional, and legal edge, postponing financial tasks because they are already overwhelmed by today's meals, tonight's studies, or tomorrow's work deadline. The routes to family financial drag may vary from hectic schedules in two-earner families to chaos created by separation, divorce, death, artificial insemination, adoption, or the choice to remain unwed. Important variables such as the number of children, accustomed standard of

---

DEFINITIONS OF A FAMILY

According to the U.S. Bureau of the Census, the definition of a *family* is: A group of two or more people (one of whom is the householder) living together, who are related by birth, marriage, or adoption.

The Census Bureau's definitions of other relevant terms:

1. A *household* is a person or group of people who occupy a housing unit.

2. A *nonfamily household* consists of a person living alone or a householder who shares the home with nonrelatives only, for example, boarders or roommates.

3. *Own children* under 18 are never married sons and daughters of the householder, including step- and adopted children.

living, and employment status create additional issues to consider as you search for your unique financial balance.

In 2000, the United States Census will allow respondents to indicate more than one category for race, for the first time recognizing the multicultural aspect of many of today's families.

VARIABLES THAT AFFECT FAMILY FINANCES

Your situation determines your needs and outlook. Key elements that can influence your actions and perceptions include the *timing* of your family's life cycle, the *choice* you had in the situation, and the level of your *finances*.

TIMING

Each family's needs are determined by where the family falls in its life cycle. If your family involves young preschoolers, your financial needs and expectations are completely different—no matter your own age or marital status—than if your children are grown and you are retired. Likewise, families that find themselves in the process of formation or breaking up experience special needs that arise from their specific point in time.

CHOICE

If you actively chose your unique family configuration, your outlook toward your family's health—financial, emotional, and spiritual—will be completely different than if your position were thrust upon you. For example, two women who set out to make a multicultural adoption may feel particularly fortunate when the child arrives, while a woman in her late 40s who has already raised her family may find herself stressed at the news she's pregnant again. Likewise, a single parent who chose the role may feel differently about it than one who had expected to coparent with a mate. A two-earner family in which both partners enjoy their careers functions very differently than one in which a spouse reluctantly returns to work as a family financial necessity.

FINANCIAL CAPACITY

While no one would argue that having money totally simplifies a family's existence, certainly a larger income and asset base opens up more opportunities for families, no matter what their other issues.

To a great extent, a family's ability to plan its future rests on the income level the family enjoys. You'll see the format in Figure 1.1 throughout the book, when we give advice tailored to specific income levels (amounts shown are always approximate *gross* incomes).

While the variables of timing, choice, and financial capacity are key points that make each of our stories different, many issues concern all families, no matter their income or configuration.

UNIVERSAL ISSUES FOR NONTRADITIONAL FAMILIES

Almost without exception, members of today's families concern themselves with a number of internal dynamics. These include lack of time, a feeling that no matter how hard one works there's never enough money, the feeling that other families are normal and we are different, and the feeling that life was simpler "before."

Externally, today's nontraditional families have become fodder for charged political debates, blamed for the problem of the moment, whether poverty, crime, the decline of family values, or "inferior" children. While studies do show a correlation between divorce and problems with children, little is done in schools,

FIGURE 1.1 4M INCOME LEVELS

4 Ms	FAMILY INCOME
MODEST	Under $50,000 per year
MEDIUM	$50,000 to $100,000 per year
MAJOR	$100,000 to $250,000 per year
MEGA	$250,000 and above

churches, or politics to support those trying to raise their children properly despite prejudices and misunderstandings.

If you follow the advice in this book, the result will be a healthy financial life shored up by firm legal underpinnings. While psychological adjustment is secondary to our main purpose, to establish those underpinnings, you must learn to modify nonfinancial areas along the following lines:

1. Change your thinking.
2. Develop new habits.
3. Recognize your options.

Change Your Thinking

Children sometimes say, "I wish we had a bigger, smaller, different"—take your pick—"family." Our response is, "We *are* a family." If you continue to think of your family as missing something rather than as complete, you'll make decisions as if the missing element will magically appear. Accept the reality that you and your family are complete as you are now.

Develop New Habits

When you go to the supermarket, how often do you study each item you buy? Most of us dash through the market, picking up tried-and-true brands. If we become label detectives, it's usually at the start of a new diet. Otherwise, it's easier and simpler to continue selecting products we know work for us. Our children have their favorites; we have ours.

When making financial decisions, we often act the same way. For example, if you take for granted that Saturday night means going out, you probably don't stop to add the cost of your movie and popcorn or the entry fee to a local club. Or if you grew up around a type of business where you didn't have to pay full price, you probably tend to discount the money you spend on the formerly discounted items. These examples illustrate the power of financial habits.

You probably have many financial habits that are so engrained you never think twice about them. From using an expensive dry cleaner to making long-distance calls during peak hours, habits are hard to break. If we had to think through each step of every day, we'd be exhausted; therefore, it's often easier to add new habits than wean ourselves from old ones.

Setting up new habits takes time and patience. If you attempt to correct all your financial misdemeanors at once, you'll defeat yourself before you start. Begin gradually. Pick one or two easy items and work on those. For example, if you buy a newspaper every morning from a vending machine, order home delivery. It's generally cheaper and, depending on your line of work, might be deductible as a business expense on your income taxes. Or if you always buy soda when you eat out, try drinking water for a month. Every time you save a dollar or two, put the money in a special place—such as your car ashtray—and use it for a special treat.

RECOGNIZE YOUR OPTIONS

Nontraditional families often feel they don't have options, even though having two parents working opens up a world of possibilities. Instead of learning to balance home and work, both working parents may fall into the trap of believing that they are stuck on a treadmill.

Perhaps you're a single mother who adopted a child alone. As you attend PTA meetings, it appears that everyone else is traveling in pairs, Noah's ark style. Look a bit closer and you'll find that the "perfect" couple is in the middle of a divorce; the "single" man in the corner actually is gay and his partner stayed home for fear of prejudice; the "grandmother" up front straining to hear is the mother of the most active child in the class. Perceptions of who you are in relation to others can color your own sense of self (and family) worth.

Likewise, in the past, men's lives were often dictated by the assumptions of being the breadwinner for a family, and careers and life choices were made accordingly. Even for men unsuited to family leadership, before the women's movement helped shift perspectives, the man of the house was stuck with the role, like it or not. Currently, role models for men in today's families are limited. Men who have chosen a nontraditional role or had it thrust upon them, like their female counterparts, must look at new ways to make choices, but often without as much guidance from those who've already been there.

The essence of financial change lies in making new financial choices. Learning to make new choices about what you have can transform your financial life.

Let's look at the choices you've been making.

Financial Fitness Quiz

This brief checklist is only a beginning. Don't worry if you must answer no to most questions. By the end of the book, you'll turn those answers into yeses or have strategies in place to achieve them.

$ Financial Fitness: Where Do You Stand and Where Do You Want to Be?

	NOW	DATE TO DO
1. Do you have a written budget?		
2. Are your credit cards under control?		
3. Do you know where to find your property?		
4. Do you have a list of all your bank accounts in one place?		
5. Are your savings enough to see you through three months?		
6. Do you have a disability insurance policy? How much? Where is the policy kept?		
7. Do you have a life insurance policy? How much? Where is it?		
8. Do you have an IRA, Keogh, 401(k), or pension plan?		
9. Is your will written?		
10. Does your will contain guardianship provisions for your child(ren)?		

	NOW	DATE TO DO
11. Have you made investments on your own?		
12. Do you have advisors you can trust?		
13. Do you have a health insurance policy for the entire family?		
14. Have you paid your student loans?		
15. Are your taxes filed up to date?		

FAMILY MONEY CHECKLIST

No matter how your family arrived at its unique status, several important financial rules apply:

- ✔ Be conservative with your money. Maintain your monthly bills, and don't spend extravagantly.
- ✔ Educate yourself. Read this book; go to support groups or seminars; find a mentor.
- ✔ Invest in yourself. Return to school for a higher earning potential, repair your psyche by seeking professional help, and keep yourself healthy.
- ✔ Avoid get-rich-quick schemes. It's okay to play the lottery occasionally, but avoid large lump-sum investments. Seek the advice of trusted advisors, including lawyer and accountant, before making major financial decisions, especially those with an element of risk.

CHAPTER TWO

Roll Call

Today 93% of U.S. families are us. We now outnumber the 7% who fit the traditional family model—one with two married parents, a male breadwinner, and children—by almost 13 to 1. Arrangements that seemed unconventional only a generation ago have now become the norm. This dramatic restructuring of the family has outpaced society's ability to deal with the changing financial and legal needs of almost every family. In this chapter we will show you the small space to which the traditional family has been relegated, as well as help you locate where you and your family now fit in. Along the way we will also clarify whom these categories actually include.

Take a look at the family tree in Figure 2.1 to put the traditional family structure—and your own—into perspective. You may not find yourself here, as Census Bureau figures do not track all of the categories that are meaningful to us. But you will assuredly find yourself in one or more of the sections that follow.

ROUNDUP OF NONTRADITIONAL FAMILIES

Even if you think of yourself as holding traditional values, or if you don't think that your family seems particularly nontraditional, in all likelihood, your family qualifies for one of the new

12 UNDERSTANDING YOUR FAMILY

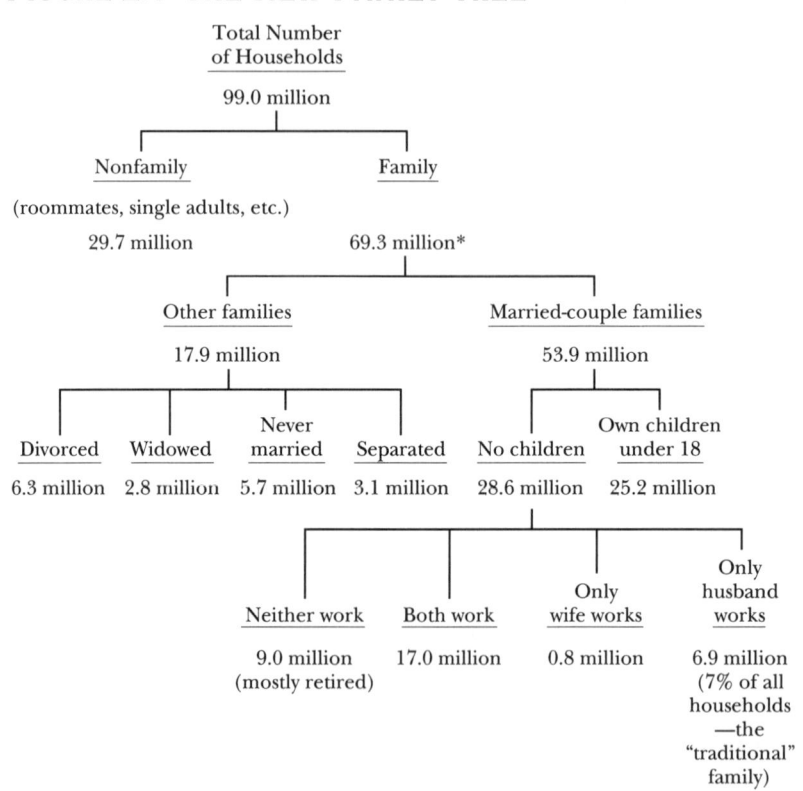

FIGURE 2.1 THE NEW FAMILY TREE

```
                    Total Number
                    of Households
                    99.0 million
              ┌──────────┴──────────┐
          Nonfamily                Family
(roommates, single adults, etc.)
         29.7 million          69.3 million*
                         ┌──────────┴──────────┐
                   Other families        Married-couple families
                   17.9 million               53.9 million
         ┌────────┬─────┴──┬─────────┐    ┌────────┴────────┐
                        Never                             Own children
      Divorced  Widowed married  Separated  No children    under 18
      6.3 million 2.8 million 5.7 million 3.1 million 28.6 million 25.2 million
                                                       ┌────────┬────────┬────────┐
                                                                            Only
                                                                Only      husband
                                                Neither work  Both work  wife works  works

                                                 9.0 million  17.0 million  0.8 million  6.9 million
                                                (mostly retired)                        (7% of all
                                                                                        households
                                                                                         —the
                                                                                       "traditional"
                                                                                         family)
```

* "Other families" and "Married-couple families" add up to more than 69.3 million because both categories take into account subfamilies—that is, married couples living within other families would fall under both "Other families" and "Married-couple families."

Source: Data from the U.S. Bureau of the Census, *Current Population Reports,* section on Family and Household Characteristics, March 1995.

family structures listed in Figure 2.2. Because many categories overlap (for instance, you could be a member of a multicultural, two-earner, blended family) you may find that your situation falls into more than one category.

TWO-EARNER FAMILIES

Made possible by the women's movement and necessitated by economic conditions, two-earner families now number over 30

FIGURE 2.2 ROLL CALL OF NEW FAMILY STRUCTURES

TYPE OF FAMILY	NUMBER IN POPULATION
Two-earner	30.0 million families
Single Parent	17.9 million
Divorced	6.3 million families (17.6 million adults)
Separated	3.1 million families (6.82 million adults)
Widowed	2.8 million families (13.4 million adults)
Never married	5.7 million families
Blended	More than 8 million families
Cohabiting with opposite sex	8.4 million adults (ages 15–44)
Cohabiting with same sex	5–9 million adults
Adoptive or foster children families	0.5 million children in foster care
Wife as breadwinner	3.8 million families
Multicultural marriages	4.7 million adults
Older parents	6.1 million families
Adult children living at home	21.7 million adults over 18 (8.5 million adults over age 24)
Grandchildren living with grandparents	4.0 million grandchildren
May-December marriages	3.3 million married couples

million and have replaced the male-breadwinner families that were the norm only a generation ago. In 1950, only 34% of women were in the labor force. Today, two-thirds of all married-couple families with children enjoy two earners. Over the past 25 years, the earnings gap between two-earner and single-earner families has widened.

- The 1995 average income for married couples was about $58,000, as compared to the 1995 average income for all families of $51,000, a 14% spread, compared to the 1970 5% spread numbers of $43,000 and $41,000, respectively. Two factors account for the widening income spread: The lower earnings of single parents, counted in the "all families" category and the rise of the two-earner family.

- As women earn more relative to men, they contribute more to the two-earner income. Payroll statistics show that the proportion of women entering better-paying jobs has increased, as the percentage of women ages 25 to 54 entering full-time jobs paying $400 a week or more rose from 15 percent in the period from 1984 to 1986 to 23% in the period from 1991 to 1993. In addition, 22% of women now *out*earn their husbands, up from 16% in 1981 (surprisingly, the first year the Census Bureau tracked those figures) to 22% in 1995.

SINGLE-PARENT FAMILIES

Whether divorced, separated, widowed, or never married, single-parent families numbered 17.9 million in 1995.

As the number of married couples with children has decreased over the past 25 years, the number of single-parent families has risen. In 1970 they constituted 40% of households. Where once the scales tipped heavily on the two-parent side (40% of households with children in 1970), they have now all but reversed.

Everyone probably remembers the loudly trumpeted outrage in 1992 of former vice president Dan Quayle at the decision of television character Murphy Brown to embrace single motherhood. His reaction elicited a lively response from the American public and from the press, both from those condemning the single-parent lifestyle and from those defending it. Quayle even took it upon himself to be the torchbearer of traditional families, expounding upon his ideas in his book, *The American Family: Discovering the Values that Make Us Strong*. The fervor with which people debated the *Murphy Brown* episode serves as evidence that single parenthood has become personally relevant to many Americans, as more and more people either *are, know,* or *have* a single parent.

The number of families maintained by women with no husband present has more than doubled—from 6 million families in 1970 to over 12 million families in 1995. (In 1970, these families accounted for 12% of families with children. In 1995, they accounted for 27% of families with children.) The number of families maintained by men with no wife present has *tripled* from 1 million families (1%) in 1970 to 3 million (5%) in 1995.

When people think "single parenthood," they most often think "divorce." The divorce rate practically doubled between 1950 and 1970 and continued to rise throughout the 1980s. In 1995, almost 9% of all adults were divorced, compared with less than 3% in 1970. Each year, reports have churned out ever increasing rates, creating such a stir that many people now fear the health of American families to be seriously endangered. In 1994, based on previous census findings, the Stepfamily Association reported that 60% of both first and second marriages fail, 66% of all marriages and living-together situations end in breakup, and 50% of children in the United States will go through a divorce by the time they are 18. The truth is, however, that the divorce rate, which took off in the 1970s, seems to be leveling off. So while historical comparisons show a great increase in the number of divorces over the past 25 years, the *rate* of increase is slowing.

In a reaction against divorce rates, some states are now adopting a new type of marriage license, called a *contract marriage,* which makes divorces more difficult to obtain. Intended to make people think more seriously about marriage, this option may or may not lower divorce rates. But even if these laws lower divorce rates, it is not clear whether forcibly intact marriage situations make for healthier families.

The category of single parents whose numbers *and* rate are increasing—and increasing dramatically—is that of *never* married parents. In 1994, 30% of births in the United States were to unwed mothers, compared with less than 4% in 1940. In 1995, a full 51% of African-American female householders with their own children had never been married, compared with 35% of Hispanics and 23% of whites.

Blended Families

Families including stepchildren (and those with a mix of stepchildren and biological children) are left out of the Census Bureau's numbers. Instead, stepchildren fall under the Census Bureau definition of *own children*. The National Center for Health Statistics of the U.S. Department of Health and Human Services does keep track of statistics on women who care for children to whom they did not give birth. In 1995, the report from the National Survey of Family Growth notes that over 6 million women, or 11% of women ages 15 to 44, have cared for or are currently caring for children they did not bear, a categorization encompassing stepchildren, children of relatives, foster children, and adopted children. (About 50% were the children of relatives, friends, or partners; about 33% were stepchildren; 10% were adopted; 10% were foster children.) In this book, the term *blended families* will be used to define those with stepchildren, since we address the situations of adopted and foster children separately.

The Stepfamily Association, drawing from previous census reports, maintains that of the 72.5% of children under age 18 living in two-parent families, 20.8% are in stepfamilies and 2.1% are children born to the current union. According to these percentages, about 10 million children are in stepfamily situations. Further studies have reached the astonishing conclusion that one out of every three Americans is now a stepparent, a stepchild, a stepsibling, or some other member of a stepfamily. In addition, by the year 2000, according to the Census Bureau, more Americans will be living in stepfamilies than in nuclear families.

Unfortunately, unlike the smoothies produced from a bunch of different fruits thrown into a blender, blended families often more nearly resemble fruit salads, with each member maintaining his or her own flavor rather than melting into a new whole. Many of the common psychological and financial glitches these families encounter account for their financial challenges.

Note: Nearly 4% (4 million) of women—one-third of the 11% of women caring for children to whom they did not give birth—have cared for or are caring for stepchildren. Women who remarry bring their biological children into the new marriage more often than the husband brings his children into the new marriage, so there ought to be more than 4 million men caring for children to whom they are not biological fathers. This would assume that more than 8 million families are blended families.

COHABITING (OPPOSITE SEX) SITUATIONS

Cohabitation is defined by the Census Bureau as "living with another person in a sexual relationship, outside of marriage." According to the Center for Health Statistics, 8.4 million adults, or 7% of the adult population, currently cohabit with the opposite sex, up from 6.2% in 1981. About half of women ages 25 to 39 have lived with men outside of marriage at some time in their lives and 11% of women ages 25 to 39, 7% of women overall, currently live with members of the opposite sex without being married.

Roughly 30% of women ages 25 to 39 cohabited before their first marriages, of which relationships 57% ended in marriage, about 33% were dissolved, and about 10% are still intact.

COHABITING (SAME SEX) SITUATIONS

Corresponding statistics are not available for same-sex couples, because researchers disagree on the prevalence of homosexuality in the population, let alone the number of cohabiting same-sex couples. But studies show that 44.5% of gay and lesbian adults are cohabiting. Depending on whether we use 6% or 10% of adults as the estimated frequency of homosexuality in the population, that percentage means that between 5 million and 9 million gay and lesbian adults are currently cohabiting. Moreover, a study has found that in 1993 there were between 3 and 8 million lesbian and gay parents, raising between 6 and 14 million children. Most of these children were the offspring of former heterosexual marriages or relationships in which one partner later came out as being homosexual, but the number of lesbian and gay couples deciding to become parents is growing.

Adoptive or Foster Families

In 1995, 500,000 women indicated that they were currently seeking to adopt a child. And of the 500,000 children in the nation's foster care system in 1994, 40,000 were up for adoption. Pairing up parents and children often leads to legal nightmares for the prospective parents, especially when the adoption is by gay or lesbian parents or parents of a race different from that of the child. And thrown into the equation, along with legal difficulties, are a host of financial concerns and emotional issues.

Two states, Florida and New Hampshire, expressly forbid lesbian and gay adoption. However, more and more homosexual couples are seeking to adopt. As of 1993, more than 200 second-parent adoptions had been granted in eight jurisdictions. Transracial adoption—the joining together of racially different parents and children in adoptive families—is also a highly debated issue. Research has tended to focus on black and Native-American adoption into white families, but of course transracial adoption includes Asians, Hispanics, and all other races. In 1972, the National Association of Black Social Workers issued a statement describing transracial adoption as "cultural genocide" and launched a vigorous campaign that prompted many states to forbid transracial adoption.

However, the influx of minorities into the foster care system is calling into question the feasibility of this policy and, in doing so, is challenging its underlying assumptions. Between 1970 and 1980, the proportion of racial and ethnic minorities in the population increased from 16.7% to 20.2%, and in general, the minority sector of the population was growing at a rate 4% faster than that of nonminorities. In 1994, more than 40% of children in foster care were black. Black children typically wait two to three *years* longer than the average 32 months that a white child waits for a family. It has been generally held that there are not enough black families willing to adopt black children, but this thinking has been contested by studies. In addition, there is the common perception, also hotly contested, that children need to be raised in a family with the same racial/ethnic background in order to develop a secure sense of self. While transracial adoption can be accompanied by even more emotional baggage than same-race adoption, both bring a new set of financial considerations to the adoptive families.

WIFE AS BREADWINNER

Four million families fall into a category that resembles a traditional family structure in all ways except one: The wife is the primary breadwinner. This is either because she is the sole breadwinner of the family (800,000 married-couple families with children) or because she earns more than her husband (22% of wives in married-couple families—or about 3 million families). Of course, some of the temporary conditions, such as a husband going back to school, will also thrust families into the female-breadwinner situation. This one deviation from the traditional family structure does indeed make a difference; it provides the wife with her own set of problems and approaches to personal finance, which we will address in subsequent chapters.

MULTICULTURAL FAMILIES

While Census Bureau figures show that 4.7 million adults live in multicultural families, they do not include those families who adopt or care for children of other races or nationalities (see "Adoptive or Foster Families"). They also do not separate Hispanic, Asian, and other ethnicities from the category of "other" race. But despite these gaps, it is undeniable that there are more interracial marriages now than ever before. In 1995, about 2.5% of men had wives who were not of the same race. Among black men, 6.7% were married to nonblack women, and 1.3% of white men were married to nonwhite women. In 1995, therefore, 2.5% of married couples and 1.4% of all households involved multicultural marriages. This compares to 0.7% of married couples and 0.5% of households in 1970. As well, the percentage of multicultural marriages that are combinations other than black/white has tripled, from 0.5% of all married couples in 1970 to 2% of all married couples in 1995.

OLDER-PARENT FAMILIES

In over 6 million American families, parents are more than 40 years older than the children. As career focus has prompted women to bear or adopt children at later ages (and modern fertility treatments have made it possible), they find themselves driving carpools and serving as den mothers at an age when their own parents were coming home to empty nests. Those who were previously married with children and now want to start families with their new spouses or partners may find themselves with a second batch of young ones at the same time their oldest children are supplying them with grandkids.

ADULT CHILDREN LIVING AT HOME

How many adolescents can recall their parents telling them, "As long as you live in *my* house, you will abide by *my* rules!"? Well, this phrase is probably being called into use more and more frequently—and on adults long past the rebellious stage of adolescence. Trends ranging from the longer period of time spent on higher education to general economic factors have resulted in almost 22 million adults over 18 years old living at home with their parents. Because more than 60% of these belong to the 18-to-24 age group, meaning that many of them live in college dormitories, one might assume that the high number of adults living at home is due to the increase in college enrollment over the years. Indeed, 53% of adults ages 18 to 24 are living at home (or in dormitories), as opposed to 49% in 1970. However, a larger jump has occurred in the number of older adults—ages 25 to 35—living at home. In 1995, 8.5 million adults over age 24 lived at home. They composed 12% of the adult population between ages 25 and 35. In 1970, however, only 8% of that age group lived at home. Many factors could account for this 50% rise. For instance, the gravitating pull of cities has drawn in more and more young adults over the past 25 years, or has kept them from dispersing if they grew up there, but rising rent costs have made them less inclined to rent their own apartments.

GRANDCHILDREN LIVING WITH GRANDPARENTS

Just as older children seem to be living at home with their parents longer, at the other end of the age spectrum the very youngest of children—grandchildren—seem to be living with their grandparents in greater numbers today as well. In 1995 there were 4 million grandchildren living with their grandparents, or over 5% of all children. This compares with 3% of grandchildren in 1970. However, not all grandchildren living with their grandparents are living with *just* their grandparents. Many are living with one or more parents as well. The number of grandchildren living with *no* parents present has decreased since 1970. In 1970 over 43% of grandchildren living with their grandparents lived without any parents present; in 1995 that figure had dropped to 37%. This means that there are more subfamilies living within another family—for example, a mother and child living with the mother's mother. The increase in this type of situation could be related both to economic conditions, such as higher rents and pressures resulting from lower incomes, and to parenting choices, such as the increased number of never married mothers. If they have children young, many of these never married women live with their own mothers until they can get themselves on their feet financially.

MAY-DECEMBER MARRIAGES

This title springs from the familiar metaphor of life as a cycle of seasons—the notion being that while one partner is just budding in the springtime of youth, the other has long been entrenched in the year's final wintry season. In 1997, 77-year-old Tony Randall and his 27-year-old wife, Heather Harlan, made the headlines with the birth of their first child. While their case may be an extreme, the census shows that 3.3 million married couples have age discrepancies greater than 20 years, which is how we have defined May-December families. When those couples have children, the resulting families can appear to outsiders as three generations rather than two.

22 UNDERSTANDING YOUR FAMILY

PUTTING IT ALL TOGETHER: THEN AND NOW

Figure 2.3 presents a statistical comparison of the various family configurations over recent decades.

FIGURE 2.3 A STATISTICAL COMPARISON OF THEN AND NOW

	Marital Status		
FAMILY CONFIGURATION	**NUMBER OF HOUSEHOLDS IN 1995 (IN MILLIONS)**	**PERCENTAGE OF HOUSEHOLDS IN 1995**	**PERCENTAGE OF HOUSEHOLDS IN 1970**
Divorced	6.3	9.1% (8.7% of all adults)	NA (2.9% of all adults)
Separated	3.1	4.4% (2.0% of all adults)	NA (2.2% of all adults)
Widowed	2.8	4.0% (6.6% of all adults)	NA (7.9% of all adults)
Never married	5.7	7.9% (27.1% of all adults)	NA (24.9% of all adults)
Interracial marriages	1.4	1.4% (2.5% of married couples)	0.5 (0.7% of married couples)
	Living Arrangements of Adults		
FAMILY CONFIGURATION	**NUMBER OF ADULTS IN 1995 (IN MILLIONS)**	**PERCENTAGE OF ADULTS IN 1995**	**PERCENTAGE OF ADULTS IN 1970**
Cohabiting, same sex	5–9	44.5%	NA
Cohabiting, opposite sex	8.4 (4.2 million women currently, 24.7 million women ever)	7.0% (10% of women in their 20s; 41.1% of women have cohabited at some time)	3.0% (1.6 million couples, 1982)*

FIGURE 2.3 (CONTINUED)

Living Arrangements of Adults (Continued)

FAMILY CONFIGURATION	NUMBER OF ADULTS IN 1995 (IN MILLIONS)	PERCENTAGE OF ADULTS IN 1995	PERCENTAGE OF ADULTS IN 1970
With parents	21.7 (ages 18 and over)	11.3% (52.6% of adults ages 18–24)	11% (48.5% of adults ages 18–24)
	8.5 (over age 24)	(11.9% of adults ages 25–35)	(8% of adults ages 25–35)
With nonrelatives	4.9	2.5%	NA
Alone	24.7	25.0%	16.7%

Presence of Children (ages 17 and under)

FAMILY CONFIGURATION	NUMBER OF FAMILIES IN 1995 (IN MILLIONS)	PERCENTAGE OF FAMILIES IN 1995	PERCENTAGE OF FAMILIES IN 1970
Married couples with no children	35.3	51.0%	44.0%
Older couples with own children	6.1	8.8%	NA
Mothers with stepchildren	1.8 (mothers ages 18–44)	3.3%	1.6%
Mothers with adopted or foster children	0.5	1.0%	2.3% (1976)*

Living Arrangements of Children (ages 17 and under)

FAMILY CONFIGURATION	NUMBER OF HOUSEHOLDS IN 1995 (IN MILLIONS)	PERCENTAGE OF ALL CHILDREN IN 1995	PERCENTAGE OF ALL CHILDREN IN 1970
With two parents	48.3	68.7%	85.1%
With mother only	16.5	23.5%	10.9%
With father only	2.5	3.5%	1.1%

FIGURE 2.3 (CONTINUED)

Living Arrangements of Children (ages 17 and under) (Continued)

FAMILY CONFIGURATION	NUMBER OF HOUSEHOLDS IN 1995 (IN MILLIONS)	PERCENTAGE OF ALL CHILDREN IN 1995	PERCENTAGE OF ALL CHILDREN IN 1970
With other relatives	2.4	3.3%	2.3%
With nonrelatives	0.7	1.0%	0.7%
Grandchildren living with grandparents	4.0	5.3% (37% with no parents present)	3.0% (43.2% with no parents present)
With adoptive mother	0.5	0.7%	1.5% (722,000 under age 18, 1982)*
In foster care	About 500,000 children in foster care system, with 40,000 children up for adoption in 1994, of which 16,000 were black.		Between 300,000 and 700,000 children in foster care system with 32,000 children up for adoption in 1978, of which 3,600 were black and 5,200 were intercountry adoptions

Workforce Status

FAMILY CONFIGURATION	NUMBER OF MARRIED COUPLES IN 1995 (IN MILLIONS)	PERCENTAGE OF MARRIED COUPLES IN 1995	PERCENTAGE OF MARRIED COUPLES IN 1970
Two-earner	30.0	55.7%	34.3%
Wife only	3.0	5.7%	1.9%

FIGURE 2.3 (CONTINUED)

	Workforce Status (Continued)		
FAMILY CONFIGURATION	NUMBER OF MARRIED COUPLES IN 1995 (IN MILLIONS)	PERCENTAGE OF MARRIED COUPLES IN 1995	PERCENTAGE OF MARRIED COUPLES IN 1970
Husband only	11.8	21.9%	33.5%
Neither in workforce	9.0	16.8%	7.3%
Wives outearning husbands	7.0	21.9%	15.9% (1981)*

* Category not tracked in 1970; earliest figures available.

CHAPTER THREE

Financial Goals and Strategies

When most of us think of financial planning, we think of the process of budgeting, paying taxes, and making investments over the long term. But before you can determine specific strategies, you must determine your destination.

True financial planning, at its simplest, centers on setting goals. The goals you set will help determine how to plan your financial life, but without these goals, the discipline of budgeting will soon succumb to daily pressures. The strategic opportunity that taxes offer soon gives way to the desire to get the 1040 behind you each year. And investing becomes a matter of watching the news and worrying about the ups and downs of the markets rather than allocating your assets and allowing them to perform long term.

With goals ever present to guide your course, you'll find working toward them palatable and even enjoyable. If you don't, change your goals. If you have set goals that don't work for you, you'll undermine your ability to achieve them. To repeat: Change your goals until they mesh with your current and anticipated emotional, economic, and family realities.

SETTING FINANCIAL GOALS

Setting financial goals sounds about as inviting as deep-cleaning your closets. But while reorganizing your closets can mean facing up to *past* clothing purchase mistakes and diet transgressions, financial goal setting empowers you to take control of your own *future* financial security.

Regardless of your age, reducing the future to a matter of dollars and cents may feel more restrictive than following the idealistic maxim of "allowing life to unfold." But by targeting and implementing realistic goals, you will take a critical step toward achieving the measure of financial security that all of us strive to reach.

PLACE YOUR GOALS IN CONTEXT

Whether you expect to consult a professional or you're a determined do-it-yourself planner, it's important for you to set financial priorities first. You're likely to be working toward several goals simultaneously, so identify your goals by time horizon: long-term (10 years and beyond), midterm (3 to 5 years), or short-term (1 to 2 years). Ideally, you'll work steadily toward your mid- and long-term goals as you complete your short-term goals one at a time.

While accomplishing short-term goals can give you a more immediate sense of achievement, it's best to focus your primary energies on mid- and long-term goals such as saving for a home or for retirement. Remember that it's never too early to start saving; in fact, you're much better off saving in small, steady increments over time than waiting indefinitely in hope of a big bonus or windfall. Even very modest savings, consistently invested, accumulate dramatically over time.

To gain perspective on your goals, use both projection and ritual. These exercises focus on the future, for goals cannot be achieved retroactively.

EXERCISE: CREATING THE FUTURE

Set aside about an hour of private time and prepare to be completely honest with yourself for maximum benefit. Answer quickly so that your deepest wishes appear without ifs, ands, or buts. Time each exercise.

1. Set out what you would like to accomplish by the end of your life. Use a checklist format—don't write a treatise. *(10 minutes)*
2. Write a short obituary for yourself as you would like it to appear. *(10 minutes)*
3. Picture the newspaper or magazine of your choice and your face on the cover in 5 or 10 years. Write the headline for the story. *(1 minute)*
4. Pick five goals, regardless of whether they seem attainable, and write them down. You may choose from your answers to numbers 1 through 3 or write new goals. *(5 minutes)*
5. Pick one of your five goals. Write down when you plan to achieve it. Make a positive statement: "By next year, I will save enough for a home down payment." Or "By next year, I will find more meaningful work." Or "By next year, my soul will be at peace and I will no longer live in anger."
   a. Write your affirmation on a three-by-five card and look at it every night before you go to bed until you achieve your goal.
   b. If you'd like to try something a little different, use the Indian "prayer arrow" technique. Write your affirmative statement on a small piece of paper and wrap it around a clean stick, stripped of leaves and twigs. Wrap brightly colored yarns around the stick and finish off your prayer arrow with a white feather, a crystal, or another semiprecious stone. Place your prayer arrow in a prominent location, preferably near your work. You'll have a tangible but subtle reminder of what you are working for, as well as the magic of the stick.

You may have noticed that not all your goals will be financial. None of us are financial goal setters in a vacuum. If your attention is focused on nonfinancial issues, then there's no point in pushing yourself in a direction you won't go. But all goals have a financial component—even spiritual ones. Spiritual goals often translate into reducing material wants or accepting present financial capacity.

WORKING THE MAGIC

While you can prepare as many affirmations or prayer arrows as you wish, the power flows from the writing-down and committing-to. For most of us, one or two goals at a time work best.

Think of it this way: By achieving a single, ambitious goal, you've worked magic.

On the other hand, sometimes people list several goals and find themselves pleasantly surprised or even startled with sudden achievement. As we have all heard: Be careful what you wish for!

FITTING DREAMS TO REALITY

Now that you have pictured your dreams in tangible form, you may be frustrated by your current financial reality. How can you close the gap between your affirmation and your actuality?

While the steps toward achieving your goals will be tempered by the realities of your current budget, you have far more control than you realize. Just think of each action you take as either a step toward your goals or away from them. Ask yourself each day: Does this thought/action/feeling take me toward or away from my destination?

ACHIEVING OLD GOALS, SETTING NEW ONES

Although your goals are personal and individual, they are necessarily colored by your age and status. If you are a younger single mother newly separated from your husband, your goals will differ from those of a widower with teenage children. Take stock as soon as you achieve a goal and set about creating a new focus.

On the other hand, if you find that you can't make headway toward your financial goal, ask yourself what other areas of your life impinge on your finances. Perhaps your health keeps you from working longer hours or friction within your family drains your energy. Yet again, your paperwork may present such a rat's nest of unresolved issues that you can't clear the clutter from your mind or your office.

If necessary, take a detour and fix your attention on intermediate steps that must be accomplished before you can solve longer-term, more challenging aims.

Every year or two, determine how your needs have changed. Keep your written affirmations, once accomplished, for comparison. You will be interested to note whether goals that once seemed so important are lower priorities later. If a goal is still important, you'll learn whether you have strayed from the original plan and then be able to rechart your course.

Give yourself space to draft your own goals. Leave your significant other and/or your children out of the equation while you set down your own goals. After all, you're the only one whose actions you can control. The time for discussion with family, loved ones, or your child's other parent is after you're clear with yourself. If you have a significant other or older children, you can ask them to draft their own goals, then come together for a family meeting and discussion of each person's goals and the steps necessary for each individual and for the family to achieve them.

But remember: Not all goals can be shared or agreed upon. Boundaries are crucial to goal setting. Let people secret their dreams until they want to share them.

SAMPLE FINANCIAL GOALS

- ✔ Save a home down payment.
- ✔ Travel around the world.
- ✔ Retire at age 40 (50, 60, ever).
- ✔ Make a million before age 30.
- ✔ Educate your children.
- ✔ Live debt-free.

Figure 3.1 presents recommended goals for each of the 4M categories.

MEANS TO THE ENDS: TECHNIQUES

Don't confuse goals or strategies with intermediate steps or techniques to achieve those goals. Techniques such as budgeting, list

FIGURE 3.1 4M FINANCIAL GOALS

4 Ms	FAMILY INCOME	ADVICE
MODEST	Under $50,000 per year	• Secure retirement. • Plan for college scholarships, grants, or loans.
MEDIUM	$50,000 to $100,000 per year	• Secure retirement. • Save for college. • Invest 10% of income. • Make modest charitable contributions.
MAJOR	$100,000 to $250,000 per year	• Secure retirement. • Save for college. • Purchase home. • Retain lifestyle by conserving discretionary expenses. • Invest 25% of income. • Contribute to charity.
MEGA	$250,000 and above	• All of the above. • Add venture investments to portfolio. • Invest 35% of income. • Share lifestyle with extended family. • Consider generation-skipping trust for grandchildren. • Make major charitable contributions (community, church, etc.).

making, cleaning your files, or drawing up your will don't qualify as goals. Some of us stop short of setting goals, being simply content to work on process. But the real-life champions set goals and keep them in sight, even if, from year to year, processing day-to-day tasks eats time, attention, and money.

For instance, if your dream were to provide college educations for your children, the first step would be to set up a college fund. If your dream were to retire in a warm climate, you would need to think of an investment strategy.

Use your first goal to complete the Make-It-Happen worksheet.

MAKE-IT-HAPPEN WORKSHEET

Today's date: _____

Describe the goal or objective in detail: _____

_____

What steps are necessary? _____

_____

_____

_____

Date to complete: _____

Complete one sheet for each family member.

THREE-PRONGED SAVINGS ATTACK

Even in the most ideal situations, when people are getting along, income is flowing in regularly, and expenses are under control, emergencies strike. Every family should plan for contingencies by saving enough to survive at least three months without additional income.

To achieve this or any savings strategy, use the three-pronged approach:

1. Stick to lifestyle choices that align with your values. Are the $150 sneakers that your child wants worth the extra hours you'll have to work?

2. Find cost-effective ways to increase your income. You may need to change jobs, get a job if you didn't have one, or start a side business.

3. Have the savings—no matter how small—deducted directly from your checking account to a savings, money market, or mutual fund account.

34 UNDERSTANDING YOUR FAMILY

These three tricks, when worked diligently, provide the financial and emotional insurance that lowers stress more than most any medicine, diet, or exercise. With savings in the bank, exposure from the downside is limited, providing the peace of mind critical to stress savers.

FIGURE 3.2 SPECIAL ADVICE FOR GOAL SETTING

TYPE OF FAMILY	SPECIAL ADVICE
Two-earner	• Make sure your individual goals don't cancel each other's out (e.g., move to Tahiti or get an apartment in Manhattan).
Single parent	• *Divorced:* Adjust goals for your own life. • *Separated:* Your financial outlook is shifting. Set small, attainable goals to avoid feeling overwhelmed. • *Widowed:* Review your changed finances and hold steady in the first months when emotions can cloud your judgment. • *Never married:* Don't allow your vision to disappear under a cloud of daily storms.
Blended	• Focus your goal setting on the permanent members of the household. • Think of your kids' other parents as wild cards.
Cohabiting (opposite sex)	• Work together on some common financial goals but retain your own dreams, needs, and desires.
Cohabiting (same sex)	• Recognize that unless your goals mesh, you need separate ones that fit your ultimate dreams. • Prepare contracts to protect both of you.
Adoptive	• Understand and plan for additional emotional and psychological support for your child. • Work ahead to prepare for the almost inevitable meeting with birth parents. • Decide if another child will be adopted and set the process in motion.

FIGURE 3.2 (CONTINUED)

TYPE OF FAMILY	SPECIAL ADVICE
Foster	• Learn to live with uncertainty. • Don't ignore parents' needs in the emotionally charged atmosphere. • Set aside educational funds that can be used for other purposes should the child be moved.
Wife as breadwinner	• If your goals include future children, plan for maternity leave, alternative income, and savings. • Return to work when both of you are comfortable. If not, set an employment goal for your husband.
Multicultural	• Discuss differences in your cultural upbringing and note how they affect your financial decisions. • Incorporate multicultural outlook into goals. • Plan to visit the countries representing your cultural heritages.
Older parents	• You will retire around the same time your children attend college. Find a balance between these important goals.
Adult children living at home	• If your ultimate goal is financial independence of your offspring, devise a plan together and check progress frequently.
Grandchildren living with grandparents	• Secure grandparents' retirement. • Safeguard the children's futures both legally and financially with solid estate plans.
May-December	• *May:* Prepare goals for the time your spouse will be gone. • *December:* Don't lose sight of the privileges of age, including resting on your achievements.

Part Two

Protecting Your Family

CHAPTER FOUR

Spending Wisely

With goals in hand, we turn to the strategies and solutions that render the goals achievable. One of the most difficult lessons today's families must learn is that, compared to incomes 25 years ago, middle-class Americans are living on less. Ironically, as real incomes have fallen compared to the cost of living, expectations about standards of living have risen.

In this chapter, we'll look at the daily changes necessary to make a good budget stick. Along with basic budgeting, we'll cover negotiating strategies for large purchases and discuss whether buying or leasing—from your home to your car—is the smarter choice for your family. Finally, we'll look at consumer laws to help conserve your hard-won income.

BUDGETING: TODAY'S STEPS TOWARD TOMORROW'S GOALS

Just setting out how much you need to save per month to achieve a given objective won't tell you how to get there. If your goal is your destination, your budget is your road map.

Another useful way to think of budgeting is to compare it to dieting:

- Calorie control is equivalent to the budget component of finances.

- Exercise is equivalent to the income component of finances.
- Genetics is equivalent to the status component of finances.

Budgeting, like calorie counting, doesn't occur in a vacuum. If your budget has to accommodate the far-flung demands of a blended family, your challenge will be as great as that of a calorie counter with a sedentary job and a sweet tooth.

Income directly affects your budget capacity and flexibility. There's no getting around the fact that a poverty line exists because there's a bare minimum income that a family of four needs to survive in today's economy. Likewise, if you exercise all day, you'll lose weight much more quickly than if you can't find time for 10 sit-ups a week.

Status—social class, race, gender, marital situation, family history, and other factors often beyond our control, including luck—works in a way akin to the genetics of weight management. Some of us will never see our teenage figures again, no matter how hard we try to exercise and eat right. Accepting one's genetics, like accepting one's luck, doesn't mean doing nothing about the other two components.

Acceptance means appreciating and enhancing the hand you've been dealt while working to improve the luck of your cards.

Daily Changes Make Budgets Work

Many of us associate the term *corporate downsizing* with layoffs, management restructuring, and slashed budgets. On the home front, families faced with increased costs, tighter time, and lower incomes often start by slashing budgets. But huge cutbacks don't work at home any better than they do in corporations, which are now learning that premature downsizing can lead to having to rehire and retrain.

A better approach: Find one to four areas that you can change in your daily, weekly, or monthly budget and work with those religiously. For example, if you have a cell phone and you use it far more than you planned, park it. If that doesn't work, disconnect it.

> ## Downsizing Junk
>
> We all know the psychological boost of downsizing junk, but consider the financial benefits. With less junk, you'll need less space to put it in, fewer items to purchase, fewer things to clean and maintain, fewer items to pack and unpack if you move, and more time to enjoy.
>
> Don't mistake feelings of guilt or obligation about gifts as sentimental value. Look at each gift or object and if you don't really cherish it, give it up. Keep the memory of the special friend who gave it to you, but don't feel guilty about losing the objects.
>
> Use the three-box method to sort it out. Put trash in one box, giveaways in another, and items that need repair in another. Consider each item in each room of your home. If an item is broken, is it worth the trouble of fixing it? Don't donate broken items to charity—with no resale value, these items will just add to their trash.
>
> After sorting, immediately go the extra step to get rid of it all. Throw away the trash, put the repair box in your car for the next errand day, and call a charity thrift shop to pick up the giveaway box.

Or, if you buy two or three new CDs every week, turn to the radio for a change.

Be sure to balance the cost of your time versus savings on smaller items. In other words, "don't sweat the small stuff." For lasting change, take it slow and easy. Learn where changes will make the biggest difference and concentrate on those areas first. And don't beat up on yourself when you don't meet your goals. Find the lesson from your setback and move on.

Everyone has secret expenses—we can't tell you yours. But you probably know what they are already.

To feel the tangible results of forgoing unnecessary expenses, try putting the money you save in a special place. Whether you choose a big, clear bottle for all to see or a separate account for this money, set it aside and see your changed habits as rewards, not sacrifices. After all, they *are* rewards—for later. The old Calvinist

Budget Worksheets: Monthly Income and Expenditures

While you may have a vague sense that you're spending more than you're bringing in, seeing the bottom-line income and expenses gives you a tangible measure of where adjustments are necessary. The following worksheets are detailed to help you remember all your expenses. Your own budget may not be so detailed, or you may find that you need to add additional categories to fit your unique situation. Convert figures to monthly amounts for easy comparison.

Monthly Income

	You	+	Partner	=	Total
1. Gross employment income*					
Salary	$____	+	$____	=	$____
Commissions	____	+	____	=	____
Self-employment	____	+	____	=	____
Other	____	+	____	=	____
Subtotal, employment	$____	+	$____	=	$____
2. Investment income					
Taxable interest	$____	+	$____	=	$____
Nontaxable interest	____	+	____	=	____
Dividends	____	+	____	=	____
Rents	____	+	____	=	____
Investment partnerships	____	+	____	=	____
Trust fund	____	+	____	=	____
Annuity	____	+	____	=	____
Other	____	+	____	=	____
Subtotal, investment income	$____	+	$____	=	$____
3. Other income					
Spousal support	$____	+	$____	=	$____
Child support	____	+	____	=	____
Subtotal, other income	$____	+	$____	=	$____
4. Benefit income					
Disability	$____	+	$____	=	$____
Social Security	____	+	____	=	____
Supplemental Security Income	____	+	____	=	____

	You	+	Partner	=	Total
Life insurance	_____	+	_____	=	_____
Annuity	_____	+	_____	=	_____
Subtotal, benefit income	$_____	+	$_____	=	$_____
TOTAL INCOME (ADD SUBTOTALS)	$_____	+	$_____	=	$_____

*Use your gross income because taxes are deducted from your expenditure worksheet, below.

Monthly Expenditures

	Current	Target	+/−
1. Housing			
Mortgage or rent	$_____	$_____	$_____
Property taxes	_____	_____	_____
Insurance	_____	_____	_____
Utilities	_____	_____	_____
Yard maintenance	_____	_____	_____
Phone	_____	_____	_____
Household purchases/supplies	_____	_____	_____
Housecleaning/household help	_____	_____	_____
Home improvements	_____	_____	_____
Other housing costs	_____	_____	_____
Subtotal, housing	$_____	$_____	$_____
2. Food			
Home	$_____	$_____	$_____
Restaurant	_____	_____	_____
Children's lunches	_____	_____	_____
Work lunches	_____	_____	_____
Warehouse club/co-op membership	_____	_____	_____
Other	_____	_____	_____
Subtotal, food	$_____	$_____	$_____
3. Clothing			
You	$_____	$_____	$_____
Partner	_____	_____	_____
Children	_____	_____	_____
Subtotal, clothing	$_____	$_____	$_____

(*continued*)

Budget Worksheets (Continued)

	Current	Target	+/−
4. Transportation			
Lease or car note payments	$____	$____	$____
Insurance	____	____	____
Fuel	____	____	____
Maintenance	____	____	____
Other transportation	____	____	____
Subtotal, transportation	$____	$____	$____
5. Dependent care			
Day care	$____	$____	$____
Baby-sitter	____	____	____
Summer programs	____	____	____
Lessons	____	____	____
Sports	____	____	____
Tutor	____	____	____
Support of relatives/others	____	____	____
Other	____	____	____
Subtotal, dependent care	$____	$____	$____
6. Education/school tuition and fees			
You	$____	$____	$____
Partner	____	____	____
Children	____	____	____
College savings	____	____	____
Subtotal, school	$____	$____	$____
7. Health care			
Well child care, immunizations	$____	$____	$____
Health insurance premiums	____	____	____
Medicines	____	____	____
Dental care	____	____	____
Eye care	____	____	____
Health care, subtotal	$____	$____	$____

	Current	Target	+/−
8. Insurance not listed above			
Disability	$_____	$_____	$_____
Life	_____	_____	_____
Other	_____	_____	_____
Subtotal, insurance	$_____	$_____	$_____
9. Recreation/entertainment			
Your club memberships	$_____	$_____	$_____
Partner's club memberships	_____	_____	_____
Children's club memberships	_____	_____	_____
Magazine/newspaper subscriptions	_____	_____	_____
Zoo/museum/park memberships	_____	_____	_____
Personal care and improvements	_____	_____	_____
Hobbies	_____	_____	_____
Movies and video rentals	_____	_____	_____
Video games, toys, CDs	_____	_____	_____
Other	_____	_____	_____
Subtotal, recreation	$_____	$_____	$_____
10. Vacations/travel			
Summer	$_____	$_____	$_____
Fall	_____	_____	_____
Christmas/winter holidays	_____	_____	_____
Spring break	_____	_____	_____
Visits to relatives	_____	_____	_____
Visits to noncustodial parent	_____	_____	_____
Subtotal, travel	$_____	$_____	$_____
11. Goodwill			
Gifts, children	$_____	$_____	$_____
Gifts, others	_____	_____	_____
Children's allowances	_____	_____	_____
Subtotal, goodwill	$_____	$_____	$_____

(*continued*)

Budget Worksheets (Continued)

	Current	Target	+/−
12. Consumer credit debt reduction			
MasterCard™	$_____	$_____	$_____
Visa™	_____	_____	_____
American Express™	_____	_____	_____
Discover™	_____	_____	_____
Gas cards	_____	_____	_____
Department store	_____	_____	_____
Education loans	_____	_____	_____
Consolidated loan	_____	_____	_____
Other	_____	_____	_____
Subtotal, debt reduction	$_____	$_____	$_____
13. Retirement plans			
IRA	$_____	$_____	$_____
Keogh	_____	_____	_____
401(k)	_____	_____	_____
Other	_____	_____	_____
Subtotal, retirement plans	$_____	$_____	$_____
14. Taxes			
Federal income tax	$_____	$_____	$_____
State income tax	_____	_____	_____
Social Security/FICA	_____	_____	_____
State disability/ unemployment	_____	_____	_____
Subtotal, taxes	$_____	$_____	$_____
15. Other expenses not listed above			
Investment payments	$_____	$_____	$_____
Petty cash	_____	_____	_____
Miscellaneous	_____	_____	_____
Subtotal, other expenses	$_____	$_____	$_____
TOTAL EXPENDITURES (ADD SUBTOTALS)	$_____	$_____	$_____

Please visit http://www.womenmoney.com to print or download an interactive version of these worksheets.

principle at work—deferred gratification—is as good at building capital today as it was in Puritan days.

SAVING: TWO UNBREAKABLE RULES

Americans save an average of only 4.2% of disposable income, compared to the average 14.9% saved by the Japanese. Savings are the first step toward almost any financial goal. Follow these two rules, even if you can stick to no others.

- ✔ Pay yourself first.
- ✔ Make savings a fixed expense on your budget. Have the money deducted directly from your account.

Figure 4.1 suggests savings goals for each of the 4M categories.

TECHNICALITIES

Most of us have tried budgeting, failed, and tried again. Choosing a method suited to your personality and the level of financial complications in your life will help keep you on track. Whether you use shoe boxes and notebook paper or sophisticated computer programs and on-line banking, your budgeting helps you gain both awareness and control of your spending. Following are some budgeting methods you might consider.

COMPUTERS

Computers have revolutionized our financial lives. Your family may number among the estimated 40% of all households with

FIGURE 4.1 4M SAVINGS GOALS

4 Ms	FAMILY INCOME	PERCENTAGE OF INCOME
MODEST	Under $50,000 per year	Save 5% minimum.
MEDIUM	$50,000 to $100,000 per year	Save 10% minimum.
MAJOR	$100,000 to $250,000 per year	Save 15% minimum.
MEGA	$250,000 and above	Save 25% minimum.

children that have home computers. If not, seriously consider buying a computer to manage your financial life.

Once you put your finances on a computer, you'll wonder how you could have managed without one. From check writing to tax preparation, sophisticated but simple programs can take the mess and guesswork out of money management.

With a computer, you can do daily bookkeeping, tap into on-line banking services such as bill payment, and even complete more sophisticated moves like trading stocks. For bottom-line bookkeeping tasks such as reconciling your checkbook and calculating net worth, start with a basic program such as Quicken™ or Quickbooks™ from Intuit (800-446-8848). While Quicken dominates the field, other popular programs include Microsoft's Money™ (800-426-9400) and The Budget Kit™ from Dearborn Publishing (800-245-2665). Since its introduction in the 1980s, on-line banking has made great strides. Almost every area of the country has something different to offer, with the latest versions providing bank-customized Quicken programs. Doing your banking and bill paying on your home computer or via the Internet can save hours of work. One bank, Security First Network Bank, operates entirely on the Internet.

If you're considering hooking up with your financial institution's home banking program, remember that you will pay fees of about $15 per month plus a charge for each transaction, whether electronic or paper.

Although technology is changing rapidly, barriers still remain:

- *The ultimate technological gap will be overcome when we can fax cash.* With home banking, you still can't make deposits or withdraw cash from home, although some business banks offer cash deferring and deposit pickup. New products to further streamline include electronic cash, magnetized debit cards, and electronic checks.
- *Electronics move at the speed of consumer-to-consumer transactions, their weakest link.* If a particular creditor doesn't have *electronic funds transfer* (EFT) capacity, upon receipt of your electronic instructions, your on-line service generates a paper

check and mails it. Delivery time will still be at the mercy of the postal system. If you time your payments tightly, on-line won't work for you.

BANK ACCOUNT BUDGETING

If you have made up and dropped many budgets, the answer may lie in instituting controls through a simplified accounts system, using more than one bank account.

Bank accounts can serve two broad budget categories: current expenses and long-term investments. With a checking account for monthly bills and a money market or interest-bearing fund for longer-term goals, you can budget by depositing to one account the amount you plan to spend on current expenses.

Caution: You will need discipline, because having liquid investment funds that are easily withdrawn can prove tempting in tight times.

THE CACHE OF CASH

Credit cards have a way of cushioning us from our financial realities. Although checks are generally thought of as cash, we may go days, weeks, or months without balancing our accounts. Overdraft protection may further provide a misleading feeling of security.

To make your spending more concrete, try withdrawing cash in your budgeted amounts by categories. If you've budgeted $150 a week for groceries, keep it in a separate envelope and use those funds to buy groceries for the week. After each purchase, stick the change and receipt back in the envelope. If you get to the checkout and you've overspent your limit, don't allow yourself to borrow from other sources of money. Instead, eliminate discretionary items from your basket. Who cares what the cashier thinks?

And believe us, we always feel superior when we plunk down a hundred-dollar bill at a business lunch and walk away from the experience debt-free.

Caution: The "cache of cash" exercise is meant to help you spend your cash in a more controlled manner, allowing you to track your spending as well as limit it. Avoid the temptation to withdraw more from the ATM and be sure to keep copies of tax-deductible receipts.

THE FLIP SIDE OF BUDGETING: BE AN ACTIVE CONSUMER

In general, we've said, "Don't sweat the small stuff." But that motto does not apply to:

- Reading the fine print
- Getting satisfaction or your money back

To make a budget work takes more than simply cutting down on expenses. You also have to make sure you don't fall into economic traps that can ruin your budget. These traps range from signing unconscionable contracts to buying shoddy, short-lived goods. By becoming an active consumer, you can save yourself more than you could imagine—sometimes even more than you can save by merely cutting expenses. We all pay dearly for failing to be active consumers, so the flip side of budgeting is: Focus on your own consumer behavior.

READING THE FINE PRINT

Even lawyers occasionally fall down in the reading-the-fine-print department. A recent newspaper story illustrated this problem. Producer Aaron Spelling, suing to obtain a replacement for his $750,000 roof, admitted, "I signed the contracts, but I don't bother reading the fine print. I leave that to my wife." If you're the producer of hits such as *Melrose Place,* you can afford to ignore the fine print and sue later.

The rest of us must pay attention. But even experts can slip up. I found myself reviewing a car insurance policy a couple of years ago and noting that I could save substantially—four or five hundred dollars a year—if I drove under the national average of 10,000 miles a year. Sure enough, when I checked my speedometer, I was well below the average. Now I take the discount for non-smoking, low-mileage drivers.

While most contracts you sign appear to be printed on Moses's stone tablets, in truth, they're documents you can—and should—amend. Anytime you find something that you don't like in the fine print, mark it out, initial your change, and ask the other side to do the same. While this technique is always valid, it may not work as well in a discount warehouse as in, say, a real estate purchase.

Just remember: The fine print is as valid as the customized information. Change it or change your mind and walk away from the purchase.

Consumer Fine-Tuning

Emily is known as "The Queen of Takeback." Follow her code: If something doesn't work, get your money back. Following are some common consumer situations and how to deal with them.

Personnel rudeness: It may not be worth the hassle unless you're a repeat customer. But sometimes, winning just for its own sake gives satisfaction.

> My sister and I rented a small boat at a local marina. The 20-year-old jock behind the counter treated us as middle-age incompetents. When we returned without a small plastic buoy, his opinion showed in the tab—$35 for a very old, very dirty, used buoy. He settled for $20. But we weren't through. We ran to a local marine supply, picked up the $9.99 buoy and returned to claim our $20 refund. Net results: Fifteen minutes spent, $10 saved, a feeling of control restored. Was this a smart battle? No, but it was our day off.
> —*42-year-old homemaker*

Product replacement: Worth the time, especially for expensive durables.

> A major national computer chain sold me a computer with an incompatible modem. When I complained, I got no results. I contacted the corporate offices of the chain and learned that the computer manufacturer was at fault. Rather than allowing corporate headquarters to slough me off to the manufacturer, I contacted the corporate general counsel's office, the lawyer most larger corporations have in-house. I insisted that the general counsel arrange a replacement machine as well as reimbursement for the independent computer consultant who had tried to solve

the problem. The chain supplied a new, more expensive computer from another manufacturer at no additional cost. That modem didn't work either. Back to the corporate offices, where I received a third upgrade which works great.

—51-year-old lawyer

Legal or product damages: From silicon breast implants to credit denials, we women have met our share of defective products and illegal consumer treatment. Complaining and/or seeking justice is definitely worth the trouble, but you'll probably need help from an attorney or a government agency.

When my doctors told me that my silicon implant was leaking, I felt I had to go ahead with the surgery. At the same time, I joined the class action suit for women with implants.

—83-year-old breast implant recipient

Whether confronting a young clerk with a negative attitude toward middle-age women or the corporate office of a national computer chain, getting results takes energy and savvy. As activist consumers, we've learned the most from friends, clients, and our own run-ins with companies. But pick your battles.

How to Complain and Get Results

If your new toaster doesn't work or your insurance policy was canceled even though you submitted your payment on time, then it's time to complain—*effectively*. In the David-versus-Goliath confrontation between consumer and corporation, it helps to have a good slingshot. The following tried-and-true techniques will help you achieve results.

1. *Prevent problems:* Establish yourself as a preferred customer. By becoming a regular and familiar client, you will receive good service in the first place.
2. *Keep records:* As a routine habit, save all copies of bills and correspondence.
3. *Set goals:* Before complaining, outline the problem for yourself and decide how you want it resolved. Simply griping without specifics can turn any situation sour.

4. *Locate decision makers:* Decide on the best person to complain to and the most effective means of communication. Most cases can be resolved by the person you originally dealt with. The situation and your judgment will dictate whether you write, call, or visit.

5. *Put it in writing:* If in doubt, record your complaint in writing at the earliest opportunity. While there's no need to write a letter if you return to the store and receive a new blender, if your car has a defective gas tank, you'll want to write to create a paper trail in case the problem isn't quickly resolved. Writing is a must when your credit is involved.

6. *Go to the top:* In some instances, you may need to speak with a higher-up if your concern is not resolved. When in doubt, start at the top. Avoid getting a "no" lower down the authority ladder. Once people have dug in their heels, it's harder for higher-ups to intervene or make exceptions. Writing to the president of the company can achieve instant results. Most helpful of all? The CEO's executive secretary, who can usually solve the thorniest of problems.

7. *Go higher than the top:* If you can't get a satisfactory resolution by dealing directly with a firm, you must turn to a professional or government organization for help. Most professionals and companies are governed by outside authorities. Examples include the state's department of consumer affairs, the state bar for attorneys, the Securities and Exchange Commission (SEC) for money managers, and the state board of accountancy for accountants. If you're unsure where to turn, the Federal Trade Commission (FTC) is always a good bet. Write to: FTC, Consumer Response Center, 6th Street and Pennsylvania Avenue, NW, Washington, DC 20580.

8. *Keep your cool:* Angry accusations will very likely elicit angry or defensive responses. Don't give the person with whom you're dealing the excuse to decide that the problem is your personality. Whatever you do, don't begin with the threat of legal action. Going to court is the last resort, not the first option, in a successful complaint process.

The Buck Stops Where? Locating the Company Headquarters

Sometimes the hardest part of complaining is knowing where to complain. Your style dictates which of these tips work for you.

- *Check the warranty card:* If you kept it, the company's toll-free number appears. However, you won't find the president's name on most warranty certificates.

- *Call 1-800:* Call toll-free directory assistance at 1-800-555-1212 and ask for the company's toll-free number. Drawback: You might be shunted to an order number rather than corporate headquarters, or the 800 listing might lead to the consumer affairs department. Beware: While many consumer affairs departments are effective, not all can achieve results that require policy decisions from higher-ups.

- *Locate the headquarters:* If you don't uncover a toll-free number but you know the company's city, you can call long-distance directory assistance at 1-(area code of city)-555-1212. Find the area code on the map of the United States in the front of your phone book.

- *Use a reference book:* Dun & Bradstreet's *Million Dollar Directory* (Bethlehem, Pa.: Duns Marketing Strategies, 1991) and *Ward's Business Directory* (New York: Gale Research, Inc., 1997) offer alphabetized company listings that include names of corporate officers. Locate them in the library. Or order the *Consumer's Resource Handbook*, a free publication put out by the U.S. Office of Consumer Affairs (Write: Handbook, Consumer Information Center, Pueblo, CO 81009).

- *The Internet:* Most large companies now offer their own Web sites where you often can find the e-mail or physical address you need. Or take advantage of the corporate directories and other resources on the Internet. Use Web browsing tools and search engines in your Internet server to locate companies by name or location.

9. *Choose your battles:* Know the opportunity cost of making and resolving your complaint. Spending $300 to solve a $100 problem doesn't make economic sense. Unless being in the right is really worth the psychic and economic hassle, you may prefer to bury your problem and move on.

In this book, we're process-oriented, so we're not going to tell you how to shop for food, clothing, or other necessities. You know how to find sales; you know what's necessary and what's a splurge. Instead, we want you and your family to learn to apply active consumerism to every consumer situation so that you can live within your budget, no matter whether your finances call for cooking more at home or eating at less expensive restaurants.

BUYING OR RENTING

From furniture to cars to sports equipment to your home, the decision about whether to purchase or lease may put your family in a quandary. Although buying can be more expensive, you may feel better that your money is going toward something. On the other hand, renting is great for those in transition, those who are uncomfortable about committing to a particular piece of real estate or item, and those who simply don't want the troubles associated with ownership.

In this section, we'll look at the costliest expenditures for most families: homes and automobiles.

Your Family's Home

If you're a family in transition, buying a house may not be the best choice. You may feel insecure about your job or your relationship, or fear that you simply can't handle the expense of maintaining your own property. In addition, since investment returns of real estate can vary, leasing may prove to be your best option in some locations.

When you feel ready, if you don't own a home, consider buying. Home ownership gives you a sense of security and stability. While the middle-class fortunes that were made with the inflation and growth years from the 1950s through the 1980s appear temporarily behind us, a home still allows you to accumulate assets for yourself, your partner, and your children.

Recently, interest rates have remained low, while the housing market, with new home sales at their highest point in 18 years, has been strengthening. In addition, trends of younger baby boomers trading up to better homes and older ones beginning to buy retirement properties have contributed to an increase in demand for high-end housing. But no matter what happens with real estate prices, there are other incentives to switch from renting to buying:

- Once you figure in the tax breaks, net mortgage payments are often less than rent.
- Your mortgage payments build equity in your home. If you rent, you'll end up with nothing to show for all those months of payments, except possibly a better credit rating.
- Your improvements and renovations increase your potential equity.
- If you itemize deductions on your federal income taxes, you may deduct: interest paid on mortgage loans up to $1 million (interest paid on mortgages incurred before October 1987 is fully deductible with no upper limit), amounts paid for property taxes, and interest on home equity loans up to $100,000. *Note:* To obtain the home equity break, you must borrow against the property, otherwise you lose the deduction. If, for instance, you use a bond portfolio as collateral, the equity line interest is not deductible. However, *never take a home equity loan and place your security at risk simply in order to take the deduction.* Many consumers fall into this trap when eager lenders sell consolidation loans to refinance previously unsecured debt such as credit cards.
- If you sell your primary residence, your profit (or capital gain) of up to $250,000 (individual filer) or $500,000 (married filing jointly) is excluded from your federal income taxes. Contrary to previous tax law, you are not required to roll over the gains into a new residence to take the exclu-

sion. However, you must have lived in the residence at least two out of the past five years (if one partner doesn't meet usage test, the other can still take the exclusion as in a couple who was separated for an extended period). Since you may use this exclusion as often as every two years, it replaces the old provision for a one-time exclusion after age 55. If unforeseen circumstances such as health or employment necessitate selling your house in less than two years, you may still be eligible for a partial exclusion of your capital gains.
- You don't have to deal with a landlord or fear losing your lease.
- Eventually, if you stay put, your mortgage will be paid off and you'll own the home outright, an important component of a solid retirement.

STEPS TO HOME OWNERSHIP

These steps make the home-buying process easier:

1. *Clean up your credit act.* Don't make a move until you've ordered copies of your credit reports from all possible agencies and corrected any errors or remedied any problems. See "Correcting Your Credit Report" in Chapter 6 for a list of credit bureaus.

2. *Prequalify.* Contact several lenders (banks, credit unions, mortgage companies) about prequalification. Since companies differ widely in promises versus delivery, prequalification gives you a commitment you can count on. Some companies will even complete the process over the telephone.

3. *Team up with an agent and an attorney.* First-time buyers should use a licensed real estate agent to assist them in the process, as well as an attorney at closing. Besides showing you prospective homes, a good agent will also show you the ropes. You'll be guided through the process of making an offer through contract (which the attorney should review before you sign), having the home inspected, negotiating

with the owners, applying for the mortgage, and, of course, the closing.

4. *Choose an agent whom you trust.* If you don't feel comfortable with the person you've chosen, find another agent. Depending upon where you live, the agent may legally represent you or the seller or both. The agent stands to make a good deal of money from your purchase. Don't use the same agent as the seller.

5. *Be your own advocate.* If you feel you've been discriminated against because of your family status, children, gender, sexual preference, or race, call your local fair housing office or the national Housing and Urban Development hot line (800-669-9777).

In addition to these general steps, several agencies offer outreach programs for low-to-moderate-income mortgage applicants. Contact the Fannie Mae Foundation for a free booklet on home ownership (800-688-HOME). Fannie Mae also has a toll-free line for information on mortgage programs and consumer counseling (800-7-FANNIE). Other helpful agencies include Freddie Mac (800-373-3343) and the Mortgage Bankers Association of America (202-861-6500). These agencies should be able to inform you about state or federal programs for which you may be eligible.

Since the traditional 20% down payment and high closing costs prove to be major hurdles to home ownership, special programs typically focus on ways to get marginally qualified people into homes. Typical programs include:

Down payment assistance: If you qualify, your lender gives you a separate loan for the down payment amount that is underwritten by the state or federal government. You must pay this loan off in a shorter amount of time, usually about 5 years, in addition to your 15-year or 30-year mortgage for the remainder of the home's purchase price.

Reduction in down payment amount: Other programs reduce the down payment amount and loan up to 100% for qualified buyers with low incomes but good credit records. (Mortgage insurance may or may not be required.)

Closing costs: You can include a clause in your contract requiring the seller to pay a percentage (typically 3%) of the purchase price toward closing costs. For example, on a $75,000 home, the seller would have to provide $2,250 toward closing costs. If the seller agrees, you can save money on the front end to cover attorney's fees, mortgage points, and other items payable upon closing.

Other measures cut costs across the board, rather than just on the front end. They include:

Negotiating with the lender: Don't be afraid to shop around for lenders with the best interest rates. Negotiate the one to four *points,* or extra fees, expressed as a percentage of the loan.

Choosing the type of loan that fits your needs: Fixed-rate mortgages are very popular when rates are low. Adjustable rates move with the market and tend to parallel inflation. Hybrids that start with a lower fixed rate then jump to variable after a set amount of time (5 or 10 years) work to get a home with lower front-end costs. Beware of balloon mortgages in which your monthly payments increase during the life of the loan.

Determining if you qualify for a lower interest rate through a government program: Some government programs can lock you into a percentage rate that's slightly lower than the going rate. If you qualify, your monthly payment could be considerably lower.

COMPARING RENTING VERSUS BUYING

While our tax system is geared to home ownership, markets of recent years have made many current and future homeowners ask the question: Would we be better off renting?

The answer is not easy. In general, real estate has represented the best and largest investment for most families. Over time, real estate overall still outperforms other investments, including the stock market. But, in the last decade, that 60-year record has turned upside down, with stocks beating residential real estate cold.

Surprisingly, however, even with housing prices flat, rents continue to rise. Market forces of demand and supply push rents up, especially as many families priced out of the home-buyers market in the 1980s remain renters. In many cities where rent control had stabilized rents for decades, rent control laws have tumbled as voters, legislatures, and courts have declined to support continued lids on rents.

Renting certainly provides flexibility. If your family finds itself in flux, you can wait to enter the housing market. Many families jumped into the market in the 1980s as they watched prices spiral daily. With inflation lower and interest rates holding fairly steady, the rush to home ownership has given way to a more measured beat. However, in some markets, real estate is heating up again. If you know you've found the area in which you want to live for several years, try to accumulate the down payment and make the move to ownership. On the other hand, if your preferred neighborhood remains out of your reach, certainly renting where schools and services meet your needs is preferable to buying in a location that you won't enjoy.

While a divorced parent may have received a house in the settlement, many families find themselves relocating to rentals. Remember, landlords are looking for the most reliable applicants. If you have a good track record as a renter or home owner, you should be able to negotiate the rent and deposits. Ask your potential landlord to take half the deposit now and to spread the rest over the next few months. Or if the landlord won't reduce the rent permanently, you may be able to negotiate by starting lower and gradually increasing over the first year. This kind of arrangement is especially helpful to families in transition.

Ultimately, though, as rents rise and lives extend, home ownership provides a way to ensure you'll have a familiar roof over your head for years to come, even if you have to pay to fix the leaks.

Your Family's Automobile(s)

When Emily's son Waldo was 12, he discovered their car's owner's manual. Looking through the drawings, charts, and specs, he realized that the manual seemed similar to the instructions that come with mechanical sets, video games, and action figures. Waldo observed, "Cars are adult toys."

As our toys have become more expensive, we've learned to consider buying versus leasing them, as we do real estate. A decade ago, most Americans' goal was to pay off the cars. But with the abolition of the consumer credit and automobile interest deductions in the 1986 tax reform, leasing suddenly became more attractive. Combined with the vicissitudes of manufacturers' overproduction of new cars and the highly competitive nature of the automobile industry today—where the U.S. manufacturer expects no more than a $2,000 profit on average per car—to remain competitive, automakers turned to leasing as a way to move new cars. Often, the interest rates charged, especially for luxury high-end vehicles, run under 2%.

DOS AND DON'TS OF AUTO LEASING

Don't choose a lease longer than three years. If you want to extend the lease for a second or even third period of time, you can negotiate a lower price for the extension and you'll know if the car is a lemon or a peach.

Knowing the car's performance personality before you renew makes a difference as the warranty ends. If you do renew, make sure to factor in repairs, since you've become accustomed to free or minimal maintenance costs.

With a high-end, reliable car, renewing a lease for two or even three cycles makes sense. As the lease winds down, you can buy the car outright and drive it for several more years.

If you do the math, this method can often prove cheaper than buying the car on payments.

Of course, with cars, as with everything else, cash is king. If you have the money to pay cash, you'll save interest. However, don't forget that you'll lose liquidity.

Choose a finance company carefully. Companies such as Ford Motor Credit or GMAC that are owned by the car manufacturers may also offer quicker approval, while if you enjoy a solid relationship with your bank, rates could prove lower there. Shop around.

When leasing, ask for extras such as free roadside assistance, free standard maintenance, repairs, and a loaner car when yours is in the shop. And negotiate for a set of manufacturer's floor mats. Leave this one until last, but don't walk out without them.

Ensure that your package includes gap insurance to pay the difference between the car's value and the amount you still owe on the lease, in case the car is stolen or totaled.

Don't underestimate your mileage needs (typical packages allow you to drive 11,000 to 12,000 miles per year). Extra miles on the odometer could cost you up to 25 cents each when you return the car. Buy extra miles at the start when they're a cheaper 8 to 9 cents a mile.

BUYING USED CARS

Since 1992, automobile dealers have sold more used cars than new ones each year. This trend is expected to continue, as the average cost of used cars is about half that of new ($11,067 versus $20,474 in 1996), technological improvements give vehicles a longer life span, and the leasing phenomenon has added a huge pool of late-model used cars to dealers' lots. Unless you intend to start with a new car and drive it a decade or more, consider used, two- to three-year-old cars.

Resale is going upscale as used-car superstore chains offer services such as free baby-sitting, computer kiosks to research vehicles, haggle-free prices, 5-day money-back guarantees, and 30-day warranties.

> *Warning:* Vehicles sold at used-car superstores can be slightly more expensive than at traditional used-auto dealers because big dealers have set prices for specific models and are not as flexible in negotiating.

Another type of car resale venue, franchised dealers, gets the largest quantity of previously leased or preowned cars. Look to dealer resales if you're going to spend a substantial sum.

The following tips apply to all used-car sales:

1. Check the blue-book value (obtain from your insurance agent, bank, or public library).
2. If you're a member of an auto club, check your member benefits. For example, the American Automobile Association (813-289-1300) offers referrals to dealerships offering discounts for members. AAA also refers members to affiliated fee-based companies that will inspect and assess used cars, whether at a dealership or through a private seller.
3. If you're not a member of an auto club, ask your mechanic or an inspection service listed in the yellow pages to inspect the car, advising you about possible trouble spots and whether the price is right.
4. Call your insurance agent for a premium quote before buying. Monthly premiums drive your cost up by as much as a third.
5. Call the *Consumer Reports* used car price service (900-446-1120). For $1.75 per minute, you can find out local prices, dealer purchase price, trade-in price, private sale price, and model reliability. Provide your zip code, model name and/or number, year, number of cylinders, mileage, and condition of vehicle.

ALTERNATIVES TO AUTOMOBILES

Vehicles are expensive to purchase, maintain, and insure. According to the American Automobile Association, motorists spend an average of $6,795 annually to own and operate their cars. And, except for a few models, they depreciate quickly. Money poured into vehicles may well be spent elsewhere. For instance, a young consultant purchased a motorcycle instead of a car and used the money he saved to capitalize a successful business.

While a motorcycle is probably not appropriate for families who need to cart their kids around, this story illustrates an important principle about transportation and downsizing in general: Use the least that is appropriate in your situation. For some, this means public transportation; for others, carpooling.

LEGAL LESSONS: USING FEDERAL CREDIT LAWS

In the consumer world, ultimate protection lies in the federal and state consumer laws. Several federal provisions in particular protect you. Keep the list handy.

The Fair Credit Billing Act: When you buy with a charge card, if the product or service isn't as promised, you have the right to request a suspension of billing without penalty while the damaged goods or poor services are corrected or credited.

Legal wrinkle: Contrary to popular belief, this privilege works best with department store cards and other credit issued by the seller. Third-party cards—such as Visa and Master-Card—are required to follow this rule only if the purchase exceeds $50 and is made within your home state or within 100 miles of your home address.

The Fair Credit Reporting Act: This requires that you notify a creditor *in writing* within 60 days if you receive an incorrect bill. The creditor has 90 days to resolve the disputed bill.

FIGURE 4.2 SPECIAL ADVICE FOR BUDGETING

TYPE OF FAMILY	ADVICE
Two-earner	• Off-budget expenses can result when time is tight and it's easier to take a more expensive quick fix for basic needs. • Determine which household chores will be divided between you and which will require hired help.
Single parent	• *Divorced:* Avoid competing with your ex-spouse for the kids' attention by purchasing them expensive gifts.

FIGURE 4.2 (CONTINUED)

TYPE OF FAMILY	ADVICE
	• *Separated:* If a divorce is pending, try to keep the house. Selling a home can be expensive and time consuming, while qualifying to purchase another one can be difficult without a spouse's income. If you fall behind in your mortgage, you have six months to bail yourself out rather than the 60 days you'd have if you were a tenant. • *Widowed:* It's hard to care about expenses when you're just trying to cope each day. Determine whether you developed poor spending habits during mourning. • *Never married:* Being on your own gives you more control over your daily spending choices, but you are accountable—there's no one else to blame when things go wrong.
Blended	• Not only do you have an ex vying for your child's attention with expensive gifts, but you have your spouse's ex doing the same. • Make sure you budget for hidden school expenses—$5 here and there can add up.
Cohabiting (opposite sex)	• Include clear budget guidelines about who is responsible for what major living expenses. • You can buy a home together if you're not married, but understand that each of you is liable for paying off the mortgage. If you break up, the burden may fall to you.
Cohabiting (same sex)	• When choosing a home, your lifestyle choices might make you more welcome in some communities than others.

FIGURE 4.2 (CONTINUED)

TYPE OF FAMILY	ADVICE
Adoptive	• You may have thought the expensive part was over when the adoption papers were signed. But variables such as the child's age and medical condition will continue to impact your budget.
Foster	• If you receive a stipend from the foster agency, determine whether you'll budget additional dollars to care for the child's needs.
Wife as breadwinner	• Working moms can be tempted to give the children expensive treats to replace the time they're not around. Try more budget-friendly techniques to show your children how much you miss them—a special note in the lunch box, a walk in the park.
Multicultural	• Members of multicultural families still find that prejudices or stereotypes can influence their negotiating power. Knowing credit rights and learning to be an active—and assertive—consumer can help.
Older parents	• Watch your daily spending to ensure that you don't chisel away at money that should be going toward your retirement.
Adult children living at home	• Adult children should contribute to the household economy by helping around the house, paying rent, purchasing groceries, and so forth.
Grandchildren living with grandparents	• If it's been a while since you raised your own flock, you may be shocked at the costs associated with child rearing. • Your housing choices may be limited by your grandchildren. For example, many retirement communities don't allow children under a certain age.

FIGURE 4.2 (CONTINUED)

TYPE OF FAMILY	ADVICE
May-December	• Your daily spending habits and money views may differ, depending on the era in which you were raised. For example, you may be a boomer married to a Generation Xer or a boomer with a Depression-era mate. If one of you is already retired, the other will have a different lifestyle (i.e., work) and different spending patterns.

CHAPTER FIVE

Tax Strategies

When Congress passed the Taxpayer Relief Act of 1997, some familiar standbys, such as the residential capital gains rollover, were altered or done away with. With its emphasis on children, education, home buying, and retirement, the new set of laws is a step toward addressing the changing demographics—and needs—of today's families.

While you will see some of the new provisions covered in this chapter as examples illustrating tax concepts or in the special advice chart that follows, other specific laws that affect you are covered in detail throughout the book. For example:

- Chapter 4, "Spending It Wisely," goes over the new *residential capital gains exclusion* in its discussion of buying a home.
- Chapter 10, "Selecting and Paying for Education," covers the multiple *education incentives* in the new tax law.
- Chapter 11, "Rescuing Your Retirement," explains the difference between regular individual retirement accounts (IRAs) and the new *Roth IRAs*.
- Chapter 13, "After You're Gone," includes information on the new provisions for *estate and gift taxes*.

In this chapter we recognize that, while such specific provisions and laws may change with the political winds, basic tax strategy exists in a framework that hasn't been changed in decades. Therefore, we emphasize how to think about—and plan—your family's taxes. Whether you're the type who likes to plan complex financial moves based on your tax outlook, or you'd rather limit your strategies to after-the-fact decisions about whether to itemize deductions or open a last-minute IRA, read on. The full spectrum of taxpayers can benefit from understanding and applying the basics of tax law.

THE FIVE TAX BASICS

The fact remains that no matter how simple or complex the current tax law looks, only five ways exist to lower tax payments for individuals. At times, the allowable uses of the five basics expand; at others, they contract. These five tax basics remain a constant through changing tax trends. Whenever you talk about taxes, you must start with these five and use them correctly to understand the effect on your own tax bottom line.

1. *Exclusions:* Income that is not taxed. (Most fringe benefits are excluded from tax, as are gifts you receive and certain insurance settlements.)
2. *Deductions:* Expenses that reduce taxable income. (Mortgage interest is deductible, while credit card interest is not.)
3. *Rates:* Tax rates determine the amount of taxes on taxable income. (By grouping your deductions together in one year, you may lower your tax rate. Creating a separate corporation can have the same effect.)
4. *Credits:* Credits to reduce the tax liability itself. (The child care tax credit and earned income credit directly reduce the tax you owe.)
5. *Deferrals:* Deferrals delay the tax. (Tax on income and interest earned in a deductible IRA is deferred until money is withdrawn from the IRA.)

The best tax strategies incorporate one or more of these savings opportunities. For example, a traditional deductible IRA takes advantage of a tax *deferral* until you fall into a lower *tax rate* when your earnings have decreased after retirement.

INCOME DEFINED

When Americans gather at holiday times, often if the talk isn't about sports, it's about taxes. Listen to a kitchen-table conversation about high taxes, and the first thing you'll realize is that most people think they are taxed on their stated income. For example, if a person's salary amounts to $60,000 a year and he hears that the tax rate is going down for incomes over $50,000, he usually assumes that his tax will go down. In actuality, people are taxed on their taxable incomes or their incomes less all exclusions, deductions, and deferrals, not their total or gross incomes.

Part of the problem lies in the way income tax law changes are reported. Rarely do news stories bother to clarify that Congress makes its changes based upon adjusted gross incomes and taxable incomes, not gross incomes.

So, the first step to understanding income taxes is to comprehend the tax code definitions of income.

Three distinct labels for income are relevant in determining your income taxes: *gross income, adjusted gross income,* and *taxable income.*

Gross income: The tax code defines *income* as follows: "Gross income means all income from whatever source derived." Gross income includes all income from wages, salaries, interest, partnerships, and businesses.

Adjusted gross income (AGI): Gross income minus certain favored 1040 page-one *deductions,* including alimony paid and deferrals of voluntary retirement programs such as allowable IRAs and Keoghs. These are favored because you do not have to itemize to receive them.

Taxable income: Adjusted gross income minus itemized or standard deductions and personal exemptions. No matter how large your total income, you pay taxes only on your taxable income. The only exception is the *alternative minimum tax* (AMT). The AMT affects high-income earners with high levels of deductions compared to their incomes (see section below).

The adjusted gross income becomes the basis for certain other deductions, such as those for medical expenses (which are deductible only by the amount that they exceed 7.5% of your AGI). Your adjusted gross income theoretically represents the money you have for housing, food, and other costs of living.

(*continued*)

> **INCOME DEFINED (CONTINUED)**
>
> So next time you engage in a casual tax discussion, be sure to clarify whether you're talking about gross, adjusted, or taxable income. Defining your terms makes a big difference to the bottom line.
>
> *Note:* Throughout the book, our 4M Income Guidelines are based on *gross income*.

Exclusions

Most people think of deductions as the easiest way to reduce their tax liability, but the first place to save money on taxes is to receive income excluded from taxes altogether. If you can increase your actual income without increasing your income for tax purposes, you are immediately saving on taxes.

Exclusions don't appear in any of the income definitions on your tax return at all. Excluded income could be cash you receive from insurance proceeds or noncash, nontaxable fringe benefits. Fringe benefits constitute a majority of the exclusions for salaried taxpayers. Within strict limits, many noncash benefits provided to employees, such as employer-provided life and health insurance, are excluded from income calculations for tax purposes. But note that certain fringe benefits are taxed even though not received in cash—for example, assigned parking paid by your employer in amounts exceeding $170 in 1997.

Excluded income, such as that provided by educational scholarships for tuition, fringe benefits, qualified residential capital gains, and interest from tax-exempt municipal bonds, is actually worth more than other income. Excluded income is earned in nontaxed dollars, and the value of this income increases with your tax rate. For example, at a 28% tax rate, if you earned an additional $1,000 in excluded income, you would save $280 that otherwise would have been paid in taxes had there not been an exclusion for the $1,000 earned. If your tax rate is 39.6%, then you would effectively be better off by $396 on the same $1,000.

In addition, state income tax savings from exclusions can be even greater.

Deductions

Depending on the type of expense or loss, deductions lower your gross income or your adjusted gross income. As with exclusions, the value of deductions varies with your tax rate. At higher tax rates, deductible expenses become cheaper. For example, if your tax rate is 28% and your deductible accountant's fees are $1,000, then you will save $280 in tax expense. Put another way, the accountant actually costs you $720 ($1,000 minus the deduction's actual value of $280 equals $720). If your marginal rate is 39.6%, then the account's real cost is $604.

The complexity of the tax code can most easily be seen by the rules surrounding deductions. Lawmakers have tried to curb abuse and limit the amount of deductions taken by taxpayers while enabling taxpayers to recognize valid expenses and losses.

Deductions are subtracted from your gross or adjusted gross income to determine your taxable income. Examples throughout this chapter illustrate the effect of deductions on your tax bill.

To obtain the benefit from large allowable deductions, taxpayers must *itemize*, or list, them. If you itemize, you file your taxes on a "long-form" 1040 and specify deductions on additional *schedules*, or forms. Personal expenses belong on Schedule A and business expenses on Schedule C (or C-EZ for certain small businesses).

If you skip itemizing, as do more than two-thirds of all taxpayers, you receive the *standard deduction*. This set amount, which may be subtracted from your adjusted gross income, is designed to ease the bookkeeping burden of itemized deductions for individuals who have minimal deductions. The standard deduction also serves to balance the benefits of deduction for low-income individuals, whose expenses are correspondingly lower than those of higher-income itemizers, by providing them with a minimal deduction to offset their income.

Any home owners itemize. Mortgage interest payments are deductible, as are real estate taxes. If you don't own a home, have student loan interest to deduct, or have very high medical or other expenses, then the standard deduction likely provides the best tax break.

COMPARING SCHEDULE A AND SCHEDULE C DEDUCTIONS

Some personal deductions taken on 1040 Schedule A are subject to a minimal floor of a percentage of your age before they are allowable as deductions. The floor is figured by multiplying the percentage by your adjusted gross income, which appears on the bottom line of the first page of the 1040. Medical deductions must amount to at least 7.5% of your AGI in order to include. Certain other miscellaneous deductions such as an employee's business-related expenses are subject to a 2% floor.

By contrast, deductions taken from 1040 Schedule C, Business Expenses, are not subject to a floor. Schedule C has two major limits: First, home office expense cannot be taken to the extent that it gives you a loss on your business income. Second, to overcome the presumption that a business is merely a hobby being used to produce a write-off, a Schedule C business must show a profit in three out of five years. This rule is not hard and fast. However, if you are a full-time, salaried person with a side business that sustains repeated losses, thus lowering your taxes, the IRS may look twice. If you start a legitimate business but it doesn't turn a profit, and if you are audited, the IRS will look to the type of business and the extent to which your business records and books look "businesslike."

DEPRECIATION

To account for the deterioration in value arising from age and use of property and equipment, depreciation is an allowable deduction. For tax purposes, depreciation expense is a deduction of the cost of a tangible asset, such as real property or machinery, over its estimated useful life.

Depreciation becomes a confusing deduction for two reasons:
1. The useful life of an asset is based on policy requirements that do not necessarily reflect reality (for example, a com-

puter may be obsolete in two years, but it may have a useful life, for depreciation tax purposes, of five years).

2. Taxpayers have a choice of depreciation schedules including *straight-line depreciation,* which deducts the same amount each year of the useful life of an asset, or the *Modified Accelerated Cost Recovery System (MACRS),* which deducts more at the beginning of the asset's useful life and less at its end. Another provision allows qualified businesses to deduct the entire cost of assets at initial purchase (up to $18,500 in 1998, to be adjusted annually until it reaches $25,000 in 2003). But a depreciation schedule is still in effect—if the item later goes out of business use before the schedule is up, a portion of the deduction must be charged back to income.

Depreciation provides an important deduction for companies and entrepreneurs, enabling a continuing stream of tax benefits for investments in machinery and equipment.

In addition to the standard deduction, all taxpayers except tax-paying dependents are entitled to a *personal exemption.* This exemption is a set amount subject to an annual inflation-based adjustment allotted to the spouse and each dependent of the taxpayer, as well as to the taxpayer.

Tax Rates

At rising, specified levels of taxable income, you pay increasingly higher tax rates. Your taxable income may be thousands of dollars less than your gross income, but the rate is still applied in incremental steps only to the taxable, not the gross, income amount. In general usage, the amount of tax paid divided by your adjusted gross income is your *effective tax rate.*

Tax Stairs

The tax rate is applied in stair-step fashion. Every taxpayer pays the same amount on the first level (or "stair step") of taxable income. Only if your income rises above the first stair step do you pay the higher tax rate, and that is applied only to the income until the next stair. (See Figure 5.1.)

The rate you apply to each stair is based on five tables, constructed according to your *filing status*. The four filing status charts are "single," "married," "head of household," "married filing separately," and "qualifying widow/er with dependent child." Filing status is not a matter of choice. One exception is married persons who choose to file separately.

The *marginal tax rate* is the amount of tax you would pay on the next dollar that you earned. For example, if your taxable income is at the limit of the lowest tax bracket (currently 15%), then your next dollar of taxable income earned would be taxed at the rate of the next tax bracket (currently 28%). Only the new income would be taxed at the higher rate; as illustrated in Figure 5.1, the base amount is taxed at the old rate.

FIGURE 5.1 PROGRESSION OF TAX STAIRS

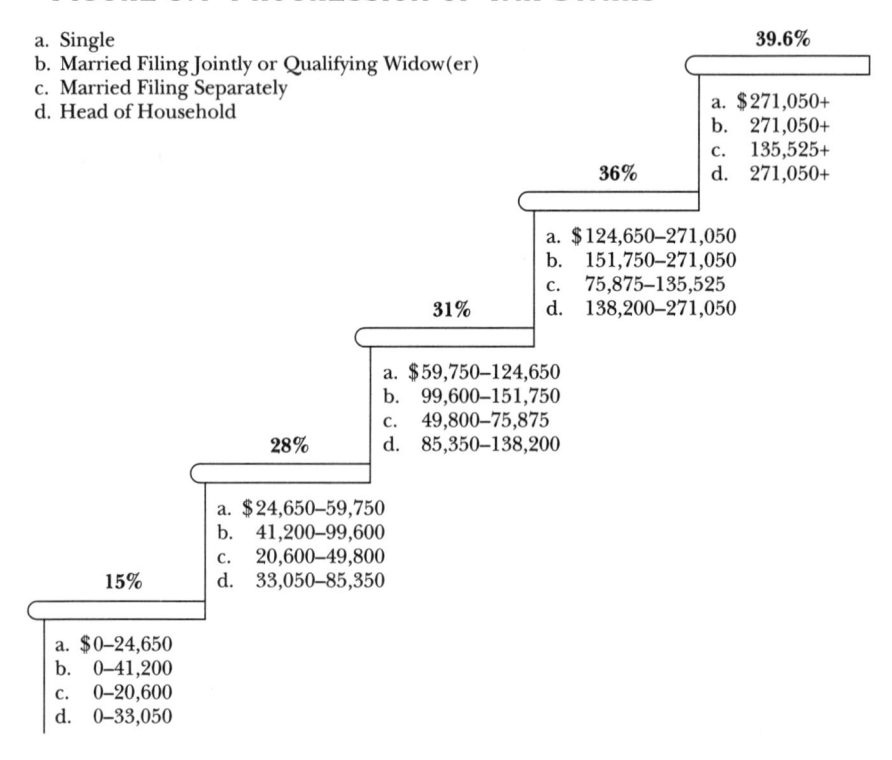

a. Single
b. Married Filing Jointly or Qualifying Widow(er)
c. Married Filing Separately
d. Head of Household

39.6%
a. $271,050+
b. 271,050+
c. 135,525+
d. 271,050+

36%
a. $124,650–271,050
b. 151,750–271,050
c. 75,875–135,525
d. 138,200–271,050

31%
a. $59,750–124,650
b. 99,600–151,750
c. 49,800–75,875
d. 85,350–138,200

28%
a. $24,650–59,750
b. 41,200–99,600
c. 20,600–49,800
d. 33,050–85,350

15%
a. $0–24,650
b. 0–41,200
c. 0–20,600
d. 0–33,050

Special note for math whizzes: Unless you are in the lowest tax bracket, your effective tax rate will differ from your marginal tax rate. For example, with an AGI of $35,000, if we assume that some of your dollars ($22,750) are taxed at 15% and other dollars ($12,250) are taxed at 28%, then all your dollars are effectively being taxed at an average rate of less than 28%. In math terms, the amount is actually (22,750 × 15% + 12,250 × 28%) ÷ 35,000, or 19.55%. Only income above the cutoff point is taxed at the next higher rate.

Once you know your effective tax bracket and marginal tax rate, you can make quick calculations about the after-tax value of additional deductions or additional income.

Your marginal rate also helps to determine whether a tax-free investment beats a taxable one with a higher total yield (see Figure 5.2).

FIGURE 5.2 EQUIVALENT TAXABLE YIELDS CHART*

TAX-FREE	TAXABLE
4.00	5.71
4.10	5.86
4.20	6.00
4.30	6.14
4.40	6.29
4.50	6.43
4.60	6.57
4.70	6.71
4.80	6.86
4.90	7.00
5.00	7.14

*At 28% marginal tax bracket, a tax-free investment equals the taxable return on the right.

THE EQUIVALENT YIELD CHART

Figure 5.2 shows the equivalent taxable yields on securities before federal income taxes. Assuming a 28% marginal federal tax rate, you can see whether yields from tax-exempt state and municipal bonds equal higher earnings from taxable investments, such as CDs.

THE ALTERNATIVE MINIMUM TAX

During the tax reforms enacted in 1986, Congress revised the alternative minimum tax, originally imposed in 1978. This tax on people with high incomes who would otherwise substantially reduce taxes with a large number of deductions applies a flat rate to these taxpayers. It also removes many allowable deductions. The AMT rate calculation is complicated. It kicks in after a certain floor of exempt income, which is dependent upon filing status. (For married filing jointly, the exempt amount is $45,000; single filers' exemption is $33,750.) After the applicable AMT exemption, the first $175,000 of income is taxed at 26%. Amounts over $175,000 are taxed at 28%. A further complication phases out the exemptions over a certain income.

Caution: The bulge in tax breaks and allowable deductions created by recent tax legislation may place a greater number of moderate-income families at risk to be subject to the AMT. If uncertain, consult a tax professional. If you know your affairs are sufficiently complex to require an AMT calculation, you should have a tax professional prepare your tax return. You would need to understand the AMT in order to make decisions about such questions as whether to make charitable contributions.

CREDITS

A tax credit is the amount that is taken directly from the tax you owe. A credit reduces your tax bill dollar for dollar and some credits are even refundable, whereas a deduction or exemption is only as valuable as your tax rate. Because of the effect tax credits have on reducing the total tax revenue received by the government, Congress is hesitant to allow them. In the past, tax credits have been allowed for foreign taxes paid, certain investments, and dependent care expenses. Beginning in 1998 a new tax credit will be applied to each child under age 17 in a family. Although subject to phaseouts over certain AGIs ($110,000 married filing jointly, $75,000 single or head of household, $55,000 married filing separately), the basic credit is set at $400 per child in 1998 and $500 per child thereafter.

The *earned income tax credit* (EITC) is commonly thought to aid the "working poor," but many single parents find they can qualify for the EITC, as do two-earner families with lower incomes. Unlike most credits, the EITC allows the taxpayer to get a cash refund even if the credit exceeds the total tax liability. Other complex computations make the child tax credit refundable under certain circumstances, yet for most it can only be used to reduce taxes owed. (See Chapter 10 for information on education tax credits.)

COMPARING DEDUCTIONS, EXCLUSIONS, AND CREDITS: THE TAX BOTTOM LINE

Although given for different reasons, exclusions and deductions have the same effect on your income tax. Both provide only a proportional reduction of your tax bill. Credits, on the other hand, provide dollar-for-dollar savings. Figure 5.3 is a quick example of how the three work, assuming you have a 31% marginal tax rate.

FIGURE 5.3   THE VALUE OF TAX BREAKS

DEDUCTIONS	
Deduction for qualified moving expenses	$2,000
Marginal tax rate	× 31%
Federal income tax savings	= $ 620

EXCLUSIONS	
Life insurance proceeds received	$2,000
Marginal tax rate	× 31%
Federal income tax savings	= $ 620

CREDITS	
Child care tax credit	$2,000
Federal income tax savings	$2,000

Deferrals

Accountants like to follow the "least and latest" rule. Pay the least amount at the latest date possible. Based on the simple financial rule of the time value of money, whereby a dollar today is worth more than a dollar tomorrow because of the interest that could be earned on that dollar today, this strategy makes sense. In tax planning there is an additional rationale: If you defer income while you are in a high income bracket, then you may be able to recognize the income when you are in a lower bracket. For example, if you deferred $10,000 that would have been taxed at 39.6% during peak earning years, after retirement the identical $10,000 might be taxed at 28%, and you would save $1,160 (the $3,960 tax that would be owed at 39.6% minus the $2,800 tax that would be owed at 28%).

Comparing Taxes

Given a variety of circumstances, the same family's identical gross income can lead to very different tax bills. Take the example of George and Elizabeth, who earn a combined total of $120,000 and file jointly in each of two years. In Year 1, George and Elizabeth both work in marketing, have no children, and take the standard deduction.

By Year 3, the couple has a baby boy, so they now have three personal exemptions. The couple has purchased a home, allowing them to deduct mortgage interest and property taxes. Now they have enough deductions to itemize on Schedule A. In addition, with the child, they can qualify for 20% of the maximum $2,400 child care tax credit. *Note:* The credit ranges from 30% down to 20% of a maximum of $2,400 of expenses. The 20% rate is reached at $28,000 AGI.

For the purposes of this simplified comparison, tax rates and exemption amounts have been left constant using 1997 amounts while social security and state income taxes have been omitted. (See Figure 5.4.)

FIGURE 5.4 COMPARING TWO FAMILIES' TAXES

	YEAR 1	YEAR 3
Gross income	$120,000	$120,000
Consulting business expenses	0	13,000
IRA contribution (deferred income)	0	2,000
Adjusted gross income	120,000	105,000
Personal exemptions (2 in year 1, 3 in year 3)	5,300	7,950
Standard deduction	6,700	0
$5,000 mortgage property interest/ taxes paid in year 3	N/A	5,000
$2,000 substantiated charitable contribution	N/A	2,000
Total itemized deductions	N/A	7,000
Current taxable income	107,800	90,050
0–$41,200 × 15%	6,180	6,180
$41,200–$99,600 × 28%	16,352	13,678
$99,600–$151,750 × 31%	2,542	0
Federal income tax liability	25,074	19,858
Child care tax credit $2,400 × 20%	0	480
Tax paid	$ 25,074	$ 19,378

In each new family configuration, the variables shown in the example above change with each set of circumstances. Since tax issues are fact-based, review the Special Advice Chart at the end of this chapter as a jog for your own search through your tax form to find other items that affect your family taxes.

As for tax strategy, don't have a child or buy a home to save taxes. The costs of raising a child far outstrip any tax benefits conferred, and buying a home should involve other issues such as your mobility, the investment opportunity, and so forth. But, as you can see from the example of George and Elizabeth, all other things being equal, these two family additions subtract a heap of taxes.

Tax-savvy people know that outside of state income tax and charitable contributions the middle class enjoys only two remaining large categories of deductions:

- Home ownership (mortgage interest, property taxes)
- Business ownership, especially a small corporation

We've seen the advantages of home ownership in the example above. To estimate the rough value of a potential mortgage interest deduction to your family in the beginning years of a mortgage, multiply the annual interest rate by the amount of the loan. Then multiply the resulting annual interest by your current marginal tax bracket (see Figure 5.5 for tax terms) and you'll have the estimated annual tax savings. In the example above, the couple saved $5,000 a year on interest and property tax deductions. At their previous top rate of 31%, that amounts to a net tax savings of $1,550.

Note: Mortgages front-load the interest, deferring the payment of principal primarily to the second half of the life of the mortgage. In later years, the interest break would decline.

As for owning a business, key advantages are the ability to deduct 100% of business costs rather than having to exceed a floor, the ability to deduct business interest, the right to deduct fees for professionals who advise the business, and many others. Home office deductions have been tricky in the past because of strict "principal place of business" rules. Starting in tax years after 1998, a home office can qualify as long as there is no other *fixed* location of the trade or business where the taxpayer conducts *substantial* administrative or management activities of the trade or business. While self-employment tax rates can be double those of regular tax rates, they are reduced by a percentage of regular income tax paid and by the aforementioned tax deductions.

In addition, if your business is incorporated into a C-Corp, for example, that does not pass through the taxes to your individual return, the income you earn and leave in the corporation is taxed at a lower rate—15% for up to $50,000 of taxable income compared to the cutoff of $41,200 for married filers and $33,050 for heads of households. The C-Corp, as compared with Schedule C of the 1040, also requires no burden of proof that the business is not a hobby. Losses can be accumulated year after year as

Figure 5.5 Tax Terms

Adjusted gross income (AGI): Income after subtracting excluded income and certain before-AGI deductions, such as self-employment taxes paid, some moving expenses, alimony paid, and business expenses. Appears on the bottom line of the first page of federal tax form 1040.

Capital gains: Appreciation realized from investments that had increased in value when they were sold (i.e., stocks or real estate). Net capital gains are usually taxed at a rate more favorable than ordinary income because, it is argued, this break encourages investment.

Credits: Dollar-for-dollar reductions of your tax liability.

Deductions: Expenses that can be subtracted from your income to determine your taxable income.

Deferrals: The portion of your tax liability that does not have to be paid until a future period.

Estate tax: Tax paid on the current value of a deceased person's total assets. In 1996, $625,000 of this amount is excluded from estate taxes, which will rise in stages until it reaches $1,000,000 in 2006.

Exclusions: Income that is not included as part of your taxable income (i.e., it is not taxed).

Filing status: Married, filing jointly; married, filing separately; single; head of household (unmarried person with one or more dependents); or qualifying widow/er with dependent.

Gross income: Income earned in any form from any source.

Income tax: Tax paid on all taxable income earned.

IRC: The Internal Revenue Code.

IRS: The Internal Revenue Service.

Itemized deduction: Expenses that may be subtracted from your adjusted gross income to determine your taxable income. These deductions, which require you to keep records of your expenses, would be taken if they exceed your standard deduction (which is often the case when you own your own home).

Loopholes: Legal, but often sophisticated, means of reducing your tax liability. The term can refer to exclusions, deductions, credits, and deferrals.

Figure 5.5 (Continued)

Marginal tax rate: The tax rate for an additional dollar of taxable income earned.

Passive losses: Losses realized from investments in which you are not actively engaged (i.e., losses from an investment in a real estate limited partnership).

Personal exemption: An annually fixed, per-person deduction that is subtracted from your adjusted gross income for yourself, your spouse, and each of your qualifying dependents to determine your taxable income.

Progressive tax: Higher levels of income are taxed at higher rates than are lower levels of income.

Regressive tax: Higher levels of income are taxed at lower rates.

Standard deduction: An annually fixed deduction, based on your filing status, which may be subtracted from your adjusted gross income instead of subtracting itemized deductions.

Taxable income: Adjusted gross income less other deductions and personal exemptions.

Tax rate: The percentage of each taxable dollar earned that goes to the government. For example, for every taxable dollar earned at a 15% tax rate, 15 cents goes to the government. Under a stepped system, different tax rates apply to different levels of income. Under current rates, if you are a single filer with $30,000 in taxable income in 1997, the first $24,650 will be taxed at 15% and the remaining $5,350 will be taxed at 28%.

---

the business develops, carried forward, and deducted in later, more profitable, years.

While business taxation is a complex area not quickly summarized, the key point to remember is this: If you are in business for yourself, be sure to work with an accountant who knows the rules for small businesses and services a number of similar clients. Also, consider using one of the simpler computer corporate tax programs, such as Turbo-Tax™, to prefigure your business tax and save yourself professional fees. Unless you know the tax code cold, then turn the computer version over to your accountant for fine-tuning, as past versions of software have contained glitches.

FIGURE 5.6 4M INCOME TAX STRATEGIES

4 Ms	FAMILY INCOME	TAX SAVINGS OPPORTUNITIES
MODEST	Under $50,000 per year	• Take full $2,000 contribution to IRAs. • Take child care tax credit. • Take earned income tax credit. • Qualify for mortgage interest and property tax deductions credit in expensive parts of the country.
MEDIUM	$50,000 to $100,000 per year	• Check all of the above. • Make 401(k) maximum contribution. • Record group health insurance premiums and other deductible expenses throughout the year. • If employer offers flexible spending account, may deduct up to $5,000 in child care expenses compared to $2,400 child care credit.
MAJOR	$100,000 to $250,000 per year	• Check all of the above. • Use mortgage-residential valuation. • Make full 401(k), IRA, and annuity contributions.
MEGA	$250,000 and above	• Check all of the above. • Look at investments with tax shelter components, so long as economically sound.

Figure 5.6 above presents income tax strategies for each of the 4M categories.

YOUR ANNUAL FINANCIAL CHECKUP

No matter what format or combination of techniques for budgeting and controlling expenditures you use, eventually the time will come for a financial review.

While most of us approach tax time with dread, use the annual roundup of numbers to review your spending. Your paperwork is out, your expenses are laid bare for you and the IRS, and, truthfully, most of today's families are too busy to spend more than a single intense period per year on their finances. Before you leave taxes behind, take time to check how you performed against your original goals and budgeting plans for the year. Use the annual numbers, rather than the monthly ones, and get a family bottom line for the year.

- ✔ Did your expenses exceed your income? If so, you know that you'll have to cut back.
- ✔ Did your income and expenses exactly match? If so, you'll need to add savings.
- ✔ If you are saving now, did you take sufficient advantage of tax incentives to put money aside for education and retirement? If not, now's the time to start.

By approaching tax time as an opportunity to strategize as well as a time to ante up, your perspective on both taxes and expenditure control changes. After all, it's your money that's going to the government—or out the door in spending you can't afford.

LEGAL LESSONS: TAX POLICY

Nowhere is our national schizophrenia over family policy more clearly spelled out than in tax policy. Hidden from view most of the time, tax policy either rewards or punishes large or small families, married or single people, single parents, two-earner, or sole-breadwinner families.

During each political tax season, the tinkering continues on family-oriented items such as the exemption for each family member (rewards high-income large families, doesn't help low-income families as much), the disparate rates among household types, the child care tax credit, the earned income credit, and now the child tax credit. The political left and right find themselves at odds, and their perspectives on tax policy rest squarely on their views about gender roles. In addition, many but not all conservative leaders see themselves as representing more affluent families. While welfare mothers are criticized for having more children, and cutoff points for government support through welfare appear periodically on the political agenda, middle-income families receive rewards from the government for the same activity through exclusions, dependent and child care deductions and credits, and now the child tax credit. In addition, like the tax system itself, much of family tax policy rests on the single-earner model, political rhetoric to the contrary.

Whether taxes shape policy or policy shapes taxes is a chicken-and-egg question best left to scholars. Certainly, when it comes to tax issues that affect families, especially working families, social change has left tax change in the dust. It took many years for a fully available child care tax deduction to develop and many more for the credit to appear, from the first glimmers in the 1940s, when only women who were the sole breadwinners, and low earners to boot, could count child care as a legitimate work expense to the credit now in place that still limits reimbursement no matter how many children a family has.

The rate charts (see Figure 5.1, progression of tax stairs) attempt to level the playing field by providing an approximately equivalent rate at each income bracket, taking into account, in theory, the size of the family.

Likewise, the standard deduction varies to acknowledge that basic household maintenance costs depend on the size and type of family. In 1997, the standard deduction for a single taxpayer stood at $4,150; for married couples, $6,900; and for heads of household, $6,050. Previously, the rate tables, in theory, recognized the differential costs attributable to running various households. For example, single people reached a higher tax bracket with less income than did a married couple filing jointly. The presumption was that a married couple will earn and use more income for their basic needs than will a single person. Today, the playing field is somewhat leveled through the combination of the standard deduction and personal exemption amounts. However, a phenomenon popularly referred to as the "marriage tax" in effect penalizes one of the most common types of today's families—married two-earners. At first glance, it seems that single filers are penalized (see table) since they have a lower standard deduction and a lower AGI will thrust them into the next higher tax bracket. In the past, when a traditional single-earner married couple was more common, these factors may have worked in favor of the married couple. However, thinking in terms of today's family with two incomes, it is more accurate to compare a two-earner married couple to two single earners, which draws attention to an obvious disadvantage for married two-earner families (see Figure 5.7).

But, no matter the filing status, an exemption or deduction is more valuable in higher brackets. In 1997, the exemption amount reached an all-time high of $2,650. For the 31% tax rate with a family of four and a taxable income of $125,000, the $10,600 in exemptions would be worth $3,300, while a family of four in the 15% bracket would receive only $1,590 worth of relief.

That effect led Congress to enact an income-related phaseout for the personal exemption (for each member of the family). In 1997, the personal exemption was phased out for adjusted gross incomes above $181,800 for joint filers; above $151,500 for heads of households; and above $121,200 for single filers.

In addition, still faced with a disproportionate tax on middle-income families, Congress and the administration passed the child tax credit, a credit to be phased out in higher income brackets but awarded to families with children.

FIGURE 5.7   COMPARISON OF STANDARD DEDUCTIONS AND RATES

	SINGLE	MARRIED FILING JOINTLY	SINGLE × 2
Standard deduction	$4,150	$6,900	$8,300
AGI to move from 15% to 28% tax bracket	$24,650	$41,200	$49,300

In order to see just how tax policy affects your own family's bottom line, as you listen to tax debates, take out last year's tax return and see whether you would qualify for new tax provisions such as the child tax credit and, if so, how much you would save in taxes.

FIGURE 5.8 SPECIAL ADVICE ON TAX STRATEGIES FOR NEW FAMILIES

TYPE OF FAMILY	ADVICE
Two-earner	• If married filing jointly, you have a disadvantage compared to two single filers or married single-earner families. • Those with children take the child tax credit. • Those with child care expenses should calculate taxes using both the dependent care tax credit and a flexible spending account offered through your employer, which may allow you to deduct up to $5,000 in child care expenses. Higher earners will benefit more from the deduction if available.
Single parents	• As a single parent, you are more likely to qualify for the earned income tax credit (EITC). • *Divorced:* If you sold your house, you each can exclude up to $250,000 in capital gains if you meet usage tests: You must have resided at your primary residence two out of the last five years. • *Divorced:* Alimony is tax deductible to the payer and taxable to the payee. If you pay alimony, you can deduct it in a very favorable position, above the adjusted gross income, the figure used to determine if you qualify for other deductions such as medical expenses. If you receive alimony, don't forget to factor in the taxes you will pay on these funds.

Figure 5.8 (Continued)

TYPE OF FAMILY	ADVICE
Single parents *(continued)*	• *Divorced:* Child support is not taxable. The payer may not claim it as a deduction and the payee does not have to report it as income. • *Divorced or separated:* Watch out for "joint and several liability" for tax bills incurred on your "married filing jointly" income tax returns from previous years. Both parties are responsible for unpaid tax liabilities they incurred together and the IRS will take them from whomever is owed a refund. • *Divorced and separated:* If you share custody of the children, the law gives the dependent exemptions to whomever has custody more than half the year. However, the custodial parent can grant the exemption to the other parent for one or more years using form 8832. Negotiate for the exemption as part of your settlement, as it also determines who may take the child tax credit. • *Widowed:* Depending on insurance benefits and your own employment status, your tax picture has changed dramatically. Consult a tax accountant. • *Widowed:* The year your spouse dies, you must file a married filing jointly return. If you qualify, you may file as qualifying widow/er with dependent child for the subsequent two years, giving you the same tax rates and standard deduction as married filing jointly, minus the personal exemption of the deceased. • *Never married:* If you provide the principal residence for your children, you can file as head of household to attain a more favorable tax bracket than a single filer.

FIGURE 5.8 (CONTINUED)

TYPE OF FAMILY	ADVICE
Blended	• Your tax outlook can be confusing because of the array of incoming and outgoing alimony and/or child support, questions about dependent status of the children, and questions about who may take certain credits and deductions. • See "Single parents" above for rules on taxation of alimony/child support and application of child tax credit.
Cohabiting (opposite sex)	• As single filers, you're at a tax advantage if you both file. • Determine if one of you can file as head of household to place you in a more favorable tax bracket. • If you can claim a child under 17 as a deduction, take the child tax credit. • If you've formed a single-earner domestic partnership in which one partner stays home to care for the children or act as a support person, the nonearner cannot be counted as a dependent unless he or she meets the test of local law. The nonearner is not eligible for a spousal IRA. • Strategically plan your charitable contributions and other deductions so that one person can take the standard deduction and the other will have enough qualified deductions to itemize.
Cohabiting (same sex)	• See "Cohabiting (opposite sex)" above.
Adoptive	• You are eligible for child tax credit if adoption is complete. • You are eligible for an adoption credit of up to $5,000 ($6,000 if child qualifies as having special needs) in the year that the adoption was complete and should review other dependent-related credits, including increased medical deductions, increased eligibility for the EITC, child tax credit, and child care credit.

FIGURE 5.8 (CONTINUED)

TYPE OF FAMILY	ADVICE
Adoptive *(continued)*	• If you meet income guidelines, up to $5,000 ($6,000 for special needs child) in employer-provided adoption assistance may be excluded from income.
Foster	• The stipend from the foster agency is not counted as taxable income. However, the child may not be claimed as a dependent. • If the foster child is eligible for the dependent exemption, you may also take the child tax credit.
Wife as breadwinner	• As a single-earner family, you won't be eligible for the child care tax credit because the IRS assumes that the nonearner will care for the children. If the nonearner is a full-time student, you may be eligible for a partial credit. • Be sure to set up a spousal IRA for the nonearning spouse.
Multicultural	• If one of you is recently from another country and not yet a U.S. citizen, you must still file federal income taxes.
Older parents	• Tap into tax savings for retirement and college planning. See sections on IRAs and 401(k)s in Chapter 11 and on tax-deferred bonds in Chapter 10.
Adult children living at home	• If your adult child is disabled, you are entitled to special tax benefits.
Grandchildren living with grandparents	• Determine whether you may claim your grandchild as dependents and therefore take the dependent exemption and child tax credits.

FIGURE 5.8 (CONTINUED)

TYPE OF FAMILY	ADVICE
May-December	• Tax-deferred retirement savings vehicles such as IRAs and 401(k)s assume a lower tax rate in retirement. Since the income of the younger spouse may push the tax bracket up in retirement, consider a Roth IRA, in which the initial contribution is made in after-tax dollars, but earnings are not taxed upon withdrawal.

CHAPTER SIX

Family Financial Emergencies

For the unprepared, an acute financial emergency can easily turn into a chronic financial crisis. And when you're already on edge financially, almost anything can set off a feeling of crisis. From missing that first Visa payment out of pure disorganization to finding yourself hounded by collectors, your responses will dictate your financial outcome.

Before you go ballistic, do an internal check and be sure that the crisis of the moment really is a crisis.

For example, on the way out the door to work, you pull your bills out of the mailbox and see that if your utilities aren't paid by the 24th, your lights will be shut off. It's the 15th, you have money in the bank, and you need to pay the bill. Is this a crisis worthy of turning around and racing into the house to write out a check? No. Do it tonight. Don't throw off your day with a minor annoyance.

On the other hand, if you open the mailbox and see that your mortgage goes into foreclosure tomorrow and you're fresh out of funds, you rightly might categorize the situation as a crisis. But wait. Foreclosures require months of work on a lender's part to throw you out on the street. Is this good for your credit? No. Can you ignore this notice? No. Will you come home tonight to find your personal belongings lining the curb? No. Toughen up. Sometimes you have to play the system. Even without money, payables often can be stretched over weeks, months, or even years, buying you time to recoup.

Learning to recognize a crisis and categorize it is the first step to solving the problem. Don't allow yourself the luxury of self-pity. Wallow in solutions instead. Solving financial emergencies works along lines parallel to the methods of battlefield medics or emergency room nurses. Find the key in *triage*—the method paramedics use to rate victims to determine who to treat first and who can wait. Work first on the dying "patients," but, recognizing that they may go anyway, turn to those you can save. If you can adopt a field nurse point of view and distance yourself from your finances, you'll find you've won half the battle.

No one is immune from economic cycles, but the first time your family hits a downturn, you'll find it especially alarming. In good times, whether as a part of a couple or as a new family, you might have lost sight of the inevitable down cycle—which hits both individuals and economies—and committed yourself to credit obligations that would be beyond your capacity in bad times.

Newly separated or divorced people find themselves particularly vulnerable to overextension. While expenses have soared and income has dropped, so, too, feelings of inadequacy rise while self-esteem drops. Shopping won't cure any of these problems, but sometimes in moments of anguish we forget ourselves and turn to binge spending as a way to stave off the feeling of helplessness. Unfortunately, out-of-control spending only leads to more problems and more depression.

For families in transition, much spending is unavoidable but can quickly drive you into financial quicksand. Unexpected medical needs; expenses necessary to provide family support and counseling; or new housing, automobile, or furniture needs to replace those lost in a divorce settlement are just a few examples.

Divorce is an especially risky time for potential bankruptcies. Ruptures in the fabric of the family, tugs-of-war carried out in the bank account as the marriage falters, and the sheer cost of setting up two families lead many divorcing couples into bankruptcy.

Before you take that step, study the pointers here. But if bankruptcy becomes the only way out, don't beat yourself over the head.

CREDIT CRISIS

While it's best to avoid being caught short, there are times when a credit crunch becomes inevitable. Credit shortages happen to our national economy, so it's not surprising that individual budgets experience them, too.

In the past when institutions faced tight money, they rarely lost their credit but simply had to pay more for it. Nowadays, counties and even the federal government can see funds dry up overnight. But after a governmental credit crisis, the penalty isn't nearly so severe as that for individuals. Once you get one or two black marks on your credit report, you quickly lose the ability to take on new credit at any price—without a systematic effort to rebuild your credit.

If faced with a credit problem, you should start with a damage assessment and tailor your response to the severity of your problem.

1. *Short-term credit crunch:* A temporary, short-term inability to meet your current obligations
2. *Medium-term credit crisis:* A loss of income set off by your divorce, unemployment, business failure, or investment losses, resulting in a need for a six-month to one-year plan to recover
3. *Credit fraud:* A serious situation in which your past exaggerations or even your spouse's financial sins—while you were married—catch up with you
4. *A deeper crisis:* When your debt so far outstrips your ability to pay that you may require bankruptcy code protection

SHORT-TERM CREDIT CRUNCH

A short-term crunch means you reasonably expect that you'll be able to bring your debts current in 60 to 90 days. Your goal here: to keep your credit and credit rating secure while you recover.

Short-term tactics include the following:

- List all bills.
- Note due dates and grace periods.
- Pay bills only at the end of the grace period—the computer doesn't know the difference, as long as the payment reaches the creditor before the late period.
- Send only the minimum due, but pay something on all your bills. Don't pay all of some bill and none of another.
- Don't charge anything on cards that are due in 30 days, such as American Express or Diners Club™.

Your immediate posture centers on convincing your creditors that you're operating as usual. If you use these credit-stretching tactics to preserve your credit rating, a short-term credit crunch won't leave you with damaged credit for years to come.

Medium-Term Credit Crisis

If the crisis extends beyond your ability to stretch your credit, you need to prioritize in a process similar to emergency room triage. For the sake of the most salvageable "patients," you'll need to let some of your credit "die."

The first cut should depend on creditors' responses: the more cooperative the creditor, the greater your benefit from paying something, however small.

- Call or write creditors with an explanation that you've met difficulties and you intend to pay your bills. Ask for their cooperation.
- Call people you know personally, such as doctors, local stores, and others where you need continuing services, and try to work out payment plans that keep the relationship alive.
- Get your credit report and monitor who's on your case. If accounts are missing from the report, the likelihood is strong that the creditor won't report you for a while.

Making the choice about what to keep current and what to let slide can be excruciating because, once you've defaulted on bills, creditors will call. If you aren't able to pay within a certain period, their efforts escalate, depending on other factors. If you have a home that can be attached or a salary that can be garnished, creditors will persist and may even take you to court. On the other hand, if your resources are scant, stonewalling may produce an end to active efforts.

The creditor may use credit-reporting services and property reports obtained from county recording offices to find your assets. However, in most instances consumers, not computers, tell creditors exactly what they need to know.

Since you're probably in a fragile state from the stresses that caused your credit crisis, stay off the phone with collectors. Use an answering machine to screen calls, and assert your key legal rights. These include the right not to be called at work and the right not to be called at all if you so request in writing.

DEBT COLLECTORS AND YOUR RIGHTS

Assert your legal rights with collectors. Collectors have no right to call you early in the morning or late at night. They have no right to call you at work once you have asked them not to in writing. For that matter, once you ask *in writing* not to be called, creditors cannot call you unless they intend to take more formal legal steps.

Creditors and collectors all too often violate these procedures, so log any calls you receive, noting the time and date, and use this evidence against the collector. Many a consumer debt has been forgiven in exchange for consumers' not suing overly aggressive collectors.

Also, get an answering machine and use it to filter unwanted calls. You have no obligation to talk to hordes of angry collectors, thereby making your mental outlook more difficult.

CREDIT FRAUD

If you puffed up your income for a mortgage application, falsified your tax returns to support a business loan application, or spent on a credit card you knew you couldn't pay, creditors can and may go after you for fraud.

Fortunately for you, fraud is one of the hardest causes of action to prove. To find fraud, the court must find four elements in concert with one another, including the following: (1) The creditor must have knowledge of a material *misrepresentation* of a past or existing fact; (2) the creditor must have *relied* on that fact; (3) the creditor's reliance must have been to its *detriment;* and (4) there had to be *intent* to induce reliance.

Right now, don't take chances. If you know in your heart of hearts you lied or if you suspect your spouse engaged in fraud, seek the help of an attorney experienced in this area of the law. You don't want to play around with fraud charges because you could land in jail and lose your children.

Also, fraudulent obligations aren't dischargeable—if proven—in bankruptcy, so there's no relief in sight from the bankruptcy courts.

There is one piece of protection you can use: Often creditors charge fraud when, in fact, legal fraud is not at issue. If a credit collection agency hounds you for unpaid bills and charges fraud, keep track of the telephone calls in a log or diary. The consumer protection laws may provide you a safe haven if collectors step overboard, because they will fear that you might countersue for violation of these federal statutes.

Again, your best recourse is to see an attorney. Remember, attorney-client privilege offers you protection. Your attorney has a legally binding reason not to reveal your confidences, and attorneys can lose their licenses if they break confidences. And if your spouse engaged in fraudulent acts, in many instances, depending on both the facts and state law, you won't be legally liable.

WHEN A CRISIS DEEPENS

According to the American Bankruptcy Institute, an industry group, the number of consumer bankruptcies filed annually nationwide exceeded 1 million for the first time ever in 1996.

If your family emergency has turned into an extended period of crisis, certainly do not rule out bankruptcy protection. But remember, many of the creditors will go away if you don't return their phone calls. Reason: After 90 days, most debts are uncollectible anyway, and collectors know that.

Considering Bankruptcy

The key bankruptcy code provisions are as follows:

Chapter 7: Asset liquidation. Used by individuals or businesses that can't pay their debts from their income. All except *exempt* possessions (usually determined by state laws) are sold and money is divided by creditors. Provides a "fresh start," but stays on record for 10 years. Chapter 7 can be filed only every 6 years.

Chapter 11: Usually used to reorganize a business while the business continues to operate. Used by large corporations, but is open to both individuals and businesses with sizable debts and assets. If you are in business and facing a financial downturn, remember that, today, bankruptcy must be considered to involve strategy and planning; therefore, you need to consult an attorney expert in this field so that you can come out as financially and legally unscathed as possible.

Chapter 12: Allows farmers to reorganize debts and keep their farms.

Chapter 13: Often called a "wage-earner" petition, allows people and small businesses with regular incomes to pay off all or part of their debts over a three- to five-year period without continuing collection measures from creditors. The upper limit for using Chapter 13 is less than $250,000 in unsecured and less than $750,000 in secured debts. (Secured debts are those in which you have pledged an asset, such as a mortgage; unsecured debts include items such as most credit and department store cards, except where you have made a major purchase such as furniture, appliances, etc.)

Although bankruptcy can give you and your family a fresh start, filing for bankruptcy itself can be costly and time consuming, especially if you have assets. All forms of bankruptcy will mar your credit report for 10 years.

On the positive side, while you're in a bankruptcy program, creditors cannot foreclose on your home, repossess your car, garnishee your wages, shut off your utilities, or proceed with any debt collection activities. Depending on the type of bankruptcy you file, most of your unsecured debt (such as credit cards) will be forgiven, but child support, alimony, fines, taxes, and some student loan obligations may not be excused. Also dependent on the type you file and the state you live in, your secured debts such as a home or car may still not be safe after the bankruptcy proceedings are over, since you must resume payments on them in order to keep them.

On the negative side, asset liquidation can leave a family with few or no assets, depending upon state law, while Chapter 13 leaves you reporting to the bankruptcy trustee, the court's representative, for a period of years.

The choice of whether to file and the decision about which type of protection to seek should be made in consultation with an experienced bankruptcy attorney who knows the law in your state and the judges and trustees in the court.

Avoiding Bankruptcy

As you can see, while bankruptcy is right for many, this cure for your financial woes can be a hard medicine to swallow. As with physical diseases, the sooner you detect your financial ailments, the greater the chance for recovery. If you catch it early enough, you may be able to handle your financial problem on your own or with the help of an agency such as Consumer Credit Counseling Service (800-388-2227), a nonprofit organization that provides free or low-cost credit counseling, help creating and sticking to a personal budget, and assistance negotiating with your creditors. But note that using this service will not protect your credit rating and it essentially operates much like Chapter 13, except your debts are *not* forgiven.

A better plan, if you want to avoid the stigma and expense of bankruptcy, is to retain a good negotiator to get creditors to take a percentage on the dollar of your debts. Called an *informal work-*

out, this process avoids the courts and often can produce results that work best for you and the creditor.

AFTER THE CRISIS IS OVER: RESTORING YOUR CREDIT

Once you have been in credit trouble, television advertisements to the contrary, no easy or quick fixes can clean up your credit. Instead, federal law provides that the credit-reporting agency or bureau can show late or defaulted debts for 7 years and bankruptcy for 10. Immediately following a credit crisis is not the time to go shopping for new credit in any case. Usually, if you have reduced circumstances, it's better to wait at least a year or two. By that time, if you've turned your credit life around and your payments are current, then you may find an individual bank officer willing to take a chance on you. But it's unrealistic to expect immediate restoral of your credit history.

However, the law does provide protections to ensure that your credit, however it looks, is reported accurately. Use the law to clean up your credit. Also, use it following a divorce to be sure you have credit in your own name.

Correcting Your Credit Report

Three major agencies and countless local feeder companies carry your name on file.

The three national companies are:

Equifax Credit Information
P.O. Box 105873
Atlanta, GA 30348
800-685-1111 or 770-375-2500

Trans Union Corporation
P.O. Box 390
Springfield, PA 19064-0390
800-888-4213 or 770-396-0961

Experian
P.O. Box 2104
Allen, TX 75013-2104
800-682-7654 or 800-392-1122

Prices vary according to state law, from $2 to about $8. If denied credit, employment, or insurance within the last 60 days, you are entitled to a free copy.

When you receive your reports, review them carefully.

- Verify that your name, current home address, employer, and (if applicable) salary are up to date.
- Ensure that individual accounts of your ex-spouse are not listed. (If you had joint accounts when you were married, they may stay on your report for some time.)
- Check for incomplete information such as paid-off or closed accounts that are still listed as open or unpaid.
- Check for accounts or other information that you don't recognize. Most commonly due to mistakes, they could also result from fraudulent accounts set up illegally by third parties using your credit information.
- Examine negative entries and determine whether they are accurate. If you suspect that a mistake may have been made, shift the burden of proof to the credit-reporting bureau by requesting that it check the listing. The bureau has 60 days to investigate your *written* complaint.
- Even if you can't dispute negative entries, make sure that they are accurate and as up to date as possible while reflecting your side of the story if that would be of help. For instance, if delinquent items have been paid off, it should be noted. You have a legal right to insert up to 100 words in your report by each entry—use it, if you think an explanation will improve your chances for credit in the future.
- Correct erroneous entries or note accounts on the dispute form that the agency supplies with your report. The process sometimes hits a snag when the creditor reporting the erro-

neous entry insists that it is correct. In that case, dispute it with the creditor rather than the credit-reporting agency.

Wherever the blame for the error may lie, it's your responsibility to find it and correct it. Save your money by doing it yourself. When the negative entries on your credit report are correct, there's nothing a lawyer or television spokesperson can do that you can't do yourself, using the guidelines above.

Figure 6.1 presents suggested amounts in liquid funds to maintain for each 4M category to avoid financial emergency.

LEGAL LESSONS: FEDERAL CREDIT PROTECTION

Knowing your rights can protect you and your family from a host of credit worries, from collectors' calls at work to money charged by thieves to your cards.

Major federal credit legislation includes the following:

Truth in Lending Act

JULY 1, 1969: Requires creditors to disclose specific costs of annual percentage rates and finance charges in dollar amounts as well as other loan terms and conditions; regulates the advertising of such terms; provides the right to cancel a contract when certain real estate is used as security.

FIGURE 6.1 4M CUSHION FOR AVOIDING FINANCIAL EMERGENCIES

4 Ms	FAMILY INCOME	AMOUNT IN LIQUID FUNDS
MODEST	Under $50,000 per year	$10,000 in savings
MEDIUM	$50,000 to $100,000 per year	$11,000 to $20,000 in savings
MAJOR	$100,000 to $250,000 per year	$25,000 to $50,000 in savings
MEGA	$250,000 and above	$100,000+ in savings

JANUARY 25, 1971: Prohibits credit card issuers from sending unrequested cards; limits a cardholder's liability for unauthorized use of card to $50.

OCTOBER 1, 1982: Requires disclosures for installment (closed-end) credit to be written in plain English and appear apart from all other information; allows credit customer to request an itemization of the amount financed if the creditor does not automatically provide it.

Fair Credit Reporting Act

APRIL 24, 1971: Requires disclosure to consumers of the name and address of any consumer reporting agency that supplied reports used to deny credit, insurance, or employment; gives a consumer the right to know what is in his or her file, have incorrect information reinvestigated and removed, and include his or her version of a disputed item in the file; requires credit-reporting agencies to send the consumer's version of a disputed item to certain businesses or creditors; sets forth identification requirements for consumers wishing to inspect their files; requires that the consumer be notified when an investigative report is being made; limits the time certain information can be kept in a credit file.

Fair Credit Billing Act

OCTOBER 28, 1975: Establishes procedures for consumers and creditors to follow when billing errors occur on periodic statements for revolving credit accounts; requires creditors to send a statement setting forth these procedures to consumers periodically; allows consumers to withhold payment for faulty or defective goods or services (within certain limitations) when purchased with a credit card; requires creditor to promptly credit customers' accounts and to return overpayments if requested.

Equal Credit Opportunity Act

OCTOBER 28, 1975: Prohibits credit discrimination based on sex and marital status; prohibits creditors from requiring women to reapply for credit upon a change in marital status; requires creditors to inform applicants of acceptance or rejection of their credit application within 30 days of receiving a completed application; requires creditors to provide a written statement of the reasons for adverse action.

MARCH 23, 1977: Prohibits credit discrimination based on race, national origin, religion, age, or the receipt of public assistance.

JUNE 1, 1977: Requires creditors to report information on an account to credit bureaus in the names of both husband and wife if both use the account and both are liable for it.

Fair Debt Collection Practices Act

MARCH 20, 1978: Prohibits abusive, deceptive, and unfair practices by debt collectors; establishes procedures for debt collectors contacting a credit user; restricts debt collector contacts with a third party; specifies that payment for several debts be applied as the consumer wishes and that no monies be applied to a debt in dispute. If you think that one or more of your rights have been violated, take action first through the channels provided for you by the laws. If you are not able to correct the violation to your satisfaction, see Appendix A for a list of agencies you can contact for help.

FIGURE 6.2 SPECIAL ADVICE FOR FAMILY FINANCIAL EMERGENCIES

TYPE OF FAMILY	ADVICE
Two-earner	• If married, it's okay to have joint accounts, but each individual should carry at least one major account in his or her own name. • If it becomes apparent that parts of your credit will have to be sacrificed, try to save joint accounts first. Then determine whether it will be possible to save one of your credit reports and let the other one get the black marks. It's better for one person to go than the entire ship, and if joint accounts are saved you'll have a start on future creditworthiness.

FIGURE 6.2 (CONTINUED)

TYPE OF FAMILY	ADVICE
Single parents	• *Divorced and separated:* Make sure you separate your credit histories if you haven't done so. Remove your name from all jointly held accounts. • *Separated:* While you can't close a jointly held mortgage, you should include equitable payment arrangements in your separation papers. If you do come to divorce, include a provision that you won't sign over the house to your ex-spouse unless he or she agrees to take your name off the mortgage. • *Widowed:* If the deceased had a lengthy illness, your medical bills could be staggering. Negotiate a realistic payment schedule for the part you must pay. • *Widowed:* If your spouse held individual credit cards, the debts may have been extinguished upon his or her death. Consult a lawyer before paying or responding to threats from the creditors. • *Never married:* Keep a regular bookkeeping appointment with yourself so you can see a crisis coming and avert it while still a crunch.
Blended	• Like two-earner families, you are susceptible to credit glitches. One of you thought the other paid that bill and, before you know it, you've got a string of late fees and minor black marks on your credit report. Get your timing down and a schedule in place to prevent financial tasks from falling through the cracks.
Cohabiting (opposite sex)	• You may have cosigned the mortgage or hold other joint accounts, but each of you should keep an individual financial identity.
Cohabiting (same sex)	• See "Cohabiting (opposite sex)" above.
Adoptive	• See "Two-earner" above.
Foster	• See "Two-earner" above.

FIGURE 6.2 (CONTINUED)

TYPE OF FAMILY	ADVICE
Wife as breadwinner	• If the husband is completely out of the workforce, he needs to build and maintain credit in his own name.
Multicultural	• See "Two-earner" above.
Older parents	• See "Two-earner" above.
Adult children living at home	• Be cautious about cosigning for your adult children if you don't truly have the resources to bail them out when something goes wrong.
Grandchildren living with grandparents	• See "Two-earner" above.
May-December	• One of you has had more time to get pluses and minuses on your credit report. Now that you share finances, use that information to determine strategy in a crisis.

CHAPTER SEVEN

Boundaries: Yours, Mine, and Ours

In this chapter, we look at issues that lie at the heart of family finances. The more complex the arrangements and diverse the members, the greater the challenge of balancing the personal, financial, and legal needs of each family member with the needs of the whole group.

Since psychological questions underlie many financial and legal issues, achieving balance often involves attending to competing emotional needs of gender role definition, blended-family dynamics, and age differentials. In addition, the "yours, mine, and ours" legal agreements you've made with current or previous partners become an important determinant in the ease of balancing the other variables.

YOURS, MINE, AND OURS: THEORY AND PRACTICE

By now, most of us are fully familiar with the notion that couples require their own financial divisions of labor. For example, in traditional families a generation ago, it was uncommon for a woman to have a checkbook. Instead, the patriarch doled out a household allowance once a week. The homemaker's challenge entailed mediating among children's lunch money, allowance, clothing, and toy demands, while using the money to put food on the table and run the household.

Since the early 1970s when women began entering the workforce in increasing numbers each year, they have gained a solid footing in the realm of family finances. In 3 million couples, women find themselves the sole breadwinners. And in 21.9% of two-earner families, the wife earns more than the husband. Finally, single-parent families headed by women now number 7% of all families—as many as the traditional family.

Now that women wield more financial power, marketing financial products to women has become big business. A headline a few years ago in the *Washington Post* said it all: "Credit for Women: Yesterday's Pariah, Today's Market." In fact, now women face an opposite challenge, that of controlling debt.

Yet women are still more likely to involve their husbands in the family financial decisions. By contrast, men often place the family financial security on the line without thinking it necessary to confer with their wives, much less allow them to exercise veto power.

Of course, both of these models leave something to be desired. A dialogue about "yours, mine, and ours" must occur in each family so that family members are free to pursue their dreams while others can enjoy a sense of security and trust that their futures won't be placed at risk.

The Theory

The theory of closeness with boundaries in complex families is hard enough to understand and even harder to put into practice. From separate toy shelves to separate checkbooks, in the frenetic mix of daily life, boundaries that seemed reasonable at quieter moments can quickly erode. Adults and children alike need to meet certain expectations, but with too much to do and too little time, who hasn't grabbed a busy member of the family and asked for just one more favor or one more advance on next week's allowance?

Each family member, no matter the age, gender, or financial capacity, must have some money that belongs solely to that individual, who exercises complete control. If another family member blows his or her own stash, the saver must not be punished for the spender's mistakes.

LEARNING FROM OUR MISTAKES

Everyone makes parenting mistakes that can have a financial impact on the family. One of the worst examples in Emily's recent life involved her son Waldo's savings account. At a moment when money was tight, she drew out the thousand dollars he had carefully saved from his allowance, thinking she'd put it back right after Christmas. Instead, months passed and she forgot about his money. In early summer, Waldo wanted to buy a new mountain bike he had eyed longingly all winter. When he finally went to check his account, he was devastated to learn the money had been spent at Christmas, even if it was on toys for him.

As a parent, especially one who writes about (and tries to apply) good financial practices, she felt her behavior was totally unacceptable. Not only had she violated Waldo's sense of security about his checking account, but undermined his faith that if he saved money, it would be there later. From an early age, this child has always carefully squirreled away part of his allowance. Suddenly, he seemed uninterested in collecting it.

She shares this painful story because it illustrates clearly how a single, thoughtless financial act can undermine years of careful teaching.

In many families, the demands made on family members by others become a source of constant contention, while in families with teenagers, finding family moments may be difficult. Between divorced parents, competition for emotions and attention sometimes proves fierce. With remarriage and the formation of blended families, relationships become even more complex.

Thinking of a calculus equation helps illustrate how individual family members' time, attention, and money demands create a ripple effect for other members. In calculus, a curved line on a graph represents a constantly changing set of vectors that impact

114 PROTECTING YOUR FAMILY

on a moving point—the locus—of the equation. Think of your basic family structure as the x-y axes (see Figure 7.1), or the grid in which individual dramas are played out. Each member of the current family or previous spouse or partner would be represented by a curve graphed on the x-y axes. While the individual curves can run parallel or perpendicular, cross or recross, no two curves can be exactly the same. The locus of each individual is, by definition, different from the locus or path of any other individual in the family. But each person's actions change the relationship between the lines.

THE PRACTICE

All but sociopathic parents want the best for their children as each parent defines *best*. But if you always put your children's needs front and center, you'll ignore your own adult requirements of nourishment and growth. Airlines' standard emergency

FIGURE 7.1 FAMILY EQUATION IN CONSTANT MOTION

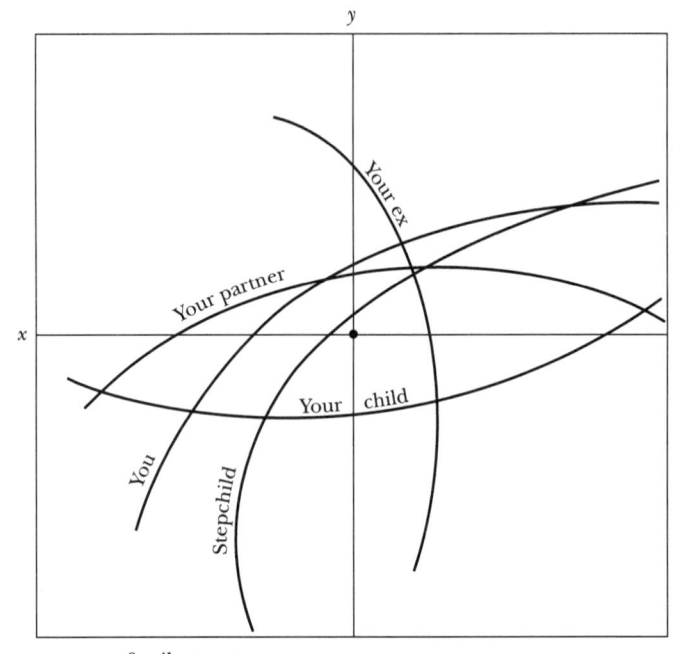

x-y axes = family structure

instructions apply to you, too. Put on your own oxygen mask first before helping the children. In addition, many of the activities suggested here can be done alone or with a partner or children.

AVOIDING PERSONAL BURNOUT

Counteract or avoid burnout by taking care of yourself regularly. Learn how to find hidden moments to treat yourself. If you have an hour for lunch, take along a novel. Read a few pages at lunch, then tuck the book away to look forward to at bedtime. If you lunch at your desk, shut the door for five minutes and call someone you miss. Spend an extra minute in the bathroom after lunch and stretch.

Looking to the natural elements for inspiration always produces instant relief. Every day, make sure you are consciously in touch with each of them, if only for a few moments.

Earth: Garden. Walk barefoot in a patch of grass. Stretch out on Mother Earth. Lie in the sand. Put your arms around a tree. Pick a single leaf and learn it. Buy a bunch of flowers.

Air: Breathe. Open a window. Stand under a tree and feel the extra oxygen. Open the car window and hang your arm out.

Fire: Light the fireplace, even in summer. Make a campfire in the mountains, at the beach, or in the backyard. Roast a marshmallow on a chopstick over a gas burner. Burn candles in the bathroom.

Water: Swim. Shower. Bathe. Surf. Wash your hair and rinse it with cool water. Drink plenty of pure water.

Jot down your own favorite techniques for staying centered and keeping in touch with your inner self:

> ### STAYING STRONG, STAYING SANE
>
> 1. **Take a moment to recharge before important events.** When you arrive at a meeting, sit in the car for an extra minute,
>
> *(continued)*

> ### STAYING STRONG, STAYING SANE
> #### (CONTINUED)
>
> close your eyes, and offer a silent prayer. The prayer might be wordless—just a moment to acknowledge that something important could happen if you are open to the possibilities.
>
> 2. Lay out everything you need for busy days the night before. Assemble all of your clothing, from underwear to jewelry, on a chair so you don't have to think in the morning. Pack your briefcase or lay out your papers if you will be working at your desk. It feels good to start and end the day with an empty desk.
>
> 3. If a negotiation or meeting turns tough or you're facing something stressful, such as meeting the principal or making a speech, take a break. Go to the bathroom, wash your face, get centered, and return only when you feel absolutely ready, even if you have to keep others waiting a few extra minutes. They won't start without you, and without the centered you, there's no point in starting anyway.
>
> 4. When the children and family come home, stop everything for five minutes. Look at the sky with your family or even alone and think of your loved ones. If you miss the sunset, pick the *l'heure bleu*, the first evening star, the moon—a cosmic yardstick against which to measure our minute concerns and put them in perspective.

REDUCE STRESS

All of us have our own personal ways to avoid stress. In a busy family setting, one of the quickest ways to build up extra costs is to use money to relieve stress. You know the scenario—time is short, so we eat out. We don't get our exercise and take our vitamins, so we get sick, losing days at work and income. Our clothes can be washed but need touch-up ironing, so we end up getting them dry-cleaned instead.

No one in this society can afford to substitute their own time for all the services they use. Each family must choose those trade-offs between time and money that are most practical, given family factors. But whatever trade-offs you choose, the starting point for saving money is not saving time—time cannot be added to or subtracted from, so it's really not possible to save it—but allocating time with less stress. To do that, pick your own best ways to build stress reduction into your everyday existence. Consider these time-saving techniques:

- *Stay off the telephone.* Screen calls. Don't answer the phone unless you're in the mood to talk. Say an immediate "no, thank you" to telemarketers. Don't talk to creditors unless you want to—the law allows you to write to them and often protects your rights only if you do.

- *Use e-mail.* E-mail has fast become the preferred medium of communication for busy people. You can answer questions when it works for you—not at the other person's convenience. As one visionary leader commented, "It's quieter and saner in cyberspace." If you don't have your own e-mailbox, get one today and exchange e-mail addresses with everyone you meet. Soon you'll find that 50% or more of your calls and letters can be accomplished electronically—faster, cheaper, and more easily.

- *Replace paperwork with electronic systems.* Running a household means paperwork, from tax returns to monthly bills. Modern heads of households juggle an average of six credit cards and write more than 50 checks per month. Put fixed payments on electronic debits either from your bank's electronic system or through Quicken or Microsoft Money. File your taxes electronically—the IRS promises your refund will come sooner if you do.

- *Get help with house and yard work.* Consider hiring help for home and yard. For working families, a regular visit from a cleaning person makes a big difference in the quality of life. If you or your children have allergies, a regular deep-cleaning works wonders. Be sure to pay Social Security and Medicare taxes for domestic help whom you pay over $1,000 per year, unless you use a service. In addition, you may have to pay federal and/or state unemployment taxes. For details, request IRS publication 926 from the IRS publication order line (800-829-3676).

- *Reduce errands.* Some people enjoy errands to the point that they make daily or weekly errands a way of life. But by ordering items that can be delivered—from prescriptions to groceries—you can save money as well as time. Errand running is an invitation to impulse purchasing. Cut it out, save money, and use the extra time to create new diversions, such as reading a good book.
- *Delegate worry to professional worriers.* If you have legal or financial problems that require addressing, don't try to solve them alone. Lawyers and accountants earn their livings by worrying *for* you and psychotherapists earn theirs by worrying *with* you. Even if you can't afford the going market rates for these professionals, you can find local community or government agencies that provide many of the same services.

So delegate real worries to others.

As for the other kind—the irrational worries about what might happen—try spiritual solutions. Whether prayer, meditation, or chanting, use an approach that works, with

---

STRESS SAVERS

1. Don't grocery shop on the way home from work.
2. Let your mail and phone messages wait at least five minutes after you arrive home.
3. Put your worries to bed a half hour before you yourself.
4. Plan ahead for difficult times (holidays, custodial visits in either direction, family parties) so that your budget and emotions are in check.
5. Lower your standards. Although picture-perfect meals and homes look good on television, they rarely make for picture-perfect families.

faith that things will work out. They usually do when we *work* toward solutions, not worry toward them.

- *Simplify, then simplify again.* Most financial terrors arise from complexity. If you're psychologically and educationally equipped to handle complex financial transactions, do so with relish. If not, keep your financial choices simple. You'll lower your risk while raising your level of satisfaction. From credit cards to tax strategies, too much strategy can be as detrimental as too little.

MAKING IT WORK: BALANCING INCOME, CAREER ADVANCEMENT, CHILDREN

Many parents feel caught in a survival struggle, working long hours away from their children simply to pay the bills. Too many think of the changed structures of today's family as imperfect, and the demands of career and family too difficult. We position either/or situations without realizing that the best way to make our lives work involves balancing income, career advancement, and children's needs. Studies show that working parents are healthy parents, emotionally, psychologically, and financially. In the attempt to place children front and center, we often overlook the obvious.

While acknowledging that income and career advancement allow us to provide more for our children, we also blame our work for taking away from the time we have to spend with our families. Yet it's easy to forget that farm families two and three generations ago worked long hours in the fields and quality time amounted to little more than mealtimes and Sunday services. The big brood necessary to run the family farm inevitably meant that children were second-class citizens in a large, extended family unit, for parents rarely set aside time to read to their children or focus on them individually.

Our ideal reality, based on a past model that wasn't all that great in the first place, creates tension as we nostalgically long for idealized images. While "mothers at home" symbolize three square, home-cooked meals, we forget the family problems that were swept under the corner of the rug, right along with the dust that would be hurriedly removed as visitors rang the front doorbell.

Alcoholism, child abuse, spousal abuse, depression, and ennui hid behind the ruffled curtains and manicured lawns satirized in *Little Shop of Horrors*. Ironically, in the 1950s, children's problems were laid at the door of "momism," or the perceived overinvolvement of mothers in raising children, with Dad relegated to his after-dinner pipe and paper. As George Santayana said, "Those who cannot remember the past are condemned to repeat it."

For most of us, as much as we might idealize the past, the present is a better place to live. By accepting new family realities, we can live at peace with our situations rather than struggle to reattain historically suspect models. The trick for balancing work and family lies elsewhere.

Rather than dreaming of traditional family structures, today's families must relearn old budget tricks. No matter what your earnings, if you spend a penny a year more than you earn, your financial life is out of balance. Working harder to make ends meet isn't the answer. Working harder to control spending scores A+.

WORKING SMARTER

Don't assume that you must work more to earn more. Instead, look at ways to work smarter, raising the returns for hours you already put in. To work smarter:

- *Be a valued employee.* You may be biding your time waiting for something better, but don't think of it as a dead-end job or it will become one. Employers and executive recruiters value consistent performance, creativity in problem solving, and positive attitudes. Develop these traits, and when it's time for a raise, promotion, or recommendation, your record will speak for itself. Another payoff is the increased sense of self-worth you get from a job well done.

- *Let your attitude work for you, not against you.* Don't wait until something better comes along to start enjoying yourself.

Change your attitude now, and your positive outlook will become a self-fulfilling prophecy.

- *Count commuting time when figuring your hourly wage.* For example, divide your salary by the number of hours spent in transit as well as on the job. If you have the option of a lower-paying job that is closer to home, savings on travel costs, child care, and quality of life could offset the decrease in earnings.
- *Consider working at home.* If the above example appeals to you, you may be a perfect work-at-home candidate. Could you telecommute to your current job, only visiting the office for meetings or to pick up work? Or would you consider a complete, full-time, entrepreneurial home-based business?
- *Use creative scheduling in your traditional job.* Ask your employer about flextime, which would allow you to arrive or depart at varying times or days. A 40-hour workweek can be achieved, for example, by working four 10-hour days or by working the traditional five days with some days being shorter or longer depending on your needs that particular day.
- *Think carefully about fringe benefits.* Many people stay in otherwise unrewarding jobs because of health insurance benefits. Look into alternative sources of coverage. Group rates are available for college students, members of national organizations such as the American Association of Working Women, and credit unions. A job with a seemingly low wage may offer hidden benefits such as profit sharing and bonus programs. Or benefits that sound great may not be right for your situation.
- *Don't be afraid to ask for a raise.* Think out your points of why your work is valuable to the company. Focus on the extra hours you work, how your productivity has saved (or made) the company money. Before you ask, see two good negotiating books: Robert Mayer's *Power Plays* (Times Books, 1996) and the Harvard Negotiation Project's *Getting to Yes* (Houghton Mifflin, 1992).

Lifestyle Choices

In subsistence societies, people often worked only so long as necessary to earn their livings, then turned to dancing, religious activities, or just relaxing for the remainder of the day. When colonial masters arrived in these societies, often the biggest challenge to building roads and bridges—the infrastructure of colonial rule and the corresponding trade route for exports—lay in keeping workers working. Colonial society found the solution in the *company store*. Operated much like nineteenth-century American mill-town stores, workers were allowed credit up to the extent of their next week's wages, ensuring that workers would be forced to return each week or face stiff debtor's penalties, or even prison.

Many of us feel bound to the company store today, sensing that we work longer and harder for unseen masters. With cash an abstraction and money reduced to electronic blips, the tangible link between money and work has broken. Bill-paying sprees have replaced Friday night payday drinking sprees.

Although families sometimes feel they work longer hours to produce the same lifestyle their parents did, studies show the reality stands in contrast to the perception. People have more, not less, leisure time than a generation ago. Certainly women have less leisure time than men, since women do more of the household and child-rearing work, but even full-time working women have more leisure time than women had in the past.

Why do we feel the time crunch? Many theories have been advanced. My favorite is that so many more items seem to be "must-haves," from aerobics class to children's lessons. Try a small town or a house with no TV for a month and suddenly the hours stretch before you. But it's clear that when we feel short of time, we often pay less attention to our money.

Make a pact with yourself and your family: Spend some time doing nothing. Let yourself and your children daydream. Don't feel that it's necessary to cram every minute with activity. You'll save money, feel freer, and be less stressed.

Figure 7.2 suggests some actions you can take to meet the needs of each family member.

FIGURE 7.2 ACTIONS TO MAINTAIN 4M "YOURS, MINE, AND OURS" BOUNDARIES

4 Ms	FAMILY INCOME	ACTIONS
MODEST	Under $50,000 per year	Boundaries blur. Work to maintain.
MEDIUM	$50,000 to $100,000 per year	Set up accounts, including savings for all.
MAJOR	$100,000 to $250,000 per year	Add trusts, savings, and investments for all.
MEGA	$250,000 and above	Finances open to complex planning, venture investments, trust funds, and generation-skipping trusts.

YOURS, MINE, OURS, AND *THEIRS:* DEALING WITH THE KIDS' "OTHER" PARENTS

You may have ended your *romantic* relationship with your ex, but your *parenting* relationship will continue. In most cases your *financial* relationship will continue. And whether you never married, are separated, or have divorced, your *legal* entanglements are likely to continue as well.

So far in this chapter, we've focused on changes you can make that will help place your individual needs in balance with those of your other family members. Unfortunately, you can exercise no such controls over your ex or your partner's ex. Remember, you can *control* your own actions, *direct* your children's actions, and maybe even *influence* your partner's actions. But if you think you can control your ex, you'll only make yourself crazy. Instead, focus on ways to encourage his or her healthy relationship with your children and maintain balance in your financial and legal arrangements.

Cultivating Constructive Relationships

The emotional and financial payoffs of getting along with the other adults in your child's life can't be overemphasized. Keep relationships cordial if at all possible (except abusive situations). When you were together, you and your ex might have disagreed about everything *except* parenting styles. Or differences over deeply held values may have continually provoked battles and contributed to the downfall of your relationship. If, like most, you disagreed before, consider how much harder it becomes to find common ground when you're no longer emotionally invested in the other parent. But being successful coparents requires your patience as well as your goodwill.

From payment of child support to holiday crises, leave the adult stuff to the adults. Avoid expressing exasperation about the actions of the other parent, at least in front of the children. Teach your children that they can love each of you without denouncing the other.

Grandparents raising grandchildren should keep the same lessons in mind when it comes to their own offspring, the children's parents. Here, the differences in parenting styles can be generational. Or old, pent-up frustrations can come up when parenting this second generation of children.

Controlling emotions in such situations proves taxing, but the adults concerned must try, for the children's sake, to keep their negative feelings to themselves. If not, remaining family ties erode and children lose important emotional supports.

WHEN ABUSE WAS INVOLVED

In cases of spousal and child abuse, sometimes the best relationship to cultivate is no relationship at all. Follow the advice of your attorney, health professional, or counselor to determine a safe course of action.

As a society, we have become more aware of the pervasiveness of abuse, which cuts across economic and ethnic boundaries. Even if you're otherwise financially capable, don't hesitate to seek out community programs aimed at your family. Studies show that the victims of abuse become abusers. Break this behavioral chain by helping yourself and your children heal.

When you or your child is in personal danger, check with your attorney about a *restraining order.* If in place, the police may exercise the order to intervene and arrest the violator. If money is tight, consider filing for a free *protective order* through your district attorney's office. Similarly, the perpetrator can be arrested on criminal charges if he violates it. If there is a future altercation in which police are called, showing the protective order is grounds for arrest.

Note: When abuse is involved, wage garnishment is the only acceptable method of collecting child support.

WHEN THE "OTHER" PARENT IS MISSING IN ACTION

Ideally, both parents are responsible for their children's well-being. But if one parent chooses to drop the ball, the kids can feel abandoned, even if you've made a new family with parent figures they love.

While you might be hurting more from the *financial* abandonment, for the children the psychological costs of a missing parent can't be measured in money. If you're a single parent and the other parent is MIA, provide strong adult role models as surrogates through close friends, relatives, or organizations such as Big Brothers and Big Sisters. Single parents should also fight for the financial support their children deserve, regardless of whether the emotional support will come with it.

Sustaining Financial Support

If your child support payments have slowed to a trickle, you're not alone. In the first place, child support is awarded to the custodial parent in only one-third of all divorces. After a year, only about three-fourths of the awards are still being paid; after five years, the figure dips to only two-thirds. How can you avoid becoming part of these discouraging statistics?

CHANGE YOUR THINKING

If you have been awarded support, you should *expect* it, but not *depend* on it. Learn to live on your family's current income. When payments come in, have them earmarked for certain projects, such as college savings or retirement investments. That way you'll

126 PROTECTING YOUR FAMILY

be able to stay even if the bottom drops out of the child and spousal support floor.

KNOW YOUR RIGHTS

If you are divorced or legally separated, learn the provisions of your settlement and keep your ex in compliance from the beginning. If the ex starts slipping a little and you treat it like no big deal, it can become a big deal. If never married, you may still be entitled to financial support. Check with your state resource office (see the blue pages of your telephone book).

From the beginning, build your case before you even have one. Memphis-based family practice lawyer R. Miles Mason suggests, "Keep a running list of the payments you *do* receive so you'll be more believable when testifying about the ones that *did not* come." Photocopy checks and list the date, check number, and amount of each payment. Cash payments should be recorded as well.

When support payments haven't been coming in on schedule, try sending a monthly bill. Having your stamped, self-addressed return envelope sitting there with the credit card statements and mortgage booklet makes it so easy to pay, it's embarrassing.

Prevent costly misunderstandings by avoiding verbal agreements about changes in alimony or child support with your ex. And never sign anything—even an informal agreement—that your lawyer hasn't approved.

If your informal tactics don't work, keep your children out of it. They should not have to act as collectors or think of you as a nag because you complain about the deadbeat parent they happen to love and even idolize. Instead, ask your family law attorney to try to enforce the agreement through writing a letter to jog your ex into paying. If that approach fails, don't wait long before filing contempt charges against your ex.

EXERCISE YOUR RIGHTS

If child and spousal support have been constantly interrupted or if they're too low, return to court to enforce your support or negotiate for more.

The longer you wait, the harder it will be to collect delinquent support. If your ex is more than a month behind in payments yet still employed, your charges may lead to wage assignment and ultimately jail time in extreme cases. In wage assignment, the employer must pay the child support directly to the county clerk (it will show as a deduction on your ex's pay stub), who will then pay it to you.

A small change (as small as $15) in salary can trigger changes in child support, but it's up to you to file a court order for the increased amount. Don't rely on the generosity of the obliger. Even if larger payments are made for a while, your ex can always fall back on the minimum requirements in your original decree. If you don't have it in writing, the spouse doesn't owe you an extra cent. It's better to get the court order for the larger amount as soon as possible. Exercise your right to monitor income by obtaining a copy of the yearly tax return.

To increase spousal support and alimony, you'll have to return to the court where you received your dissolution or to a new court if you have changed residencies. Marital law is very much state law based. Under the constitution, each state can and does make its own laws that reflect, among other things, historical antecedents and current social and economic outlooks. To complicate matters further, local courts have their own rules and procedural requirements.

As with the initial divorce process, you and your former spouse will have to provide a detailed budget picture, including your income from earnings; other income such as interest; your assets such as house, furniture, and art; monthly living expenses, including rent, utilities, food, transportation, child care, and health costs; and debt.

The judge determines how much support each parent should be paying. If state formulas show that your ex's contribution should be higher, then you're likely to obtain more support. However, if your former spouse has taken on new family obligations or is earning less, whether from a change of jobs, starting a business, or even an illness, this information becomes a variable in the equation.

Depending on the changes that have occurred on the other side, you could find yourself with a smaller award. If feasible, ask your attorney to run the numbers first. But since your spouse is sufficiently uncooperative as to warrant a return to court, he or she may be hard to pin down outside a courtroom about financial changes. While you'll certainly know if more children are in the family photo album, it's less likely you'll know the size of your ex's paycheck or debts.

LEGAL LESSONS: DOMESTIC AND MARITAL PROPERTY RIGHTS

Whether a divorce, a formal separation, a division of assets in a domestic partnership, or even in settling an estate, if you've lived through a legal disentanglement before, you know that the way you set up property rights can have a major effect on the outcome. If you don't set up ownership to reflect your preferences—or to protect your special relationships—the court will fall back on state laws in dividing a couple's or the decedent's assets.

To further complicate matters, state law varies tremendously between community-property and common-law states. If parts of the family live or own property in different states, they are likely to have different expectations and different rights. A similar situation can occur when a couple divides time between a primary residence in a separate-property state such as Tennessee and a community-property state such as Arizona. Since the couple may own property or have family in both states, if one spouse dies, additional confusion can arise over estate and burial rights.

Any general legal discussion serves to point you in the direction of issues to identify. To know your own rights, which are fact-dependent, look to competent local counsel and to the general information provided by state, county, and local bar associations and attorneys general.

If you're in a committed relationship but can't or don't plan to marry legally, you should formalize your financial expectations in writing to protect both of your interests. Even same-sex couples who are denied legal marriage can exercise contractual rights by drawing up agreements reflecting their understanding of income and property arrangements. If you enter the relationship later in life, preexisting financial and familial obligations must be considered as well.

If you plan to marry, remember that your romantic alignments are also legal and financial ones. Act accordingly. Seek financial and legal advice right alongside the premarital counseling.

TYPES OF MARITAL PROPERTY

Understanding the basics of property ownership in marriage helps you determine how to take title and how to protect your rights. Our states follow two types of property law, one derived from English common law and the other from Roman law and the Napoleonic code or civil law. There is now a hybrid called the *Uniform Marital Property Act* that has been adopted in Wisconsin, which operates much like community property. Write your state attorney general for a booklet on marital property rights.

SEPARATE-PROPERTY STATE

If you live in a common-law or separate-property state, the general rule is that each spouse has the right to manage and dispose of his or her own earnings. The property each of you brought to the marriage belongs to you individually, as does any subsequent inheritance.

If one spouse dies and does not leave a will, the surviving spouse would be entitled to between a third and a half of the property of the deceased, depending on state law. Your right to continue to live in the family home would depend on how title is held.

If you divorce, you cannot count on being awarded half the marital assets. Most separate-property states have moved to a system of equitable distribution, under which the assets are divided proportionately according to the ages of the two spouses, their individual earning capacities, the number and ages of their children, and other criteria set by law in various states. This system is usually better for women than the old common law, under which the wife's claim to any property not specifically in her name was limited.

COMMUNITY-PROPERTY STATES

In the nine community-property states (California, Texas, Arizona, Nevada, New Mexico, Louisiana, Idaho, Washington, plus Wisconsin), each spouse owns an undivided 50% interest in the community property—for example, all earnings and property acquired during the marriage, excluding individual inheritances and property each brought into the marriage. In general, even if you keep all your earnings separate, your spouse is entitled to half of them. If you buy property, your spouse will have half-interest unless you make a specific written exception. The control of community assets, including your individual salaries, varies from state to state. Traditionally, although the wife owned half, management of the community was vested in the husband. Since the early 1970s, community-property laws have been changed to allow equal-management rights in most states. California went one step further and gave either spouse the right to commit 100% of the community property. In theory, if you lived in California and your spouse earned $100,000 a year, you would have the right to spend all of it down to the last penny—and vice versa.

In community-property states, each spouse also has the right to will his or her half of community property to any heir of choice. Thus, if you want to protect your tenancy in the family home (which is usually community property), you had better make sure that your spouse does not will an interest in it to someone else.

Upon the dissolution of a marriage in community-property states, half of the community property and assets goes to each spouse unless there is a legal agreement to another arrangement. Separate property (acquired outside the marriage either in time or by operation of law, such as inheritances) stays the same.

LEGAL CHECKLIST FOR COUPLES

Whether you're married now, planning to marry, or living together, couples of every sort should sift through the following legal checklist. You may consider drafting a formal contract with the help of your lawyer or you may sit down for a casual chat with your significant other. Either way, or anywhere in between, cover these topics both in discussion and in writing.

- ✔ *Assets:* List your assets completely and be prepared to provide full documentation, for example, a trust deed for real estate or an official appraisal for jewelry. Specify which assets are to be included or excluded from marital property.

- ✔ *Liabilities:* List all debts and clarify how these will be paid. Generally, each of you is solely responsible for liabilities incurred before marriage, but you should both know the debt load that the other carries. Specify which credit cards you intend to keep separate and which accounts will be shared. Some cautious marital candidates even check their future spouse's credit reports before they tie the knot.

- ✔ *Will:* Each partner should have a will specifying what to leave to his or her children. To protect the children, clearly state the individual you want as their guardian. *Note:* You may name a separate guardian for the child's physical custody and finances.

- ✔ *Money management:* How do you run your bank accounts? In some states, simply keeping the money in a separate account does not obliterate your partner's interest unless you specifically agree in writing. You may have other points of money management that concern you. Your discussion of legal matters is an appropriate context in which to bring up your concerns.

- ✔ *Property title:* Learn about the property laws of your state with specific reference to control of property during marriage and disposition of property on dissolution of marriage. (See below.)

- ✔ *Quality of life:* If there are issues that concern you, such as housekeeping responsibilities, religious practices, and so on, you can include a statement of intent in your formal or informal agreement, although, except for religious preferences for children, other desires will not be legally binding. While many couples work these out over a long period of time and responsibilities shift as circumstances shift, going through a formal agreement process represents an ideal time to set out your current and future expectations about these issues.

PROPERTY TITLES AFFECT YOUR RIGHTS

Watch how you take title to property. Consult your attorney to make sure that your title is held to reflect your intentions about ownership.

Marital Property

Available only to legally married couples. Marital property titles protect spousal rights and include:

Community property: Applicable in Arizona, California, Idaho, Louisiana, Nevada, New Mexico, Texas, Washington, and Wisconsin. A spouse may will away one-half of the marital property. However, if a spouse dies *intestate* (without a will), the surviving spouse may be entitled to all of the community property in preference to other heirs.

Tenancy by the entirety: Available in some of the remaining 41 common-law states. Provides an automatic right of survivorship, meaning that the surviving spouse owns the property. Property held as a tenancy by the entirety cannot be willed to another. And, in contrast to *joint tenancy* (below), neither spouse can destroy this right of survivorship by selling his or her interest.

General Property Titles

These are available regardless of marital status. The most common are as follows:

Tenancy in common: Two or more owners. Can be freely willed. Selling or willing an interest does not affect others' ownership.

Joint tenancy: Provides an automatic right of survivorship, like tenancy by the entirety, except that if one party sells his or her interest, the joint tenancy reverts to a tenancy in common.

FIGURE 7.3 SPECIAL ADVICE ABOUT WHAT'S "YOURS, MINE, AND OURS"

TYPE OF FAMILY	ADVICE
Two-earner	• Be sure to save enough to cover loss of one job. • Make sure your time is carefully budgeted.

Single parents	• *Divorced:* Plan carefully to protect yourself in future relationships.
	• *Separated:* Balance your own needs with those of your children and your estranged spouse.
	• *Widowed:* Learn the stages of grief and how they affect your—and your children's—outlooks.
	   1. Shock, denial
	   2. Anger, guilt
	   3. Bargaining
	   4. Depression
	   5. Acceptance
	• *Never married:* If you are actually living with the father but chose not to marry, check your legal rights of common-law marriage.
	• *Never married:* Establish paternity and obtain child support, if applicable.

Blended	• Don't try to be a perfect family, and realize that you can't choose the actions of the kids' other parents. Act, don't react. • Legal battles with your or your partner's ex may wreak havoc.
Cohabiting (opposite sex)	• Reduce your legal and financial arrangements to writing. • Develop good financial habits, as chances are you'll marry eventually. • You may face legal parent and guardian issues.
Cohabiting (same sex)	• See "Cohabiting (opposite sex) above. • School-age children will face questions. • Use the "two dads/two moms" approach.

Figure 7.3 (Continued)

TYPE OF FAMILY	ADVICE
Adoptive	• From infants to teenagers, children who join your family will have a range of expectations and scheduling needs.
Foster	• Respect the children's own personal boundaries, especially including habits and values from other homes.
Wife as breadwinner	• Stay-at-home dads may feel left out on career and family fronts since they're usually not privy to built-in networks cultivated by stay-at-home moms for decades. • Even if her career is fulfilling, the wife as breadwinner may carry hidden resentment that the husband isn't toeing the line.
Multicultural	• Help your children identify with their cultural heritage. • Subscribe to appropriate magazines and newspapers; assist with book, movie, drama, and music selections; attend cultural festivals; and visit the home country.
Older parents	• You know your parenting skills are all the better for the wisdom of your age, but sometimes you wish you had a little more energy. Take time when you need it and you'll be renewed and ready to face your special challenges as an older parent. • Hire baby-sitters, tutors, and drivers if you can afford to.
Adult children living at home	• When intergenerational value systems about money clash, agree to disagree. • Plan an exit strategy.
Grandchildren living with grandparents	• School-age children may be sensitive to inquiries from their peers. • Help your grandchildren prepare answers to such concerns.

FIGURE 7.3 (CONTINUED)

TYPE OF FAMILY	ADVICE
May-December	- While one partner is free to travel or pursue hobbies, the other may be wrapped up in the nine-to-five working world. - If you have children, they may be embarrassed if other kids think the older parent is a grandparent.

CHAPTER EIGHT

It's Never Too Early

Your children's wants and needs can pull against what you know is best for their future. But if you get them on your side, they can become the most zealous supporters of your financial strategies.

When *teaching* your children about money, cultivate healthy attitudes and fiscal responsibility. In *talking* to your children about money, don't plant seeds of insecurity by confiding all your financial woes. Strike a balance between the security they need and the honesty they deserve.

HEALTHY MONEY ATTITUDES

First, children should understand that money is a tool. The way it's used determines its effects. While it's not the root of all evil, it's also not the answer to all your prayers.

Our increased reliance on electronic forms of payment—checks, debit cards, credit cards—has eroded our concept of the time/money/goods-and-services exchange.

To form healthy attitudes toward money, it's essential that children understand the relationship between earning and spending. In the context of your family financial goals, this understanding will encourage them to make temporary material sacrifices. They'll be less likely to feel like the poor cousin today when they are working toward tomorrow's financial rewards.

TEACHING CHILDREN ABOUT MONEY: THEORY AND PRACTICE

Unfortunately, the closest our schools come to teaching money management is mathematics word problems or social studies discussions of capitalism. Never mind real-life skills in earning, taxation, or savings.

Yet the *Atlanta Constitution* recently reported that American children receive nearly $15 billion a year in gifts, allowances, and money for odd jobs. They spend most of it on clothes, food, and games—not surprising when the adults around them are doing the same. Sometimes the best way to change your kids' financial habits is to change your own.

But if you're less into the "osmosis" approach and feel your children's financial habits need intervention, understanding their developmental stages can be key. Whether you are teaching your children the fundamentals of money management or sharing details about your family finances, you should be sensitive to their changing needs. While honesty is in order at all stages, there's no need to elaborate. If the child wants to know more, the child will ask.

The following guidelines provide both a *theory* and a *reality* for what children are ready to hear about your own family finances and what they're ready to learn about money management. But knowing your child—and knowing that everyone falls somewhere between the theory and the reality—is the key to raising fiscally responsible children.

INFANTS AND TODDLERS

Theory: Since children under age three are sensitive to disruptions in their familiar routines, you may find a correlation between your financial woes and their behavior. Although very young children may not understand money problems, they'll pick up on your cues. Try to speak to them in reassuring tones even when you are the one who needs reassurance.

Young toddlers are ready for a foundation of financial understanding. Take advantage of teachable moments at the bank, grocery store, or department store by describing your money transactions in simple words. For example, "We are letting the bank hold our money for us, so it will be safe until we need it." Help children learn the names of coins and bills. And, no matter how unpleasant, don't give in to the proverbial toy store tantrum. If you give in, you only teach them to throw a tantrum next time they want something.

Reality: Do you really want to burden kids at this age with thinking about money? Let them enjoy their freedom—they'll learn soon enough. Just steer clear of expensive stuff they can grab.

PRESCHOOL CHILDREN

Theory: Three- to six-year-olds can fear abandonment. Reassure your preschoolers that you'll always try to be there for them but if you're not there they will be taken care of. Focus on where they would go and who would take care of them in your absence.

There's no reason to burden them with financial concerns unless they directly affect the child. If you have to downsize by moving to a less expensive residence, the children have a right to know why they're moving or changing schools. In a true crisis such as a job loss, it's important to be honest without scaring the children.

Three- to six-year-olds can also grasp the value of money. A small weekly allowance (especially if earned by doing light chores) can reinforce the relationship between earning and spending, as well as introduce budgeting.

Reality: All kids care about at this age are sweets and toys. So set limits, but don't ruin their lives with budget talk.

SCHOOL-AGE CHILDREN

Theory: Because 6- to 12-year-olds seem more mature, we can be tempted to overconfide in them. But at this age, they are apt to feel responsible for their circumstances. They may blame themselves and clam up about their own problems because they don't want to worry you further.

In school, your child is learning about money denominations and how to make change. When shopping together, reinforce school lessons by asking your school-age children to estimate how much change they'll get back from the cashier and by helping them count the returned change.

By school age, a regular allowance is a wise investment in your child. If you haven't done so already, open a savings account for your school-age child. Introduce the concept of interest and be sure to go over each statement and make special trips to the bank for depositing. If your bank still uses passbooks, let the child be responsible for keeping track of it.

Reality: As children grow older, they become a series of wants. As soon as one want is satisfied, they find another. Make them save and pay for what they want.

Teenagers

Theory: Teenagers naturally disengage from the family identity, seeking greater independence. However, during times of transition they may align strongly with the family either out of insecurity or out of a need to compensate for a missing parent. In the alternative, teenagers may slip into the background, unnoticed. While your attention is turned to other, more pressing, demands, your teenager might be on the road to trouble, which can be costly to your wallet as well as your heart.

Depending on your relationship with them, teens can be constructively involved in the family finances.

Show them where to find important papers such as your will, insurance policies, and power of attorney documents. Involve them in your financial planning, especially concerning their own futures. However, resist dumping adult information in their laps.

If you permit your teen to work for extra money, be sure to lay firm ground rules. Work should never interfere with school—the greatest investment you can make in your child is a successful school experience. Although valuable lessons can be learned from working, avoid a trade-off with the child's future. If you do permit work, require a certain percentage of the teen's paycheck to be saved for larger goodies and a certain percentage to be put in a special college savings account.

Teens with money from allowances and jobs need checking and savings accounts. Make them joint accounts if you want to keep tabs on your child's transactions. But don't bail them out if they overspend. Let them be accountable for their actions now, so they'll be responsible for their actions later.

Reality: Forget it. No matter what you do, independence is the issue here. So, whatever they want, tell them they can buy it when they can earn the money.

Young Adults

Theory: During the college years you can begin opening adult lines of communication about your finances. Whether you have planned for college expenses or are frantically scrambling for your options, it's time to start passing the financial baton to your offspring. Clarify expectations: Will the student work during these years to supplement what you've saved? Will you take out student loans? Who is expected to pay back the loans? How many years will you foot the bill?

If the young adult is not entering higher education, you must decide how long you're willing to support him or her. If your offspring is living at home, draw up an informal agreement about living arrangements. Will the child contribute to rent? Groceries? Home and yard maintenance? How will he or she entertain friends? Who will provide a means of transportation, insurance, and so forth? If your child is away from home, be clear whether moving back home is an option or whether you're willing to supplement the child's income.

But before your child leaves home, prepare him or her for the temptations of cash machines on every corner and a dorm mailbox full of preapproved credit cards. If you're still offering support, open a student checking account that allows the parent to make deposits from another city. If you haven't done so already, walk your child through the basics of writing a check and reconciling the account.

Reality: By now they know the truth, that resources never equal wants. But try to give them as much peace as you can during their college years, the last time most of us don't think about money every day.

Figure 8.1 presents pointers for teaching children about money in families that fall into each of the 4M categories.

FIGURE 8.1 4M POINTERS FOR TEACHING CHILDREN ABOUT MONEY

4 Ms	FAMILY INCOME	ALLOWANCE POINTERS
MODEST	Under $50,000 per year	• Even if the budget is tight, each child should have a small regular allowance. • Encourage saving for larger items.
MEDIUM	$50,000 to $100,000 per year	• Give larger allowances but set guidelines for college savings, gifts to family and friends, and charitable contributions.
MAJOR	$100,000 to $250,000 per year	• All of the above. • For older children, include clothing, gas, and entertainment money in allowance and require them to budget. • Introduce children to investing with penny stocks or help them choose a socially responsible mutual fund (no tobacco stocks, etc.) with small minimum investments.
MEGA	$250,000 and above	• All of the above. • Require children to work for a portion of their allowance. • Prepare children to deal with trusts or inheritances if any.

GETTING THE KIDS ON YOUR SIDE

Families work something like sports teams. The parents wear many hats—owner, coach, cheerleader—and the kids are the players. Ask any coach, and he or she will tell you that a team's winning streak has more to do with hard work than luck. Your family team can be a winner if you cultivate harmony in the ranks (confront sibling rivalry) and find the correct balance between offensive (preventative) and defensive (responsive) moves.

THE PARENT'S PART

When a sports team is on the defensive, the best it can do is respond to what's coming at it. When it's on the offensive, it is in control but it has to work to stay that way. You—and your kids—need both types of skills to succeed in life.

First, show your kids that you are a team player. If divorced or estranged from their other parent, put the children's needs first even when it's easier to put down the ex-spouse. Respect your children's rights as individuals even when you don't respect their actions or behavior.

Next, show *your kids* how to be team players. Combat sibling rivalry by finding individual time to spend with each child. By modeling respect for their rights, you show them how to respect the other children in the household—especially important in blended families.

Finally, teach your kids both the defensive and offensive skills they need to succeed. Even if your family consists of only two people, make time for regular family meetings. Planning a family vacation, making decisions about expenditures, or renegotiating allowances in the supportive environment of a family meeting gives your kids a chance to tackle real problems and work as a team. You'll be surprised at the observations and solutions they devise.

THE FAMILY'S PART

Don't think you have to follow a formula for your meetings. After all, a trademark of today's families is diversity and no plan is "one size fits all." But, as with business meetings, family meetings go more smoothly if you set an agenda, even if it's written on the back of a used envelope. Adapt the following 4Ps checklist to your own situation.

- ✔ *Participation:* Under what circumstances will family members be excused from the family meetings? If you expect the children to follow these guidelines, make sure you follow them to a T yourself.
- ✔ *Progress report:* Review issues from previous meetings and steps taken toward the objective.
- ✔ *Planning:* Set new objectives based on family members' needs.
- ✔ *Prescription:* Make assignments or agree to a new protocol.

Even the most recalcitrant children can be roused into enthusiasm about issues that affect them and the ability to make changes in their own lives. Start with an issue that's dear to their hearts, make connections, and build from there.

FIGURE 8.2 SPECIAL ADVICE FOR TEACHING CHILDREN ABOUT MONEY

TYPE OF FAMILY	ADVICE
Two-earner	• The best way to teach your kids about money is to model sound financial habits—a tall order when everyone is already swamped with career and domestic chores. • Take advantage of life lesson opportunities such as a trip to the grocery, a summertime lemonade stand, or volunteer work at church or in the community.
Single parents	• *Divorced and separated:* It's okay to be honest with your children about your new financial picture. But keep it simple and on a level they're emotionally ready to handle.

IT'S NEVER TOO EARLY **145**

FIGURE 8.2 (CONTINUED)

TYPE OF FAMILY	ADVICE
	• *Widowed:* If you received a great deal of life insurance, your children may be confused and guilty about the new abundance and the loss of a parent. Explain that the money is not meant to replace the parent, but that he/she loved them and wanted them to be taken care of if something ever happened. • *Widowed:* If your spouse wasn't adequately covered, you may be struggling to make ends meet at a time when you are overwhelmed with grief. Children may feel abandoned in the sense that the parent is missing and they're facing a financial struggle. Assure your children that their feelings are okay and you'll make it. • *Never married:* Let your children learn about working with partners and financial give-and-take. Show them how you handle your finances and discuss how it might be different if your family included a second parent.
Blended	• Try to coordinate rules about allowances, etc., with the kids' other parents. But keep consistent money systems in your own household even if the kids live in chaos the rest of the time.
Cohabiting (opposite sex)	• See "Two-earner" on previous page.
Cohabiting (same sex)	• See "Two-earner" on previous page.
Adoptive	• If your children came from a different economic environment, they may have never had their own allowances to work with or felt that they had abundance in their lives. Be patient while they learn the lessons that come with access to money for the first time.

FIGURE 8.2 (CONTINUED)

TYPE OF FAMILY	ADVICE
Foster	• See "Adoptive" above.
Wife as breadwinner	• Take advantage of National Take Your Daughter to Work Day (and take your sons sometimes, too) to help your children understand what you do when you're not with them and especially show your daughters their own possibilities.
Multicultural	• Use your heritage as a springboard for teaching your children money values.
Older parents	• Your children were not around during the tough times when you were building your professional identity and setting up your home. While they should enjoy their abundance and prosperity, they should also learn that hard work is behind it.
Adult children living at home	• If your young-adult children are living at home while pursuing a higher education, you can still teach them valuable money skills. Make sure they have checking, savings, and credit cards in their own names. Don't bail them out if they get in over their heads—instead, show them how to bail themselves out.
Grandchildren living with grandparents	• If it's been years since you raised your own flock, you may be shocked at the high price of raising children.
May-December	• The older spouse may have an earlier family of children from which to draw experience. If not, your children will benefit from having parents with a range of financial experiences.

Part Three

ENRICHING YOUR FAMILY

CHAPTER NINE

Investments for Changing Times

Just as in life you don't want to put all your eggs in one basket, in investing don't put all your money in one asset or asset class. Real estate, stocks, bonds, jewelry or precious metals, a car, a savings account—you probably have a mix of at least three of these assets in your investment portfolio already. This mix, or *asset allocation*, should be adjusted periodically in response to life and income changes, family structure, and age.

In this chapter we'll explore the process of asset allocation and how we can use it to spread our investments more productively, with information on the risks and benefits of common investment options. We'll also look at the types of advisors that best meet your needs.

HOW MUCH MONEY SHOULD YOU PUT WHERE?

Periodically you should verify that the allocation of your assets works best for your needs. Take into account your age, net worth, earning prospects, personal circumstances, and risk preferences. Investing for a comfortable retirement 25 years down the road is very different from saving for your children's college or conserving a cushion to sustain you during a possible layoff. For instance, with a well-paying job that you're confident will continue, you can take a more aggressive position than someone who has decided to make a career change at midlife or is nearing retirement age.

INVESTMENT CRITERIA

When you review your mix of investments, address six areas of concern:

1. *Diversification:* How well have you spread out your wealth? Is all of your money in one stock, or is your portfolio balanced by shares in a number of different companies? Better yet, is your money spread out across stocks, bonds, real estate, and other assets?

2. *Risk:* Although nobody wants to take excessive financial risk, analysts have found that risk is inescapably tied to growth. Have you invested aggressively enough—taking on enough risk—to meet the investment returns you seek?

3. *Growth:* Are your investments expected to grow fast enough to meet your investment goals? If you are skittish about putting any of your money at risk and instead stick with conservative, fixed-return investments, in a period of high inflation, you won't earn enough to keep even.

4. *Liquidity:* Do heavy investments in real estate or venture capital restrict access to your funds? Are your investments liquid enough to meet your short-term needs?

5. *Tax consequences:* Would tax-preferred investments, such as municipal bonds, give you a higher overall return than other investments? If you're in the upper tax brackets, a tax-exempt investment adds about 2% to your effective returns. In other words, a tax-exempt investment with a 5% return will have the same earning power as a non-tax-exempt investment with a 7% return.

6. *Cash flow:* When do you need your money? Can you afford to wait until your bonds mature or your stocks increase in

value or do you need income each year to supplement your current earnings?

These variables, combined with personal sentiments about maintaining specific investments—such as your parent's house or your husband's long-time stocks—will influence your ideal asset allocation.

Allocation Guidelines

Although a good advisor should customize your asset allocation to match your personal needs, most planning professionals start with general allocation guidelines. Such guidelines commonly depend on your net worth. (If you are married, you should consider your net worth and your investment goals jointly with those of your spouse.) In the cases outlined below, we will look at the standard investment approach and then consider how your personal circumstances may require a different approach.

No matter how small your savings, an analysis of your asset allocation can be a helpful planning tool. After studying the standard asset allocation models, use your own data to create a personalized pie-chart profile. Either sketch the chart by hand or use a software program such as Quicken or Excel™ to simplify your task. Then compare your investment mix to the standard allocation models.

Modest Portfolios

If, like most people's, your investment pool is under $50,000, focus on basic priorities such as providing for your retirement and your children's education. Figure 9.1 shows the standard conservative and aggressive models for moderate portfolios.

Typically, you would be advised to follow the conservative model, creating a portfolio that will stand up to inflation, involving a mix of stocks, bonds, and cash instruments (savings accounts, CDs, and money market accounts). But your real-life circumstances may warrant a more aggressive approach. If you are young, anticipate a rising income, *and* are disciplined enough to stick to a budget, you can afford to introduce more risk into your investment profile to reach for larger returns.

FIGURE 9.1 STANDARD ASSET ALLOCATION MODELS FOR *MODEST* PORTFOLIOS

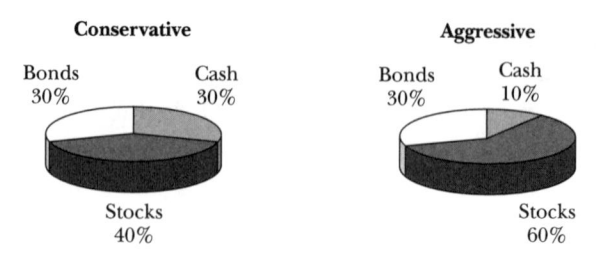

Conservative
Bonds 30%
Cash 30%
Stocks 40%

Aggressive
Bonds 30%
Cash 10%
Stocks 60%

For example, if you don't need to supplement your income with dividends or bond interest payments now, you might consider investing more heavily in stocks. If you choose to invest in stocks, be sure to diversify your holdings—not only across companies, but also across industries.

If you are not an experienced investor, consider investing in equity (stock) mutual funds to diversify your stock holdings. Pick equity mutual funds designed to meet your criteria for growth or income, keeping in mind that you are still exposing yourself to risk because of the stock component. Or look at special interest mutual funds that offer competitive returns while allowing you to invest with your social or environmental concerns in mind.

Finally, be careful not to keep too much of your money in low-return cash instruments. Depending on your job security and spending patterns, you should not keep more than three months' salary in your checking and savings accounts combined.

MEDIUM/MAJOR PORTFOLIOS

If you aren't a home owner already and you have an investment pool of more than $50,000, seriously consider using a portion of the money for a down payment on a home. Our legal system has always favored property owners, making substantial tax deductions available to them. As shown by Figure 9.2, most advisors suggest that those with moderate portfolios may conservatively invest up to half of their portfolio in real estate.

However, as indicated by Figure 9.3, your own portfolio may look very different from these standard allocation charts. For

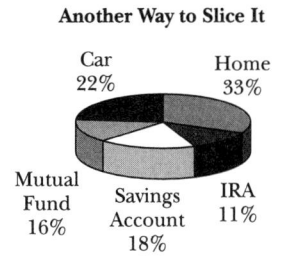

FIGURE 9.2 STANDARD ASSET ALLOCATION MODELS FOR *MEDIUM/MAJOR* PORTFOLIOS

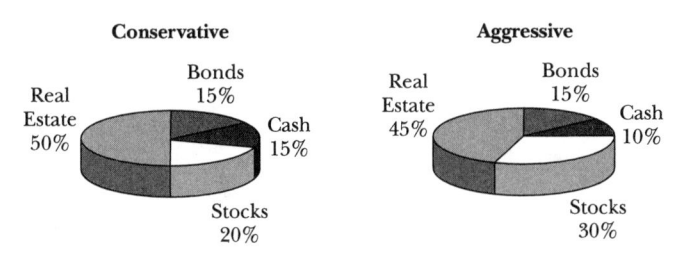

Conservative
- Real Estate 50%
- Bonds 15%
- Cash 15%
- Stocks 20%

Aggressive
- Real Estate 45%
- Bonds 15%
- Cash 10%
- Stocks 30%

example, your car may actually make up a significant portion of your net worth, and your home equity might amount to far less than half your portfolio value. (In asset allocation you consider only the amount of net equity in your home or the amount you've paid on principal plus any capital gains indicated by your appraisal value.)

You probably also have at least a small percentage of your net worth tucked away in a retirement account. Technically, an individual retirement account (IRA) is not a type of asset itself, but rather an account containing well-diversified assets. Nonetheless, consider your IRA an important slice of your asset pie, whose growth you want to cultivate over time.

MAJOR/MEGA PORTFOLIOS

The standard guidelines (as shown in Figure 9.4) for asset allocation in major/mega portfolios are usually best suited for investment pools of more than $250,000. Interestingly, real-life investment portfolios valued at more than $250,000 are more

FIGURE 9.3 TYPICAL ASSET MIX

Another Way to Slice It
- Car 22%
- Home 33%
- Mutual Fund 16%
- Savings Account 18%
- IRA 11%

Figure 9.4 Standard Asset Allocation Models for *Major/Mega* Portfolios

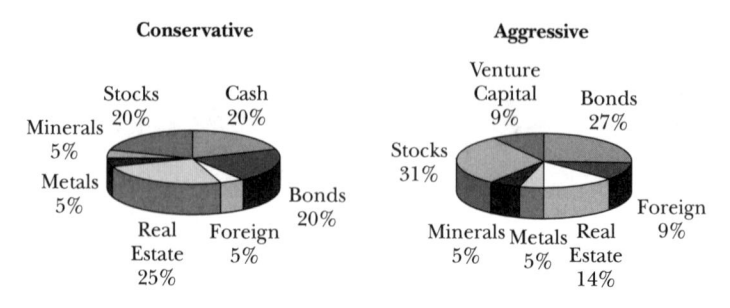

Conservative
- Stocks 20%
- Cash 20%
- Minerals 5%
- Metals 5%
- Real Estate 25%
- Foreign 5%
- Bonds 20%

Aggressive
- Venture Capital 9%
- Bonds 27%
- Stocks 31%
- Minerals 5%
- Metals 5%
- Real Estate 14%
- Foreign 9%

likely to follow the standard asset allocation guidelines for medium/major portfolios. The flexibility you have with a portfolio of this size enables any number of suitable asset allocations. For example, consider purchasing real estate outright. Even the most conservative major/mega investor can afford to add metals or minerals to his or her asset mix. And with our increasingly global economy, international investments belong in every sizable portfolio. Venture capital allocations of 5% to 10% belong in aggressive portfolios, while inexperienced investors might limit such investments to a smaller portion of their total portfolio, regardless of the initial appeal of the investment opportunity.

4M INVESTMENT GUIDELINES

Investment styles are set in families. Like religious and political choices, after rebellion in our teens and 20s, most of us return to family investing styles. If you grew up in the south, your investment of choice is land. If you grew up in the cities of the eastern seaboard, you probably prefer stocks. If you grew up in Los Angeles, you may prefer fancy cars. Or, if you're a Westerner, cattle and ranches loom large. Recognize and work with family investment styles—there's no point in pulling against them. If a couple prefers different investments, then each should have some of their respective preferences.

Figure 9.5 lists some suggested investments for each of the 4M categories.

Figure 9.5 4M Investment Guidelines

4 Ms	FAMILY INCOME	INVESTMENTS TO CONSIDER BEYOND RETIREMENT SAVINGS
MODEST	Under $50,000 per year	• Inflation-indexed Treasury bond funds. • Equity mutual funds. • Bond mutual funds. • Find low entry investments; have minimum monthly investment drawn directly from your bank account.
MEDIUM	$50,000 to $100,000 per year	• Equity funds. • Bond funds. • Global funds.
MAJOR	$100,000 to $250,000 per year	• Direct equity and bond investments. • Global funds. • Additional venture capital investment.
MEGA	$250,000 and above	• All of the above. • Venture, collectibles, gold, minerals, etc. • Consider hiring a money manager.

WHICH INVESTMENTS ARE RIGHT FOR YOU?

When most people think of investing, they think of stocks, bonds, and mutual funds. They may even hold investments in these classes without understanding their relationships—for example, that a mutual fund can contain stocks (equity mutual fund), bonds (bond fund), a mix of stocks and bonds, or none at all (in the case of currency funds).

Looking at the Stock Market

"Invest in the stock market for the long term."

"Over time, the stock market outperforms all other investments."

How many times have you heard or read these two phrases? They have a blind side: The market *can* stop advancing and contract. The stock market *isn't* right for everyone.

Ever since the October 1987 Wall Street crash, when the stock market lost a fifth of its value in one month, stock market indexes have relentlessly climbed higher overall. In 1996, experts predicted the Dow Jones Industrial Average would top 7,000 by the end of 1997. But the market one-upped them as it sometimes topped 8,000.

Coupled with this dizzying performance, the public's reliance on stock-oriented media for investment advice has contributed to stock market hype that has kept the public heavily invested.

But for stock prices to climb, money must continue to pour into the market. Share prices rise faster than economic growth when people place a greater share of their assets into the market. At some point, people reach the limit on how much money they can put into stocks. For instance, a big pension fund decides it will allocate a maximum of 60% of its assets to equities. Once it reaches 60%, it doesn't have any more money to invest in stocks. When that happens with enough investors, the market's ascent will slow.

When experts begin suggesting the market will become more volatile, it's not such a good time to buy stocks—or leave your money in stocks—unless you can put money in for the long haul. Volatility is a frequent feature of stagnant markets because, as the market slows, speculative money begins swarming to the slightest move as traders strive to maintain high earnings. The result is that any trends are amplified, both for individual stocks and for the market as a whole.

If you can't handle the short-term risk or may need to draw on your money to meet expenses, you are not a good candidate for direct stock investments. But only you can decide whether you belong in the current market. Look at the percentage of your assets in the market, your age, and your tolerance for risk. If in doubt, get out. You can always buy back in later.

💲 If you do get burned on a stock investment, remember that you can deduct up to $3,000 of capital losses from your ordinary income each year. If your capital losses exceed your capital gains by more than $3,000, the surplus amount can be *carried forward*, or deducted against capital gains in future years. Each year the carryover is deducted first against new capital gains and then up to $3,000 against personal income and may be carried forward until exhausted in this manner.

💲

HOW LONG IS "LONG TERM"?

Many investors have internalized the litany: "Invest in stocks for the long term." But just how long is "long term"? Five years? Fifteen? Thirty? According to John Maynard Keynes, creator of the policies and practices known as *Keynesian economics* that pulled the United States out of the 1930s depression, "In the long-term, we'll all be dead."

Ironically, real estate was historically considered a long-term investment; the stock market a short-term, liquid investment. That formula has been turned on its head as more and more people have been drawn in by the lure of seemingly ever higher market prices.

But a closer look shows that from 1940 to 1990, the median value of residential real estate grew from $2,377 to $79,100, or 33-fold. The stock market, as measured by the Dow Jones Industrial Average, grew from 150 to 2,800, only 18-fold, in the same years. So in the really long term, as Scarlett O'Hara's father said in *Gone With the Wind*, "It's the land, Katie Scarlett."

EQUITY MUTUAL FUNDS: A SAFER WAY TO INVEST IN STOCKS

Despite our cautions about the stock market, we recognize that mutual funds—in particular, equity mutual funds—are the most common entry ticket into the investment arena.

If you want to get into the stock market, but you don't know what to buy, equity mutual funds offer diversification. While you may not have the money to invest in 100 different companies, a mutual fund has the financial muscle to spread money around. A well-balanced portfolio protects you from the risk associated with an individual company by offsetting one company's losses with several other companies' gains. Funds also have full-time employees who spend their days poring over company reports and watching trends to make informed stock choices, something you probably don't have time to do.

Of course, you have to pay the fund for handling your money, but the fees—usually 1% or less—buy the safety of diversification and the fund manager's expertise. Fees charged by mutual funds are discussed below.

Ask four questions before putting money into a fund:

1. Does the fund's investment objective meet my needs?
2. How has the fund performed over the past 1, 3, 5, and 10 years?
3. How is the fund structured?
4. What fees are associated with it?

INVESTMENT OBJECTIVE AND PERFORMANCE

With more mutual funds on the market today than individual stocks, there's sure to be a fund to match your investment needs. While clues will be found in the classification of the fund (aggressive growth, growth and income, etc.), you need to check the individual fund's history to see if it lives up to its name. For example, a particular "aggressive growth" fund may actually grow more slowly than another fund labeled "balanced."

Figure 9.6 gives the average yearly return over 10 years for different types of funds. Look at the "best" and "worst" years to give you an idea about the volatility of each type.

A classification not included on the chart, *index funds* structure their portfolios to mirror an index such as Standard & Poor's 500. However, with index funds, timing is everything: If the market advances, the value of your investment rises; if it declines, the value falls.

FIGURE 9.6 INVESTMENT OBJECTIVES AND PERFORMANCE

FUND CLASSIFICATION AND INVESTMENT STRATEGIES	RISK LEVEL	10-YEAR AVERAGE	BEST YEAR	WORST YEAR
Aggressive growth: Seek to achieve the highest possible growth.	very high	13.3%	53.6%	−8.3%
Small company stocks: Invest in companies that have less than $1 billion in stocks.	high	13.2%	50.1%	−9.3%
Growth funds: Seek less risky growth than aggressive growth funds.	high	12.9%	37.1%	−4.7%
Specialty utility: Invest in utility companies.	low	10.9%	14.7%	+3.2%
Specialty gold: Invest only in precious metal stocks.	highest	4.3%	11.8%	−5.6%
Growth and income: Pursue a blend of growth and dividend income.	moderate	12.0%	28.7%	−4.6%
Equity income: Try to achieve the highest possible dividend income.	low	11.5%	27.4%	−6.4%
Mixed income: Mix dividend and bond income.	low	10.2%	24.0%	−4.5%
Balanced: Usually blend 60% blue-chip stocks with 40% government or highly rated coupon bonds.	low	11.4%	27.7%	−2.8%

Table originally published in *Emily Card's MoneyLetter for Women,* January 1997, vol. 1, no. 4. Used with permission. Subscriptions $29 annually (12 issues). For a free sample or more information, call 310-285-8088 or write Subscription Department, 1158 26th Street, Suite 450, Santa Monica, CA 90403.

Finally, while it's a good idea to check the fund's performance over the past 1, 3, 5, and 10 years, be forewarned that the past does not always predict the future. Changes in fund management and market conditions beyond the fund's control may also affect performance.

STRUCTURE: OPEN END OR CLOSED END

Open-end funds are the most common type. They issue as many shares as people want to buy and then invest the money into their portfolio. Let's say they have 1,000 shares and you have 1 share—your share is worth 1/1,000 of their portfolio. You can sell the shares back to the fund at any time.

There is usually a minimum initial investment, often ranging from $500 to $2,500. The minimum subsequent investments are usually in the $100-to-$500 range but can be as low as $25.

Closed-end funds issue a set number of shares, like any company, and then use the money to invest. Unlike open-end funds, you are buying part of the mutual fund company, instead of a portion of its portfolio. If you do buy shares in a closed-end fund, remember that the value will fluctuate according to market perceptions just like any other stock.

A closed-end fund could be attractive if some panic in the market has pushed the share price below its *net asset value* (NAV). For example, a fund with 1,000 shares and a portfolio worth $1,000 has an NAV of $1 per share. If the share is selling for 90¢, it may be a bargain. But be careful, the market may know something you don't. Its portfolio may be overvalued or the manager may have a poor track record.

HOW MUCH WILL IT COST YOU? LOAD OR NO-LOAD

A *load* is basically a sales commission you pay a broker for selling you shares in a fund. In exchange for the load, the broker gives you advice. *No-load* funds are sold directly by the fund company to the consumer. You still must pay operating expenses, but you avoid paying a commission. If you buy the fund through a broker or investment planner, you will probably pay a load. There are four main types of funds:

Front-end loads: Charge 3% to 5.75% of the money before it's invested.

Back-end loads: Charge 5% or more when the money is withdrawn. Some funds have sliding withdrawal loads that decrease over time to discourage investors from pulling their money out during market downturns.

Level loads: Deduct some percentage of earnings, usually 1% or less a year, to cover sales and marketing. These loads are often hidden in sales and marketing expenses, called 12b-1s. While 1% a year may seem insignificant, over 20 years it adds up to 20%.

No-load, or funds with no commission: With more than 2,000 no-load funds, you can probably find a good fund without paying someone to sell it to you. But watch out: What is advertised as a no-load fund may have a sales and marketing fee hidden in its operating expenses.

PICKING A WINNER

When adding a new fund to your portfolio, make sure its stock positions don't overlap with those of your current holdings. Shoot for a few carefully chosen funds that give you holdings in a variety of industries and among companies with a range of growth expectations. In addition, look at the fund's ratio of expenses to earnings and check its track record from one of the sources listed below.

All funds have operating expenses. The question is what percentage of its earnings go to paying overhead? You can find this ratio from fund literature and from fund rating services. Expenses shouldn't be any higher than 1% or 100 basis points.

Many funds report their earnings or costs in *basis points*. Just remember, a basis point is 1/100th of a percent. For example, 50 basis points is 0.5%. But the measurements are meaningless unless you compare them. A fund with low overhead yet a poor return could earn a net return far less than that of a fund that seems more expensive but earns terrific returns.

Ask your broker, advisors, colleagues, and friends about their experiences with funds. Check magazines such as *Mutual Funds, Money, Business Week, Forbes,* and *Fortune.* Research individual funds in the following sources:

- *Morningstar Inc.* is the well-known rating guide, which you can find in your public library. They also sell two software packages of information on individual mutual funds: *Ascent,* $95 for the program and quarterly updates, will cross-reference funds with up to 70 search criteria; and *Principia,* $195 with quarterly updates, will cross-reference up to 98 criteria. Their number is 800-735-0700.

- *The Domini 400 Social Index*^{SM} (617-547-7479) tracks the performance of socially responsible stocks, much like the S&P 500 tracks industrial stocks—with one major difference. It screens out companies involved in alcohol-, tobacco-, and defense-related products and includes those with good track records for fair employment and protecting the environment.

- *The Investor's Guide to Low-Load Mutual Funds,* 15th edition, by the American Association of Individual Investors, $24.95, rates over 800 low- and no-load mutual funds. You can find it in the business section of many bookstores. If you can't find it, you can call 312-280-0170 to order the book. You might also be interested in finding out about becoming a member of the association.

For no-load funds, check:

- Mutual Fund Council Directory of 100% no-load mutual funds, 212-768-2477, or the Mutual Fund Education Alliance's Directory, 816-471-1454.

INVESTING IN BONDS

When the stock market becomes jumpy, people turn to bonds as a safer way to invest. With bonds, you get what you pay for. If a bond is offering a higher-than-market return, the risk will be greater.

Just remember, you can't make 20% returns on anything and be safe. While many less-developed countries might promise great returns on their government bonds, they won't necessarily be able to pay you back. That's why they have to offer such high rates to attract capital.

The same goes for high-yield corporate bonds. If they're offering rates that are too good to be true, they are. In the 1980s they became known as *junk bonds* for a reason.

The real use of the bond market is security, which can come in two ways. One is to generate reliable income for something along the lines of a trust fund, retirement fund, or scholarship endowment. The other is to provide a relatively short-term but very safe moderate return on money. For instance, if you want to stash some money to be used in three years, put it into bonds. A three-year Federal Treasury Note would be perfect. If you keep a bond to maturity, you are assured of getting the full face value back as well as a return while holding it. You will know exactly how much you will get back and when, if you buy a newly issued bond.

When choosing the length of time for maturity, consider social trends and economic factors. For example, with Social Security facing reorganization as boomers begin to retire, long-term (20- to 30-year) Treasury bonds could prove less rewarding than medium-term (5- to 10-year) Treasury issues.

INTEREST RATES AND BOND PERFORMANCE

The Federal Reserve sets interest rates to achieve economic objectives. As a side effect, these interest rates can affect the return on the bond market. When interest rates rise, it's good news for those buying bonds because they can lock in at higher rates. However, the existing bond market falls, as new bonds will now give a higher return and older bonds will sell for less.

Some tips on timing: Since interest rates normally rise with inflation, watch for inflation warning signs such as three consecutive months of a 1.5% or greater rise in the core Producer Price Index of monthly inflation, accompanied by stronger monthly employment figures and rising wages.

When the Fed adheres to low short-term interest rates and a falling federal government budget deficit, interest rates should stay low, which means new purchase bonds are not as attractive. But, if interest rates rise, lock them in with bonds. If they rise further, you can always sell the bonds for a small penalty and purchase new ones. A woman who bought long 18 years ago has enjoyed a 15% annual return—pretty good money if you can get it today.

> ## BILLS, NOTES, AND BONDS
> U.S. government debt goes by different names depending on when it matures:
>
> *Bills* = 1 year or less
> *Notes* = 1 to 10 years
> *Bonds* = 10 to 30 years

INFLATION-INDEXED TREASURY BONDS

In 1997, the U.S. Treasury began selling inflation-indexed bonds in an effort to protect investors' money from the eroding effects of inflation. Auctions are held quarterly. Each time, an interest rate will be set at time of issuance and adjusted for inflation at maturity. For example, the first $7 billion in 10-year securities was auctioned in January 1997 with a 3.45%+ inflation interest rate. If inflation is 3% at time of maturity, the return will be 6.45%.

Individuals can purchase the $1,000 bonds through the Treasury Direct program. Or, for a fee, they are available through banks or brokers. In addition, some brokerage houses offer mutual funds based on these bonds. While more expensive than buying direct, buying through a fund offers liquidity since you don't have to wait for a specific bond to mature in order to withdraw your investment. For more information contact a branch of your regional Federal Reserve Bank or call the Treasury Department's Bureau of Public Debt at 202-874-4000.

Going Global

As boundaries between countries soften and the global marketplace grows, individual investors should tap into new opportunities for profit abroad by adding an international component to their portfolios.

Just as with domestic stocks, start with a mutual fund before attempting to select and invest in individual stocks. You will find global and international mutual funds with stock, bond, or a mix of stock and bond holdings.

Global funds may hold both domestic *and* offshore holdings. If you already own plenty of domestic stocks and you're aiming for a certain percentage of pure global in your portfolio, consider an international fund.

International funds tend to concentrate on non-U.S. holdings. Like global funds, they can take advantage of buying and selling stocks with an eye to trends in world markets and currency values.

Since industry usage of the terms *global* and *international* is still in flux, look beyond a fund's name and check its actual holdings before deciding whether it meets your needs.

A Currency Primer

Currency values can give you clues about other countries' economies in relation to the U.S. economy—important when deciding where to make your global investments. They can also impact the returns of your current holdings, as fund managers must convert your U.S. dollars to purchase foreign stocks and convert back again when the stocks are sold.

The currency exchange rates highlighted in daily news reports provide a basic measure for tracking the global marketplace. Learning to track the movements of Japanese yen, German deutsche marks, French francs, and British pounds can be an important step in your entry into the global investment environment.

Understanding what is being compared by the various exchange rates is the key to decoding their meaning. *Foreign currency to dollar* rate tells you how many American dollars it takes to buy a single unit of the foreign currency. For example, if a dollar is "at 1.647 against the pound," it means that you must pay approximately $1.65 for a British pound.

(continued)

> ### GOING GLOBAL (CONTINUED)
> *Dollar to foreign currency* rate is the inverse ratio, giving you the number of units of foreign currency you could get for each dollar. When you hear, "The pound is at .6621 against the dollar," you know you'll get .66 pounds for each dollar.
> There's no official close of the global currency market (currency trades are being made somewhere in the world 24 hours a day). For simplicity, U.S. news organizations have chosen to report the rates as they stand at 3 P.M. eastern time. In addition, the U.S. Federal Reserve hot line (212-720-6693) provides the "Noon Buying Rates," an approximation of the daily rates at which national banks are buying the major currencies.

MAKING A DIFFERENCE WITH SOCIALLY RESPONSIBLE INVESTING

The same business practices that make certain corporations good for their employees, their customers, and the community often make them sound financial performers, too. Scrupulous management can give a company inherent value that stands up to the downward pressures of a falling market.

To locate *socially responsible investments* (SRIs) in stocks or mutual funds, check out the Domini 400 Social Index^{SM} (see previous section on mutual funds).

To learn more about the field, check out books such as *Investing With Your Conscience* by John Harrington (John Wiley & Sons, 1993) and *Investing for Good* by Amy Domini (HarperCollins, 1993).

In addition, look for a financial advisor who specializes in SRIs. "When choosing a money manager, ask about their track record in the socially responsible investment field," advises Boston-based money manager Jay Bragdon. His company, Conservest, "has been doing environmentally screened portfolios since 1973." In 1994, Bragdon paired with Harvard MBA Geeta Bhide, to form his new firm, Walden Capital Management, which also serves clients with social concerns.

DIRECT VENTURE CAPITAL INVESTMENTS

If you want to add venture investments to your portfolio, join a socially responsible investment fund or club to tap into opportunities that have been screened for social criteria. Or list yourself as an investor with an *angel* network—a service that matches investors with investment opportunities (see Appendix B for organizations).

Remember: Never invest more in venture than you are willing, and can afford, to lose. And, do your own due diligence, or checking, on the validity of the legal and financial representations of the entrepreneurs.

WHY SHOULD YOU USE A PROFESSIONAL ADVISOR?

Your accountant handles your taxes, your lawyer advises you on specific transactions, but who watches out for your big picture? Your bottom line? Unfortunately, if you're like most, you take a do-it-yourself approach with your finances and much of your information comes from the media.

But often financial reporters have little hands-on investment experience. A savvy 31-year-old Wall Street writer who interviewed Emily admitted, "Most financial writers live in Manhattan on modest salaries. Investing is something we want to do, but so is sailing around the world. Rent, food, credit card debts, and graduate school loans come first." Understandably, these writers work from theory rather than practical experience. For example, today's 30-year-old reporters have never experienced a major downturn in the market to temper their enthusiasm about its growth.

When you read the financial press or watch financial shows on television, remember that most of the material is written by Generation Xers. Bring your own experience to bear when investing. And turn to competent financial advisors for your big-picture advice. Not only will you gain from their expertise, but you will learn more about your own finances, consolidate accounts, simplify your bookkeeping, and follow performance of your investments.

The 411 on Financial Planners

Financial planners come in many varieties and specialties, but the financial planning industry is largely unregulated. In most states, virtually anyone can work as a financial planner regardless of education or training. And since all but a very few financial planners work on commission (good intentions to the contrary), biased information is almost an inevitable result.

Protections

Get your financial planning advice and your investment purchase services from two different professionals. Find and use one of the *fee-only* planners (see National Association of Personal Financial Advisors in Appendix D), who will put together a customized strategy and financial plan for a fee. Don't allow a stockbroker or insurance agent to create a financial plan and then sell you his or her recommended investments.

Hiring a Money Manager

Money managers will work to maximize your after-tax wealth in a manner that fits your risk profile. In contrast to stockbrokers and insurance agents, whose advice ultimately must be underwritten by product sales, money managers work for you, the individual investor.

If your investment pool approaches $200,000, you will probably benefit from hiring a money manager. Because transaction costs can be prohibitively high for investment pools lower than $100,000, most managers set investment minimums ranging from $100,000 to $500,000.

However, if your portfolio stands to grow through inheritance, a manager may take you on with an eye toward future business. The higher fees you'll pay on the front end may save you the costs of poor investment decisions made on your own. If you come into a large lump sum through inheritance, divorce, or widowhood, you will especially benefit from professional advice. But be sure to check references carefully. Money managers typically have broad trading and custodial powers over clients' funds.

Consider the following when making your selection:

- *Fees:* Generally, fees should be 1% to 1.5% for investments of $100,000 to $250,000 and should fall as the amount invested rises. Depending on the manager, when the portfolio reaches $1 to $5 million, the fee should be negotiable.
- *Style:* Your investment style and that of your money manager must mesh. Because it is almost impossible to really get a feel for someone's style by phone, meet in person. Few money managers are willing to travel far for any but the most well-heeled clients; therefore, expect to go to them or pick a local money manager.
- *Reputation:* The money manager should be well-established. A long track record of positive performance is much more important than a brief spectacular one.

FIGURE 9.7 SPECIAL ADVICE ON INVESTMENTS FOR CHANGING TIMES

TYPE OF FAMILY	ADVICE
Two-earner	- As with credit accounts, you'll hold jointly held investment accounts. - Keep individual accounts as well.
Single parent	- *Divorced:* You probably divided your investment assets as part of your divorce. Make sure your asset allocation matches your current scenario. - *Separated:* With your life in flux, it may be difficult to tend to your regular investment plans. If you think your separation may lead to divorce, become familiar with your marital assets and how they should be divided.

FIGURE 9.7 (CONTINUED)

TYPE OF FAMILY	ADVICE
Single parent *(continued)*	• *Widowed:* If you or the children received life insurance benefits, consider hiring a money manager. At first, protect the value of your principal. When you're ready to begin investing, go slowly. Don't jump into anything until you explore what may be accomplished with the amount you have to work with—which may range from simply supporting your children through majority to providing for future heirs. • *Never married:* As a single parent, your investment objectives include ensuring children's needs in your absence as well as securing your retirement and their education.
Blended	• See "Two-earner" on previous page.
Cohabiting (opposite sex)	• See "Two-earner" on previous page.
Cohabiting (same sex)	• Because your relationship is not legally recognized, jointly held investments are one way to strengthen your financial ties and provide for your loved ones.
Adoptive	• If you were childless before the adoption, make sure your investment objectives and existing portfolio address your new priorities.
Foster	• See "Adoptive" above.
Wife as breadwinner	• See "Two-earner" on previous page.
Multicultural	• Explore socially responsible investment opportunities that relate to your heritage.
Older parents	• If you have an established investment portfolio, revisit each investment in terms of how it serves your retirement and education objectives. • If you don't have an established portfolio, get busy. See Chapters 10 and 11, on education and retirement, respectively.

FIGURE 9.7 (CONTINUED)

TYPE OF FAMILY	ADVICE
Adult children living at home	• If your adult children are living at home because of a medical condition, invest wisely to see that they'll be taken care of in your absence.
Grandchildren living with grandparents	• See "Older parents" on previous page. • If you have already secured your retirement, invest with an eye to providing for the children in your absence.
May-December	• While you will share parts of your portfolio, each individual should hold an asset mix that is appropriate to his or her age.

CHAPTER TEN

Selecting and Paying for Education

From infant child care through college, the inescapable truth remains: Many parents sacrifice future security for the sake of their children's education. Our own parents were able to rest secure in the knowledge that the public schools they funded through their property taxes would educate their children, at least up until college. Colleges offered many more merit-based scholarships than today. And the extended family offered support up and down the generational ladder, often with homes to return to at retirement or with the loss of a spouse.

Today's education landscape looks quite different and, while baby boomers can be faulted for failing to save in their early years, no family today can escape the inevitable crunch between educational expenses and saving for the future of the parents.

THE CHILD CARE CHALLENGE

If you're more worried about where your child will go for day care than college, you're not alone. Every budget season, Congress debates the best way to deliver affordable child care to the American family. Finding high-quality affordable child care is one of the toughest challenges you'll face as a family.

More progressive employers have begun to recognize the value of helping employees with child care and even backup child care. As you seek employment, put child care front and center when you look at fringe benefits.

While it's hard enough to find a fit for an only child, parents of more than one face a seemingly unconquerable financial burden and a dizzying array of scheduling conflicts. Because of differences in their ages, it's rare to find a single solution that works for all.

If you find an excellent situation that costs more than you have budgeted, don't automatically rule it out. Knowing your child is well cared for will help motivate you to save in other areas. If possible, choose an arrangement first by its suitability for your child and second by its effect on your pocketbook.

Start by obtaining a copy of your state's child care licensing requirements. But even if a center meets the standards and comes with a shining recommendation from your friends, it may not be right for you and your child. Follow your intuition.

Child Care Centers/Preschools

Many parents feel safest with an accredited day care center that is affiliated with a larger organization, such as national franchises or centers found in churches or universities. Full-time day care facilities are desirable because they offer longer hours (usually 7 A.M. to 6 P.M.) as well as the knowledge that the center provides backup when the child's teacher is sick.

As a rule, the younger the child, the less available are day care spaces. Because infant care is so labor intensive, spaces that are available may be as much as 20% more expensive than for older children. Expecting parents should get on waiting lists before the baby is born and be prepared with home care or a relative to watch the child if the space doesn't open up in time.

Once children reach about three years old, families with a little more flexibility (for example, if one of the two earners works part-time or at home) may opt for a preschool with extended-care hours before and/or after school. Plan ahead for summer vacation and winter breaks by coordinating family vacations or enrolling the children in day or overnight camps.

$ In 1996, the American Camping Association reported that the typical age of the youngest campers had dropped to seven years old, while some camps took children as young as five or six. Psychologists credit children's decreased emotional dependence to the looser structure of two-earner families. David Elkind, author of *The Hurried Child*, advises parents looking for a camp to look for fun, age-appropriate activities with a low counselor-to-camper ratio.

Source: Mike Madden, "More Overnight Camps Welcome Younger Kids," *USA Today*, June 11, 1996.

$

AT A CAREGIVER'S HOME

Home care situations range from a stay-at-home mom taking in an extra couple of children to a fully licensed, state-accredited private day care facility. While many home care situations are excellent, potential problems include a lack of backup if the provider is ill, failure to meet state licensing requirements, and an increased likelihood of abuse because there's no one around to check up on them.

AT YOUR OWN HOME

You may overlook nanny services that care for your children in your home because you think this option is more expensive. But nanny services may be particularly suitable for families with more than one child because services typically charge a base rate for one child and a smaller fee for each additional child, making the per-child average more manageable. The children stay in a familiar home environment and have one-on-one interaction with their caregiver, and the parents save valuable commuting time. If you desire more peer interaction for your children, insist that the nanny take them to regular play groups.

The same thinking applies in considering an au pair. However, remember that work visas allow international au pairs to stay only one year. You must also pay travel expenses, food, health insurance, and a small salary. In addition, recent high-profile cases illustrate the importance of screening your child care applicants. Don't rely solely on the referral agency.

$ In 1997, government regulations for au pairs required a weekly stipend of $128.25, child care responsibilities of no more than 45 hours per week, a complete weekend off each month, and two weeks of paid vacation during the exchange year.

Source: United States Information Agency.

$

For multicultural families, a carefully chosen au pair could provide a unique opportunity for children to learn about their cultural heritage. In addition, a family seeking a male role model can request a male au pair.

If you pay your in-home caretaker through an agency or referral service, you won't have to worry about taxes. But if you hire an independent nanny or baby-sitter, you must pay Social Security and Medicare taxes for anyone you pay over $1,000 per year. You may also be required to pay federal (and sometimes state) unemployment taxes. Call the IRS publication order line (800-829-3676) to request IRS publication 926, Household Employers tax guide.

Relatives

Even when you pay them, it's much harder for you to make demands about the way relatives treat your children. Dialogue about expectations so they don't feel taken advantage of and you don't feel like you're stepping on their toes. Turning to family may provide a temporary solution when you're in transition and making other arrangements.

Kids on Their Own

You are the best judge of your child's readiness, but children are generally ready to spend short amounts of time on their own by age 10 (i.e., while you run to the corner to buy a paper or for an hour after school). However, don't expect a child under age 12 to care for younger siblings. Here's a checklist for families with kids on their own:

- ✔ Give your child the usual list of emergency numbers as well as a number where you can be reached and the number of an adult friend. Have your child check in with you as soon as he or she arrives home from school.
- ✔ Periodically go over safety rules such as "stop, drop, and roll" if your clothing catches fire, watch for unusual circumstances when first arriving home, leave immediately if an intruder is suspected, and never alert callers that there's no one else home.
- ✔ Show your child the first aid kit and how to use it. Leave a signed and notarized authorization form for emergency medical treatment.
- ✔ Set strict guidelines about activities you will or won't allow, whether friends may visit, whether appliances may be used, and what time to arrive home.

You as the Provider

If you've considered providing child care in your home, you know you'll save money on your own day care and commuting costs while filling a need for others. But remember, the trade-off for spending your days with your children in this way is little vacation time and little or no flexibility in your schedule. Form a network with other home providers to serve as backup for one another in case of illness, emergencies, or vacations. Before you get started, consult state laws and check the library for books on the topic.

Backup Child Care

Odds are your primary arrangements will fall through at some point or another. Prompted by the cost of parental absenteeism, many large companies are buying memberships in special drop-in day care centers that require only a 30-minute advance warning. Contact Lipton Corporate Childcare Centers (202-416-6875) to see if your company might be a candidate.

Although you'd prefer to be with your child when he or she is ill, sometimes you simply don't have that option. Some hospitals offer a special room or unit for sick-child day care. Don't wait until your child is sick. Call now to request information or to pre-register.

ENSURING A BRIGHT FUTURE

According to the 1996 Economic Report of the President, each year of formal education after high school adds 5% to 15% to a worker's annual earnings later on. Other census data support the fact that college is the key to higher earnings and an enhanced quality of life. More and more parents are coming to realize that the road to college starts *before* kindergarten. And the grammar school years set a learning and behavioral foundation that continues through high school and beyond.

Private Schools

Although many excellent public schools still exist, others just can't seem to meet children's needs. Parents may feel an unpatriotic twinge just *considering* pulling their children from public schools. Yet when they see their progeny falling through the cracks, they feel they have no other choice—that is, if they can afford the private school option.

Pilot public school voucher programs notwithstanding, private school tuition is beyond the reach of most parents struggling to provide for their own future retirements and children's college education. Scholarships and financial aid are rare, but don't discount them as a possibility. On the plus side, while paying private school tuition may reduce the amount you can put aside for college, the enhanced education may increase your child's qualifications for college scholarships.

SPECIAL EDUCATION

Federal law requires that public schools provide equal education opportunities for special needs children. If a public school is not able to adequately provide for your child's needs, the federal funding that would normally go to the school may follow your child to another, more suitable situation (i.e., a private school). Or so the theory goes.

Originally intended for children with disabilities such as hearing or vision loss, precedent-setting court cases have opened the door for parents of learning-disabled children to exercise this option as well. Since you may be in for an uphill struggle, start with the least drastic measure and document every step of the way, in case, as one mother put it, "things turn nasty."

STEP ONE: WORK WITH YOUR SCHOOL

Perhaps your child's school has suitable programs but your child isn't in the proper niche. Meet with teachers, principal, and guidance counselors. Make sure the problem has been correctly identified through proper testing.

STEP TWO: REQUEST A TRANSFER

If the problem persists, request a transfer to another school within the system. But survey the situation thoroughly or you may simply be going back to step one.

STEP THREE: CONSIDER LEGAL ACTION

If you feel you've exhausted your school system's capabilities and they're still not meeting your child's needs, consider legal action to have your child's funding channeled to a private school.

COLLEGE: GETTING THE MOST FOR YOUR MONEY

Set the expectation early that children will attend college and keep periodic attention focused on this goal. By raising family consciousness, encourage help from gift givers who will typically contribute to the college fund in addition to regular gifts. Put aside money—whatever you can afford—regularly. Require children and teens to contribute a portion of their allowance or job earnings. Complete a couple of special projects early on, invest your profits, and make compound interest work for you. Later, if money isn't sufficient, enlist your child's school guidance counselor for help in applying for scholarships, grants, and loans.

EDUCATION TAX CREDITS

The following credits may be used to directly reduce your income tax liability if you fall within the guidelines (however, if the credits exceed your liability, they are not refundable). Both credits are phased out incrementally for families earning $40,000 to $50,000 AGI (single filers) or $80,000 to $100,000 (joint filers). Since you can't use the credits simultaneously or in combination with the distributions from Education Investment Accounts (see page 185), calculate your taxes with different scenarios to see which option offers the most savings.

- You can claim a *HOPE Credit* equal to 100% of the first $1,000 you pay of qualified tuition and 50% of the next $1,000, for a total of $1,500 per student per year. Students (including yourself, your spouse, or your dependents) in their first two years of an undergraduate degree or certificate program are eligible.

- The *Lifetime Learning Credit* can be used to reduce your tax liability by 20% of qualified tuition and fees you pay on behalf of yourself, your spouse, or your dependents. For tax years between June 30, 1998, and December 31, 2002, up to $5,000 in qualified expenses are eligible, resulting in a maximum credit of $1,000. For tax years after December 31, 2002, up to $10,000 of expenses will result in a maximum credit of $2,000.

COLLEGE SAVINGS WORKSHEET

Step 1: Determine How Much Your College Will Cost.

   A. What year will your child start college? _____

   B. Look up the year on the College Cost table, below, and enter the amount you'll need. _____

Step 2: Determine How Much You Need to Save.

   C. *How much are you prepared to invest now as a lump sum?* _____

   D. *How many years until your child enters college?* (Subtract the current year from the year you entered in line A.) _____

   E. Find the number you entered on line D in the College Savings table below, and enter the corresponding number from the Growth Multiplier column. _____

   F. *How much will your initial investment be worth when your child enters college?* (Multiply the amount you entered in Line C by the multiplier in Line E.) _____

   G. *How much more money (total) do you need to set aside?* (Subtract the amount in Line F from the amount in Line B.) _____

Step 3: Determine Your Monthly Investment.

   H. Find the number you entered in Line D in the College Savings table, below, and enter the corresponding number from the Monthly Divisor column. _____

   I. *How much will you need to set aside monthly?* Divide the amount in Line G by the divisor in Line H and enter the result. _____

Step 4: Consider an Alternative Savings Plan.

Don't be discouraged if the amount in Line I is more than you can afford to set aside. Instead, determine what you *can* afford and how much it will grow.

(continued)

COLLEGE SAVINGS WORKSHEET
(CONTINUED)

J. Enter the amount you can comfortably save each month (in addition to the initial deposit you listed in Line C). _____

K. Divide the amount in Line J by the amount in Line I and enter the result. _____

L. *How much will my additional deposits have grown by the time my child enters college?* Divide the amount in Line K by the amount in Line G and enter the result. _____

M. *What is my total return from my initial investment and subsequent monthly investments?* Add the amount in Line L to the amount in Line F. _____

N. *What amount of supplementary funds (i.e., grants, loans, scholarships, student income) will be necessary to fund my child's education?* Subtract the amount in Line M from the amount in Line B. _____

College Cost Table

YEAR CHILD WILL ENTER COLLEGE	PROJECTED COST OF FOUR YEARS AT PRIVATE COLLEGE	PROJECTED COST OF FOUR YEARS AT PUBLIC COLLEGE
1998	$101,267	$40,503
1999	108,041	43,217
2000	115,280	46,112
2001	123,004	49,202
2002	131,245	52,498
2003	140,039	56,015
2004	149,421	59,769
2005	159,432	63,773

(continued)

COLLEGE SAVINGS WORKSHEET
(CONTINUED)

College Cost Table

YEAR CHILD WILL ENTER COLLEGE	PROJECTED COST OF FOUR YEARS AT PRIVATE COLLEGE	PROJECTED COST OF FOUR YEARS AT PUBLIC COLLEGE
2006	$170,114	$ 68,046
2007	181,512	72,605
2008	193,673	77,469
2009	206,650	82,660
2010	220,495	88,198
2011	235,268	94,107
2012	251,031	100,432
2013	267,850	107,140
2014	285,796	114,319
2015	304,945	121,978

The above table projects total 4-year costs, including tuition, fees, and room and board. It assumes a 6.7% inflation rate in college costs, based on the previous 10-year average inflation rate of private school tuition.

College Savings Table

YEARS UNTIL ENTER COLLEGE	GROWTH MULTIPLIER	MONTHLY DIVISOR
1	1,137	13,275
2	1,196	27,241
3	1,258	41,932
4	1,324	57,388
5	1,393	73,647
6	1,465	90,752

(continued)

COLLEGE SAVINGS WORKSHEET
(CONTINUED)

College Savings Table

YEARS UNTIL ENTER COLLEGE	GROWTH MULTIPLIER	MONTHLY DIVISOR
7	1,541	108,746
8	1,621	127,676
9	1,706	147,590
10	1,794	168,540
11	1,888	190,579
12	1,986	213,766
13	2,089	238,156
14	2,198	263,815
15	2,312	290,808
16	2,432	319,205
17	2,559	349,079
18	2,692	380,507
19	2,832	413,568

The above table assumes a constant amount put aside each month, the maturities coinciding with the four years your child will be attending college, the reinvestment of all earnings, and an average annual rate increase of 6.7%.

Source: Worksheet adapted from planning materials for the CollegeSure™ CD offered by College Savings Bank, Princeton, N.J. (800-888-2723). Individual results will vary if funds invested in other vehicles.

SAVINGS OPTIONS

However you come up with the money, your choice of investments can make the difference in whether the money you've put aside is enough to meet the objective. Consider the following savings options.

EDUCATION INVESTMENT ACCOUNTS

These tax-favored investment vehicles are popularly known as "education IRAs" since they operate in a similar fashion to IRAs. Taxpayers may contribute up to $500 per year per beneficiary (child) less than 18 years of age, with a phaseout of the eligible contribution occurring at AGIs of $95,000 (single) or $150,000 (married filing jointly). In this case, divorced or never married parents can earn a higher combined income and still make the full contribution for their common children.

The child may then take tax-free distributions of earnings for qualified postsecondary education expenses. A formula is applied to distributions of the original contribution to determine whether they are also excluded from the child's taxable income. These exclusions cannot be taken in the same tax year as a HOPE Credit or Lifetime Learning Credit (see page 180).

If the child does not use the entire amount accumulated, the remainder may be rolled over tax-free into another family beneficiary's (a child's or grandchild's) account in addition to the recipient's own $500 annual limit.

STANDARD SAVINGS ACCOUNT

A good start, but at typical savings rates—usually less than 4% annual percentage rate (APR)—you'll barely keep your money's value in the face of inflation. In addition, the liquidity may prove too tempting to you or your teen.

SAVINGS BONDS

The traditional college standby can still work, but changes in the Treasury laws have lowered your potential return. One plus: Interest earned on Series EE bonds purchased after 1989 is excluded from your federal income taxes, provided that the bond proceeds are used to pay higher education expenses.

SPECIAL BANK PRODUCTS

Check into bank products geared toward college savings. One of the best examples, the College Savings Bank in Princeton, New Jersey (800-888-2723), offers a product called the CollegeSure

CD. The special CD guarantees returns that are equal to the percentage of rise in average college costs, even if they soar above the rate of inflation. Therefore, you could make a lump-sum investment today of the average amount of four-year costs to attend a state college (for 1998, about $40,000) for your one-year-old child. By 2015, the year your child enters college, the mature CD would yield the approximately $115,000 it's projected to cost by that time.

Since most parents can't make large lump-sum investments, CDs are sold in one-year *units,* which can be purchased (and subsequently mature) over a four-year period. For those who can't afford an entire unit, guidelines help parents determine how much to invest monthly to meet the objectives.

Interest earned on such products is not tax-sheltered. Parents may consider opening them as a custodial account, which will make the first $650 in interest tax-free, the second $650 taxed at the child's rate (15%), and any additional gains taxed at the parent's rate until the child reaches age 14 and can file his or her own income taxes (figures are 1997 amounts and subject to annual inflation-based adjustment).

MUTUAL FUNDS

Look for a fund that encourages college savings by allowing smaller investments (such as $50 monthly) and easier payment methods (electronic funds transfer straight from your bank account).

TRUST FUNDS

Depending on the type of fund, it may be virtually impossible for a student to access this money until college. If divorcing, your marital dissolution agreement can require your ex-spouse to start and fund an educational trust. Consult your accountant and/or lawyer to decide what's best in your situation.

INDIVIDUAL SCHOOL SAVINGS PLANS

Some states or school systems allow parents to prepay at today's tuition rates but require the student to attend a specific school or system. But you just can't predict what your child will do that far in advance. Even if you get a refund later, you will have tied up your money for many years with no investment returns.

However, if this type of plan appeals to you despite the limitations, recent tax law expanded the definition of qualified state tuition programs and the way they interact with other educational tax incentives:

- If not used by the designated beneficiary, such accounts can now be rolled over and used by an expanded menu of family members, including siblings or their spouses.

- Amounts paid into these programs and later used for qualified expenses are eligible for the HOPE and lifetime learning credits.

- Proceeds from U.S. savings bonds used to purchase qualified tuition plans are excluded from the beneficiary's taxable income.

- Contributions to qualified tuition programs of up to $10,000 annually may be made on behalf of any individual and remain excludable from gift taxes. The recipient of the gift is not required to pay taxes on the gift.

Alternative Funding Sources

Unless your child is a star athlete or academic, it's up to you to locate scholarships, loans, and grants for which you might be eligible. Additionally, you and your child should decide how much money the child will contribute to the funding of his or her own education.

Private Scholarships

Consult guides such as the *Worldwide College Scholarship Directory* (Career Press, 1995) for scholarship listings. In addition, visit your school's scholarship office and find out about unique local opportunities such as scholarships from service clubs. Internet searches can also reveal hidden opportunities.

UNIVERSITY SCHOLARSHIPS

Start making inquiries early in your child's junior year of high school. Getting your scholarship paperwork in early can make a difference in the award amount. Most colleges offer the following types of scholarships:

Academic: Based on ACT/SAT scores, grades, and student involvement in extracurricular activities.

Adult: Adult scholarships typically seek adults who showed merit in high school and have work or other credentials that indicate a commitment to education. Could be an option for older children still living at home or for yourself.

Alumni: If you have friends or relatives that were alumni, your child may be eligible.

Departmental: Check with the college of your major for special scholarship opportunities. This source is especially important for graduate students.

Minority: Some universities use scholarships targeted to minorities to bolster their multicultural array.

Sports: If your child is a candidate for a sports scholarship, you've probably dealt with recruiters and the like already.

GOVERNMENT GRANTS

Although it may seem troublesome to apply for government grants, the potential payoff is well worth it. Don't discount Pell grants as a source of funds. Single parents and parents whose legal status is single (such as same-sex couples) must show only their own incomes when applying, which may increase their chances of qualifying. Remember, grant money that's left after tuition is paid is considered taxable income.

Unfortunately, most families make just a little too much money to get the grants, yet don't have enough to fully fund their children's education without jeopardizing their own retirement. For those who couldn't put enough away, student loans are the next option.

STUDENT LOANS

Your student loan may come either directly from the government via your school or through a private lender but guaranteed by the government. In either case, your school determines your eligibility and disperses the funds. Figure 10.1 charts available loan types. In addition, order the free booklet, *The Student Guide: Financial Aid from the U.S. Department of Education* (800-433-3243, Federal Student Aid Information Center, P.O. Box 84, Washington, DC 20044-0084).

> ### DEDUCTING STUDENT LOAN INTEREST
> The interest portion of student loan payments is deductible from your gross income under the following circumstances:
> - You were not claimed as a dependent on someone else's taxes (but you can use deduction for interest payments made on behalf of *your* spouse or dependents).
> - Loans were used to pay for qualified education expenses (tuition, fees, room and board, etc.) for a student enrolled at least half-time in a qualified postsecondary program.
> - Deduction can be used for interest payments made during the first 60 months in which payments are required.
> - Maximum deduction is $1,000 in 1998, increasing $500 per year to a maximum of $2,500 in 2001 and thereafter.
> - The deduction is phased out incrementally for AGIs of $40,000 to $55,000 (single filers) or $60,000 to $75,000 (joint filers).

THE STUDENT'S CONTRIBUTION

Your child will take college more seriously if asked to contribute. At a minimum, give your child some responsibility for meeting the paperwork deadlines. If the student will contribute financially by working, guide him or her into a job experience that will be beneficial in the long run.

Figure 10.1 Student Loans

	INTEREST	REPAYMENT	SUBSIDY	AMOUNT
Stafford Loan for undergraduate student	Variable, not to exceed 8.25%	6-month grace period after student graduates, leaves school, or drops below half-time enrollment	Need-based. Government pays interest until repayment begins or during authorized periods of deferment. If not subsidized, student must begin paying interest immediately or allow it to be capitalized.	Depends on need, years in school, years left to complete the program, and whether parent is eligible for PLUS loan
PLUS Loan for parent of undergraduate student	Variable, not to exceed 9%	Begins 60 days after the final loan disbursement is made	Not unless parents apply for a deferment (time period with no payments) or forbearance (reduced payments). A student may obtain repayment assistance for the parent by serving in the military.	Yearly limit equal to the cost of attendance minus other financial aid for which the student is eligible
Consolidation Loan for student or parent	Depends on previous loans	Depends on previous loans	Used to combine several loans or renegotiate the repayment terms of a single loan.	Depends on previous loans
Federal Perkins Loan for graduate or undergraduate student with exceptional need	5%	9-month grace period before repayment begins and up to 10-year payoff	Subsidized as with Stafford Loan, above. In addition, loan origination and insurance fees are waived, although late charges still apply.	Amount still needed after other financial aid has been exhausted

Saving on College Costs

- *In-state tuition:* If your child's college of choice is a state school in another state, consider establishing residency in that state. Save about 50% over the life of a four-year degree and even more if your child continues for graduate-level work. Once you've enrolled as an out-of-state student, most schools won't let you switch over to in-state tuition unless you are a permanent resident.

- *Faculty and staff discounts:* University faculty and staff benefits usually include reduced or free tuition for employees and their children. Families with both parents and children in school would benefit the most from this discount and could make changing jobs worthwhile. If a noncustodial parent is working at a university, your children might still be eligible for benefits.

- *Living arrangements:* There are pros and cons for every type of living arrangement, but in pure economic terms living at home can't be beat and accounts for 60% of our "children living at home" category. If the choice is between no college at all or living at home and attending the local college, there's no shame in the latter choice. For those who are going away to school, weigh carefully the options of dorm versus apartment living. Many schools require freshmen to live in a dorm and buy a food plan. But if free to choose, an apartment with roommates can be more economical and comfortable.

- *Transportation:* Vehicles are expensive. After paying insurance, bank notes, and repairs, there may be nothing left for gas money! If the student will be living on campus and not holding down an outside job, consider public transportation or a bicycle as viable options.

- *Hidden expenses:* Many classes have hidden expenses that could drain hundreds of dollars from your wallet. Before registering for art or lab-type classes, find out if supplies are included in tuition.

- *Tuition ceilings:* Typically, a certain amount of tuition is charged per semester hour earned, up to a ceiling, which is the flat rate paid for full-time tuition. Most colleges consider 12 semester hours to be full-time enrollment, but they'll allow

(continued)

SAVING ON COLLEGE COSTS
(CONTINUED)

students to enroll in more classes (up to about 19 hours) without paying any additional tuition. If 18 credit hours seem like a tough academic load, remember that in high school your child was accustomed to six or seven classes daily plus extracurricular activities. The amount you save on tuition this way may mean that your child will have to work less on outside jobs and will graduate sooner.

- *Greek life:* There's just no getting around the expense of sororities and fraternities. An alternative? Encourage your student to get involved with another group experience, such as a campus religious organization, student council, activities council, intramural sports, or clubs associated with favorite hobbies.

Work-study programs aren't lucrative, but they keep your child on campus and in a supervised situation. Other pros include learning job skills and making university contacts. Apply for work-study by checking the appropriate box on the general financial aid application. There is no choice at first about where your child is placed, but once a student is accepted, a transfer to a position that is closer to his or her field of study can be requested.

$ Fifty-six percent of full-time students hold down a job.
$

Some parents encourage off-campus jobs only during school vacations, to avoid interference with academic pursuits. Others feel that keeping a regular work schedule during school teaches the student to budget time wisely and may take some focus away from partying. Either way, look for jobs that are flexible, part-time, and close to campus. Carefully weigh the hidden benefits of a job more closely related to the child's field of study even if it doesn't pay as much. If your child isn't working, encourage him or her to schedule a couple of hours each week in a volunteer organization.

WHEN MORE THAN ONE OF YOU ARE IN SCHOOL

Although sending yourself and your family through school at the same time is not a task for the weak at heart, it's a winning investment in your family's welfare. We saw earlier the effects of higher education on quality of life, but you should note the special rewards for an adult who goes back for career renewal, as a beginning to a new life.

CAREER ENRICHMENT

If your employer pays for eligible non-graduate-level educational expenses, you do not have to count this contribution as part of your income. Although this exclusion previously existed for courses beginning prior to July 1, 1997, recent tax law extended it to courses beginning before June 1, 2000.

ADULT STUDENT DEVELOPMENT OFFICE

If your school has such a department, it can be invaluable in walking you through the paperwork and finding programs to match your needs. Ask for a list of adult-oriented, for-credit classes such as how to use the university library, night classes, or extended three-hour classes held only once a week to save trips to campus.

STUDENT HOUSING

Though quality and availability vary, adult student family housing can be a real bargain for families in transition. Because of the high percentage of single-parent residents, many have evolved informal support networks for carpooling, baby-sitting, and meals.

OTHER STUDENT BENEFITS

A student activity fee is built into tuition, enabling discounts all over town, from movie theaters to bookstores to city attractions. You may be able to attend school lectures, art events, theater, and, of course, sports functions for free.

Of course, more serious services are available as well. For instance, group or individual personal counseling may be available free to students and their families. Career placement offices offer seminars and job search help. Don't overlook the departmental study centers, where you or your child can get free tutoring from interns and graduate assistants.

Figure 10.2 Special Advice on Selecting and Paying for Education

TYPE OF FAMILY	ADVICE
Two-earner	• Experiment: Build your budget around one earner's income. Channel your second income into retirement, education, and estate building.
Single parent	• *Divorced:* If provisions for college savings were made in your divorce settlement, check periodically that your ex is complying. If no provisions were made, open a dialogue about how you will handle this important topic. • *Separated:* If you are negotiating a divorce, determine who will pay what share of the children's education. • *Widowed:* Your financial picture will vary depending on the circumstances of your spouse's death and the adequacy of health and life insurance coverage. • *Never married:* If unable to put as much aside as you'd hoped, set up a college fund for each child and ask close friends and relatives to contribute on birthdays or holidays.
Blended	• See "Two-earner" above.
Cohabiting (opposite sex)	• For financial aid forms, the parent who claims the child as a dependent is the one whose income is counted in eligibility calculations.
Cohabiting (same sex)	• See "Cohabiting (opposite sex)" above.
Adoptive	• If the children are older, you won't have as much time to set aside savings. Set aside as much as you can, but look to supplementary sources as well.

FIGURE 10.2 (CONTINUED)

TYPE OF FAMILY	ADVICE
Foster	• For foster families, programs in most states end at majority and don't cover college-age young adults. • Give the young person a head start in life by helping in school selection, admissions, and financial aid.
Wife as breadwinner	• If children are still young, organize a traditional college savings plan. • If children are older, begin setting aside money more aggressively if you can afford it. • In either case, ask your stay-at-home support person to wade through all the loan, grant, and scholarship paperwork with the college-student-to-be.
Multicultural	• Plan ahead with sound investments, but don't forget to check into minority scholarship funds if applicable.
Older parents	• Don't think the trade-off between your retirement and the children's education means all or nothing. If you're able to contribute anything, the kids can supplement with scholarships, grants, loans, and even working if necessary.
Adult children living at home	• If you're allowing your young-adult children to live at home rent-free (or for reduced rent) while they complete an education, you're making quite a contribution already.
Grandchildren living with grandparents	• See "Older parents" and "Adult children living at home" above.
May-December	• See "Older parents" above.

CHAPTER ELEVEN

Rescuing Your Retirement

The realities of longer life spans, shrinking Social Security reserves, and healthier senior populations are changing our retirement assumptions from those of the previous generation. With a longer life span after retirement, the money you've put away must last longer. With less income from Social Security, you must make up the difference with your own investments or suffer a decline in lifestyle. A healthier senior population means many are working longer before retirement or continuing in part-time positions after retirement, out of choice or necessity.

How must your current lifestyle change in order to overcome your retirement hurdles in the face of these odds? Focus on the following retirement checklist:

- ✔ Estimate your approximate living expenses for retirement. A general rule of thumb says that you will need about 80% of your preretirement income.
- ✔ Make sure you are adequately covered by disability and health insurance, including long-term care.
- ✔ List all benefits that you already have coming, such as Social Security, pensions through work, or plans you've set up for yourself such as IRAs.
- ✔ Make informed choices about your retirement investments. If you must change jobs and you have a vested pension, roll it over into a tax-sheltered investment.

✔ Manage your retirement investments according to your stage in life. When you are younger, for example, you can afford to invest in stocks, which have a higher return overall but may also drop at times. Your younger age gives you time to ride out the low points. As you near retirement age, shift a greater percentage of your investments into more stable vehicles such as CDs.

OVERCOMING YOUR RETIREMENT HURDLES

For any given income, estimates show if you save 10% annually, it will take forty years to have enough to retire, even when supplemented by Social Security. Forty years! If you feel the pressures of family life, where every penny goes to current expenses, consider the alternative. If you don't drop everything and start saving now for retirement, you could find yourself working until *you* drop.

The lucky few who *are* planning for retirement 40 years in advance can expend energy regularly and steadily—as if running a long marathon—to make it to their destination. But for the rest of us, retirement is more like a sprint to the finish line—expending every ounce of energy and focus for that final push. Whether your own race to retirement is a sprint or a marathon, you must overcome three hurdles:

1. *A place to live:* If you're already a home buyer, you're off and running. If not, you must set aside funds to cover your rent in retirement.

2. *Social Security benefits:* If your records aren't accurate or your work patterns have been erratic, you may not receive the entitlement you are expecting. Know the rules, periodically review your records, and make informed choices about your work patterns.

3. *Living expenses:* If you don't have a company pension (and who does these days?), take advantage of tax-sheltered investments now to ensure an adequate income in retirement.

More Than a Room of Your Own

The truth is, most of us wish to have more than a room of our own in retirement—at least as long as we're able. The only way to ensure that you won't be crashing with your kids is to plan ahead. Buy a home now or set aside funds for renting later. In either case, be sure you've got adequate long-term care insurance if the time comes that you are no longer able to take care of yourself.

Buying a Home

Earlier in the book, we discussed the tax and investment benefits of residential real estate. From a retirement perspective, local market conditions and your ability to pay withstanding, purchasing a home is the most significant contribution you can make to your future security.

Historically, although the stock market is often touted as the best performer, real estate has actually outperformed all other classes of investments overall. And *residential* real estate provides you the opportunity for both tax shelter *and* growth. The interest and state property taxes are deductible on your federal income taxes and the equity gives you an opportunity for low-interest and tax-deductible interest loans. On the growth (investment side), you don't have to worry about being taxed on your capital gains up to $250,000 if single and $500,000 if married filing jointly upon sale as long as you lived in your primary residence at least two out of the last five years. You can continue taking this exclusion indefinitely once every two years. This provision started May 6, 1997 and replaced the one-time waiver of the capital gains tax previously allowed to those over 59 years old.

Finally, if you're closer to retirement and don't yet own, consider that a fixed-rate mortgage gives you a buffer against inflation. Your monthly payment will remain stable while surrounding rent costs continue to rise. These reasons alone may give you the impetus to buy.

Planning to Rent

If you choose not to buy because local real estate conditions aren't rosy, or you're not able to buy because you've been permanently priced out of the housing market, you must move to a second strategy—investing money now so you can rent later.

Your dual challenge: paying rent for your current digs while putting aside a large enough nest egg to ensure that you have a future nest in which to live. Gauge the amount you'll need to set aside by estimating the amount you pay now plus inflation (multiply times 3% per year). Although there isn't an exact correlation between rents and inflation, rents, in general, rise parallel to the inflation rate, so it's safe to use as an estimate.

When you consider the number of years you'll need to pay rent during retirement, this task can seem daunting. A key strategy is to put your home-replacement fund in investments that have growth potential, so they, too, will rise with inflation and keep pace with rising rents.

Figuring zero inflation, for $12,000 rent a year (or $1,000 a month) at 10% interest, you would need a fund of $120,000 on top of your investments that will cover other living expenses, to defray your annual rent of $12,000.

Depending on your age, the number of years to retirement, and your expectations about retirement lifestyle, you need to add a target for rent replacement to your current growth strategy. Obviously, if retirement is years off, this component can be a small amount. But if retirement is near, you must make this an absolute priority.

BENEFITING FROM SOCIAL SECURITY

Opinion polls show that while people nearing retirement trust in the strength of the system, Generation Xers believe that Social Security will disappear before they retire. But as long as political support for the system remains strong, Social Security will continue in some form.

In 1997, the Social Security Advisory Council published a report offering options for congressional consideration (see Appendix D to order). Not even after years of study and debate could this panel of experts come to a consensus about how to keep Social Security going at its current benefit rates. Budget discussions have frequently looked at the possibility of reducing cost-of-living allowances and shifting the age at which payment commences. But the report advised Congress to consider more drastic ideas such as taxing benefits that exceed what the worker paid into the plan, investing a portion of the Social Security endowment into the stock market, gradually reducing benefits, mandating an additional 1.6% payroll contribution toward a retirement account in which the worker chooses the investments, converting a percentage of the current 12.4% payroll contribution to a defined-benefit plan, and placing contributions of those under age 25 in a *personal security account* subject to regulatory restrictions.

While many of these options sound unattractive, consider the alternative—returning to the type of fear and uncertainty that previously plagued old age.

Government change is slow. It may be years before *any* proposals are adopted and years still before the effect on your bottom line. Be proactive. Watch out for your future interests by contacting your representatives. But for now your best defense is to learn the current rules and work them to your benefit.

CHECKING YOUR REPORT

While Social Security payments can be an important component of your retirement, for most the income will not be sufficient to live on. Instead, think of it as an important supplement. Since your benefit level as an individual retiree is calculated from your earnings and the number of years you've been employed, the Social Security administration keeps a running tab on these variables. Periodically check up on them to ensure that the account is accurate.

To order your report, request a *statement of earnings* (form SSA7004) from your local Social Security office or from the Commissioner of Social Security, 6410 Security Boulevard, Baltimore, MD 21235. A few weeks after you return the completed form, you should receive a review of your work life and earnings as recorded by the Social Security Administration. A 24-hour toll-free hot line can shortcut the process (1-800-772-1213).

WORKING THE RULES

Following is a sampling of Social Security rules that can impact today's families.

Divorce

If you divorced after having been married for 10 years or more, you're entitled to draw on your former spouse's account (formerly, 20 years of marriage was required). If you have earned your own Social Security through employment, you have a choice of the higher benefits: your own or half your former spouse's. More than one spouse can claim retirement benefits; your former spouse's remarriage will not affect this right.

Age

If born before 1938, the retirement age for maximum benefits is age 62. For retirees born after 1938, the retirement age is increased by two months for each year up to the maximum benefit retirement age of 67 for those born after 1960. A retiree born any time may take early retirement at age 62, but the benefit is decreased to 70 percent of the maximum paid at age 67.

Work Patterns

Under current law, if you reach age 65 in 1994 or later, you'll need to have been employed for 10 years or 40 quarters to collect your full retirement benefit. If you're 55 and haven't been contributing fully to the Social Security system (by deducting Social Security taxes from your paycheck), you should make a point of doing so even if you must pay additional self-employment tax. To keep this part of your retirement solid, keep abreast of the changes in retirement rules such as selecting the age at which you will retire. In so doing, you'll receive the full benefit from this pillar of your retirement plan.

SECURING YOUR INCOME

Today, fewer workers can count on a company pension with sufficient vested benefits to overcome the living-expenses hurdle. Regardless of whether you have a company pension, you should invest in tax-deferred retirement vehicles to ensure the type of income you need for a comfortable retirement. Employed people can contribute to 401(k) plans or 403(b)s if employed by a nonprofit company, *self*-employed people must set up their own Keoghs or SEP-IRAs, and everyone can contribute to individual retirement accounts (IRAs) and annuities.

EMPLOYER-SPONSORED RETIREMENT PLANS

If you are lucky enough to be partially or fully vested (see sidebar) in a *defined-benefit* retirement plan, you're part of a fading demographic. These plans are what we think of when we hear the word *pension*. The company promises to pay a set amount upon retirement based on an employee's salary and number of years at work. Important points about defined-benefit plans include the following:

- If you are close to being fully vested, watch your timing if you are considering changing jobs. It may be worth the extra wait to go for the full pension.
- If you are partially or fully vested and you leave your job, some companies insist on keeping tabs on your pension and paying whatever benefits are owed you at the time you retire. Others will give you the option of taking your vested amount with you. If given the option, roll it over into a tax-deferred account.
- Some classic pensions have a spousal provision in which you may take reduced benefits in return for a pension going to your spouse if you die before retirement. If your partner or spouse does not have sufficient retirement savings, consider taking this option. The only risk is a reduced benefit to you if you don't die, but the alternative—a loved one left penniless—is far worse.
- A portion of your defined-benefit pension may be insured by the Pension Benefit Guarantee Corporation even if the company goes bankrupt.
- Unless you waive your right at divorce, federal law entitles you to a minimum of 50% of the accrued vested benefit in

your spouse's plan. Technically, it is considered a survivor's benefit. If you are going through a divorce, have your attorney draft a QDRO (Qualified Domestic Relations Order, pronounced "quadro"), which will direct the retirement plan administrator as to what payments are to be made to the divorced spouse.

$ ARE YOU VESTED?

To be vested is to have a nonforfeitable right to money your employer contributed to your retirement plan on your behalf. After you've worked for the firm a certain number of years, you become fully vested and the money your employer contributed to the plan is yours when you retire. Typically, that's five years. Some companies have a gradual vesting policy, so that you own 20% of your benefits after three years, 40% after four years, 60% after five years, 80% after six years, and 100% after seven years.

More common are employer-sponsored *defined-contribution* plans. These plans set the size of the employer and/or employee contributions and pay out whatever yield the investment has accrued. They allow the employer to make tax-deductible contributions while the employee contributes pretax dollars. A common variety of defined-contribution plans are 401(k)s, which your employers may offer even if they also provide a regular pension.

Typically, participation in a 401(k) involves employees voluntarily diverting pretax salary to the fund. Employers may match all or a portion of the contribution. If, for example, the company contributes 50 cents to each dollar contributed by the employee, the investment return is already 50% before even being invested.

In addition, 401(k) funds are *portable* by law, meaning upon leaving an employer, you can either withdraw them (paying taxes on interest and contributions), or roll them over tax-free into another tax-advantaged account. An employer may limit your access to their matching contributions in some cases (i.e., if you haven't met company vesting guidelines).

People employed by IRS code 501(c)(3) organizations—public school systems and certain nonprofit educational, charitable, literary, scientific, and religious organizations—are eligible for a similar salary-reduction plan under IRS code 403(b). The plan for nonprofit employees offers tax benefits similar to those in the 401(k). In addition, the employer has the option to contribute an additional amount in the employee's name to increase the employee's retirement benefit.

Both salary-reduction plans offer tax benefits to the employer as well as to the employee. You contribute a certain portion of your income (in 1997, the legal ceiling was the greater of $9,500 or 13% of your gross income). The maximum reduction is indexed for inflation annually and announced by the IRS.

$ **Generally, if you can afford to do it, think in terms of funding your 401(k) to its maximum amount and then making a nondeductible contribution to an IRA if you still have extra funds to commit.**
$

RETIREMENT PLANS FOR THE SELF-EMPLOYED

If you're self-employed and can afford to save more than the $2,000 upper limit on an IRA, take advantage of a Keogh plan. Or you may consider a SEP-IRA in lieu of both.

A Keogh plan is a pension fund for any person who reports earnings from self-employment, regardless of how small. Generally, there are three situations in which you might encounter a Keogh: as an employee, as a self-employed person, or as partner or member of a board of directors.

If you're employed by someone else, your employer may contribute to your Keogh plan. If so, he or she is required by antidiscrimination laws to contribute the same percentage of your income to your Keogh as your employer contributes to his or her own Keogh. Usually, this contribution comes from the employer and not from your salary.

If you're not self-employed, this is the only way a Keogh may apply to you.

If, however, you are the sole proprietor of a business, you may set up a Keogh for yourself. There are two basic types of Keogh plans: *defined-contribution* plans and *defined-benefit* plans. With defined-contribution plans (a discussion follows), you contribute a certain amount of your income, which is fixed by law. On the other hand, a defined-benefit plan allows annual payments according to your predetermined retirement income needs. This plan works best if you have ample discretionary funds and are fairly close to retirement.

Defined-contribution plans are the most common types of Keoghs. They offer two options, depending on your payment plan. If you fix an annual percentage of income to be contributed when you first open the account, you may contribute up to 20% of your earned income with a $30,000 maximum. However, if you want to have the option of paying differing percentages each year, you may contribute up to 13% of your earned income.

Partners and members of boards of directors (and self-employed people who employ others) may also open Keoghs. However, remember that if you employ others, you must match percentages with their salaries, potentially making a Keogh very expensive.

With Keogh plans, no matter what type, you determine whether the funds will be released in a lump sum or in installments. You also decide how you want the funds invested—in a money market, variable universal life insurance policy, an interest-bearing bank account, or any combination of these. However, you do have certain limitations with your Keogh, like those on IRAs. For instance, you are generally not allowed to withdraw money without a penalty until age 59½ or until you become disabled. And you must begin withdrawing money from your Keogh plan when you reach age 70½ even if you haven't retired.

The calculations in Keoghs are complex, so it's a good idea to seek professional advice if you're considering this plan.

Another option is the *simplified employee pension,* or SEP-IRA. Like regular IRAs, SEP-IRAs offer tax-sheltered contributions and interest income. The maximum yearly contribution is up to 15% of your gross income, not to exceed $22,500 in one year. The simplified paperwork required often makes it a good choice for self-employed persons who do not have any other employees and are not concerned about being able to take loans out against their funds.

But the SEP-IRA is not for everyone. If your small business offers any other type of pension benefits, you may not use a SEP-IRA. In addition, if you use a SEP-IRA, you must offer the same benefits to your qualifying employees as you offer yourself. Qualifying employees are those to whom you've paid at least $400 in a given year and have worked three out of the previous five years, so depending on your circumstances, you might be required to cover a lot of people.

INDIVIDUAL RETIREMENT ACCOUNTS (IRAS) AND ANNUITIES

Aside from annuities, individual retirement accounts are the ubiquitous tax-favored investment vehicle. Taxpayers now have three IRA varieties from which to choose:

1. Deductible IRA
2. Roth IRA
3. Nondeductible IRA

Any earner (as well as a nonearning spouse in a single-earner household) may sock away up to $2,000 per year in an IRA (or divided between one or more different types). Your own best choice depends upon income, age, and other circumstances.

The *deductible IRA* is generally still the best option for eligible taxpayers who meet the income guidelines. It gives you an immediate $2,000 deduction on this year's taxes and a deferral of taxes on both your original contribution and earned interest. You pay taxes only upon withdrawal—presumably when you're retired and subject to a lower tax rate. Since your contribution was made in before-tax dollars, your effective earnings are boosted from the start and compound interest does a nice job on your untaxed earnings. In addition, you may set up the IRA as late as April 14 and it will still count as a deduction against the previous year's taxes.

In 1998, those earning up to $30,000 AGI (single filers) or $50,000 (joint filers) can take the full deduction. For those with higher incomes, the deduction is reduced in increments until no deduction may be taken for those earning over $40,000 AGI (single filers) or $60,000 (joint filers).

If you're covered by an employer-sponsored retirement plan you cannot open a deductible IRA (consider opening either a Roth IRA or a nondeductible IRA instead, see below). Married couples note: Previously if *one* spouse was covered by an employer-sponsored plan, *neither* could take the IRA deduction. Starting in tax year 1998, if one spouse is covered by an employer plan, the other can still take the deduction, providing they meet income guidelines.

While you can begin taking withdrawals from your deductible IRA as early as age 59½, you are *required* to begin taking withdrawals after age 70½. In addition, you are not allowed to contribute to a deductible IRA after age 70½. If withdrawal guidelines are not met, a stiff 10% tax penalty is levied *in addition* to income taxes you'll pay on the withdrawal amount at your current tax rate.

In contrast to the deductible IRA, contributions made to a *Roth IRA* (first available in tax year 1998) are not deductible. In exchange for making your initial contribution in after-tax dollars, your earnings accumulate tax-free and no taxes are due upon qualified withdrawal—a boon for those expecting to remain subject to a high tax rate upon retirement.

At income thresholds of $95,000 AGI (single filers) and $150,000 AGI (joint filers), a Roth IRA is a good option if your AGI makes you ineligible for a deductible IRA. In this case, eligibility for tax-free earnings is phased out in increments up to AGIs of $110,000 (single filers) and $160,000 (joint filers).

A final difference in the Roth IRA that can make it appealing to some is the greater flexibility of withdrawals and contributions. Qualified (nonpenalized) withdrawals may begin as early as five years after the initial contribution, provided at least one of the following qualifiers is met: You are 59½ years old, disabled, a beneficiary of the estate that holds the IRA, or using the withdrawal for the purchase of your first home. *Caution: The greater ease of withdrawal may place retirement funds at risk.*

In contrast to the deductible IRA, the Roth does not require you to begin making withdrawals at any age and there is no limit on the age at which you may open or contribute to a Roth—a plus to those who expect greater life spans and wish to continue amassing retirement funds after age 70½.

If you feel a Roth would offer greater benefits for your situation, you may roll money over from existing IRAs into a Roth, but you must report any previously deductible contributions as income, paying taxes at your current rate. For the tax year 1998 only, you may roll a lump sum over yet divide it into fourths, spreading the income (and paying the taxes) over a four-year period instead. This provision is meant to keep the lump sum, which would otherwise falsely inflate your income, from propelling you into a higher tax bracket. In tax years 1999 and beyond, you will be required to report all previously deductible contributions as income in the year in which they are rolled over.

But what if your AGI or participation in an employer-sponsored retirement plan disqualifies you for all or part of a deductible or Roth IRA? You can still place either your entire $2,000 (or the portion that was ineligible for the "premium" IRAs if your income fell in a phaseout range) into a *nondeductible IRA.*

Although your initial contribution is made in after-tax dollars and your earnings will be taxed upon withdrawal, you can still enjoy the benefit of your earnings accumulating tax-free for the years they remain in the account—considerably boosting your returns and making it a worthwhile option. There are no income requirements for nondeductible IRAs, but rules regarding contributions, withdrawals, and penalties are the same as those for deductible IRAs.

Finally, if you have already maxed out your 401(k) and IRA contributions but still have funds to allocate for retirement savings, consider an *annuity.* An annuity is a contract bought from an insurance company, and the holder pays a set sum of money. This money (plus interest) is then paid back at a predetermined date for either a set period of time or for the life of the contract holder.

You can cash in an annuity at any time, although there's a penalty for early withdrawal. The smallest annuity available is usually $2,500. The insurance company will apply charges that include a sales fee. You receive a tax break with a *deferred* annuity because the interest accrues with taxes deferred until withdrawal at retirement.

RETIREMENT PLANNING WORKSHEET

1. Estimated annual income you will need to retire (80% of pre-retirement income).

   Self $_____ + Partner $_____ = $_____

2. Annual Social Security benefit. (Call the Social Security Administration at 800-772-1213 and request Form SSA 7004.)

   Self $_____ + Partner $_____ = $_____

3. Annual pension income. (Get estimate from your employee benefits officer of the annual amount due you at age 65.)

   Self $_____ + Partner $_____ = $_____

4. Projected annual income from pension and Social Security. (Add lines 2 and 3.) $_____

5. Shortfall between what you need and what you have. (Subtract line 4 from line 1. If line 4 is larger than line 1, you are in the enviable position of having met your most critical long-term goal and can turn your attention to planning for other goals.) $_____

6. The minimum amount you will need in your retirement fund at age 65 to cover line 5 and meet your retirement goal. (If married, multiply line 5 by the appropriate joint multiplier from the table below; if more than five years difference in your ages, use single multiplier for the younger partner's age. Otherwise, use appropriate single multiplier.) $_____

(continued)

RETIREMENT PLANNING WORKSHEET
(CONTINUED)

7. The value of your current investments.
   a. IRA/Keogh plan　　　　　　　　　　　$_____
   b. 401(k) or other employer-sponsored savings plan
   　　　　　　　　　　　　　　　　　　　$_____
   c. Other assets (stocks, bonds, CDs, mutual funds, real estate, insurance cash values, etc.)　$_____
   TOTAL current investments. (Add lines a, b, and c.)
   　　　　　　　　　　　　　　　　　　　$_____

8. Value of current investments at retirement age, adjusted for inflation. (Multiply Line 7 by Factor C from the table below.)
   　　　　　　　　　　　　　　　　　　　$_____

9. Additional capital needed to meet your retirement goal. (Subtract line 8 from line 6.)　　$_____

10. What you need to save each year to meet your retirement goal. (Multiply line 9 by Factor C in the table below.)
    　　　　　　　　　　　　　　　　　　$_____

Table 1 Expected Retirement Age (S = single, J = joint)

	55	60	62	65	67	70
S	13.06	11.26	10.62	9.71	9.16	8.38
J	24.54	13.59	12.81	11.72	11.05	10.11

Table 2 Years to Retirement

	5	7	10	15	20	25	30	35
Factor B	1.34	1.50	1.79	2.40	3.21	4.29	5.74	7.69
Factor C	.167	.112	.072	.041	.026	.017	.012	.008

(Assumes 6% savings return)

An interactive version of the retirement planning worksheet can be found at http://www.womenmoney.com.

LEGAL LESSONS: BORROWING FROM YOUR 401(K)

Most companies write their 401(k) plans to allow you to borrow money from them at market interest rates (though the purpose of the loan may be restricted to purchasing a home or paying tuition bills, for example), so you don't feel your money is trapped until age 59½.

- Any time you withdraw money from a 401(k), you're going to be taxed.
- If you need to withdraw 401(k) funds before age 59½, you may have to prove hardship (medical reasons, for example) and meet other requirements. And, with certain exceptions, you'll pay a 10% tax *penalty* on the amount withdrawn.

FIGURE 11.1 SPECIAL ADVICE FOR RESCUING YOUR RETIREMENT

TYPE OF FAMILY	ADVICE
Two-earner	• Keep separate retirement plans, but if your spouse is one of the rare employees who are still entitled to a traditional pension, weigh the options for a partial spousal benefit in case the covered employee dies first.
Single parent	• *Divorced:* If your retirement plans got divided as part of the divorce proceedings, you may be starting at ground zero. But remember, the earlier you start, the less you have to put away to enjoy a secure retirement. • *Separated:* Retirement plans can be some of the largest assets in a marriage. If a divorce is pending, make sure the settlement includes an equitable division of retirement benefits.

FIGURE 11.1 (CONTINUED)

TYPE OF FAMILY	ADVICE
Single parent	• *Widowed:* If your spouse received an employer pension, you may be entitled to certain benefits of which you were unaware. If your spouse was receiving Social Security, you may be entitled to survivor's benefits. Otherwise, you should roll over all of your spouse's retirement assets into your own retirement accounts. • *Never married:* When the buck stops with you on every financial and legal front, you carry a big weight on your shoulders. Unfortunately, here again you must make it happen for yourself if it's going to happen at all.
Blended	• See "Two-earner" on previous page.
Cohabiting (opposite sex)	• Since you're not legally married, you won't receive survivor benefits from your partner's Social Security or pension plans and will each need to see to your own retirement funds.
Cohabiting (same sex)	• See "Cohabiting (opposite sex)," above.
Adoptive	• Bringing more children into your life can throw off the balance of your carefully crafted financial plans. Review retirement goals and projections to ensure that you can still set aside the amount you will need.
Foster	• See "Adoptive" above.
Wife as breadwinner	• Take advantage of the new tax law that allows the nonearner to make a full IRA contribution each year.
Multicultural	• See "Two-earner" on previous page.

FIGURE 11.1 (CONTINUED)

TYPE OF FAMILY	ADVICE
Older parents	• If you're still renting your home, make sure your retirement investments include a rent replacement strategy. • Remember, your retirement is a priority, even if it means the kids have to supplement their college funds with a little elbow grease of their own.
Adult children living at home	• If your adult children are already struggling, it's hard to ask them for contributions. But if they are a drain on the family economy, you could be placing your retirement in jeopardy.
Grandchildren living with grandparents	• See "Older parents" above.
May-December	• Your spouse may already be receiving retirement benefits but still supplemented by your income. Make sure your own retirement benefits are adequate so that you can retire together in style.

CHAPTER TWELVE

Insurance Trade-offs

All families can overlook proper insurance coverage—they may fail to periodically review and update their plans, feel they can't afford coverage, or put their dollars into coverage that isn't tailored to their needs.

But some families are especially vulnerable to insurance problems. Two-earners may think they're covered under company plans but may actually hold insurance portfolios that contain gaps or overlaps. Cohabiting partners struggle to get family members covered under group plans—or forget to change beneficiaries to reflect their important relationships. Single parents and families in transition are sometimes exposed to dangerous gaps in coverage. Careful planning is especially important when a lack of assets or a supporting partner means insurance money is the only protection you can offer your children in case of your illness or death.

This chapter will help you assess your health, disability, and life insurance needs to make sure you're adequately covered without being overinsured. Other types of insurances will be addressed, as well as strategies to get the most out of your insurance dollars.

START WITH WHAT YOU HAVE

Take an inventory of all the policies you now have as well as those for which you might be eligible under group rates. You may be surprised by hidden policies that you weren't even aware of. Most of us think immediately of our employee benefit packages and move on to member benefits for unions, professional organizations, credit cards, bank accounts, colleges and universities, the military, and any other organizations that count us as members.

With your inventory in hand, note where you're duplicating or overlapping coverage and where you think you might have gaps. Duplication often happens from a combination of ignorance of

INSURANCE REVIEW WORKSHEET

INSURANCE TYPE	COMPANY/ POLICY NUMBER	INSURED PERSON/ CAR/ADDRESS	BENE- FICIARY	AMOUNT OF PREMIUM	COVERAGE
Health					
Policy #1	_____	_____	_____	_____	_____
Policy #2	_____	_____	_____	_____	_____
Policy #3	_____	_____	_____	_____	_____
Life					
Policy #1	_____	_____	_____	_____	_____
Policy #2	_____	_____	_____	_____	_____
Policy #3	_____	_____	_____	_____	_____
Disability					
Policy #1	_____	_____	_____	_____	_____
Policy #2	_____	_____	_____	_____	_____
Policy #3	_____	_____	_____	_____	_____
Automobile					
Policy #1	_____	_____	_____	_____	_____
Policy #2	_____	_____	_____	_____	_____
Policy #3	_____	_____	_____	_____	_____
Home-owner's					
Policy #1	_____	_____	_____	_____	_____
Policy #2	_____	_____	_____	_____	_____
Policy #3	_____	_____	_____	_____	_____
Other					
Policy #1	_____	_____	_____	_____	_____
Policy #2	_____	_____	_____	_____	_____
Policy #3	_____	_____	_____	_____	_____

what you have and what you fear you may have left unprotected. There's no easy way to see what insurance you really need. The basic rule is that you want to insure to protect both your income and assets against loss. You'll have to play the odds, knowing that you'll never be insured for all possibilities. Instead, attempt to determine the most likely calamities and hope, of course, that you'll never have to cash in on your premiums. It's a grim exercise to attend to all the terrible things that could potentially mar your life. But worse yet is to be left with nothing if fate should deal you a bad hand.

BUILD YOUR FAMILY'S FOUNDATION

Your family's health, disability, and life insurance will form the foundation of your insurance portfolios. Following are some issues to consider as you make your selections.

Health Insurance

If you're covered under an employer's plan or your children are covered under the ex-spouse's plan, you may not have much choice about your coverage. However, almost everyone faces insurance choices at some time—whether you are between jobs, an employer offers several plan options, or an employer offers none at all. If you're not currently faced with a choice, familiarize yourself with the basic issues to get the most out of existing policies.

Just as federal income taxes are skewed in favor of a traditional family, insurance policies are cheaper for "coverage by the dozen." Typically, family plans cover a spouse and any number of children for a flat rate. The more children, the less costly per person. But when the parents aren't legally married (and don't work for a progressive company), they are forced to purchase much more expensive individual policies for family members.

If you must purchase individual policies for family members, look for membership in organizations that might make you eligible for group insurance. In addition, try to cover each person's legal children under that person's policy rather than purchasing

GETTING THE MOST FOR YOUR HEALTH INSURANCE DOLLAR

	OPTION A	OPTION B
1. Type of plan (PPO, etc.).	____	____
2. Ease of use. (Will you or your doctor file the claims?)	____	____
3. Are your current doctors participating providers?		
a. Primary care physician	____	____
b. Specialists	____	____
4. Does the policy require preauthorization or referrals from your primary care physician?	____	____
5. Are the designated facilities conveniently located and well regarded?		
a. Local urgent care center	____	____
b. Hospital	____	____
6. How does the policy rate in areas of coverage that are important to you and your family? *Note whether any areas are excluded.*		
a. Annual physical exams	____	____
b. Chiropractic services	____	____
c. Consultations with specialists	____	____
d. Drug and alcohol treatment	____	____
e. Equipment rental or purchase (crutches, wheelchair, etc.)	____	____
f. Emergency room visits	____	____
g. Family planning services	____	____
h. Home health care	____	____
i. Hospice care for the terminally ill	____	____
j. Immunizations or allergy injections	____	____
k. Inpatient hospital services	____	____
l. Long-term care	____	____
m. Maternity services	____	____
n. Mental health services	____	____
o. Prescription drugs	____	____
p. Rehabilitation services	____	____
q. Skilled nursing facility instead of a hospital	____	____

(continued)

Getting the Most for Your Health Insurance Dollar (Continued)

	OPTION A	OPTION B
r. Surgical care	_____	_____
s. Treatment for chronic conditions	_____	_____
t. Treatment for preexisting conditions	_____	_____
u. X-ray and laboratory services	_____	_____
7. What are the costs and benefits?	_____	_____
a. What is the monthly premium?	_____	_____
b. What is the deductible?	_____	_____
c. How much is the coinsurance payment?	_____	_____
d. What is the coinsurance percentage or the percentage you must pay after you meet your deductible but before you reach your out-of-pocket limit?	_____	_____
e. What is the maximum out-of-pocket or the total amount you will ever have to pay for an illness including deductible, copay, and coinsurance?	_____	_____
f. What is the annual maximum benefit (if any)?	_____	_____
g. What is the lifetime maximum benefit?	_____	_____

something separate for the kids. If it is not possible to get the kids on a parent's insurance, look at well-child insurance policies sometimes offered through the schools. Especially good for older children who don't require regular checkups, the insurance covers only major medical and hospitalization. Out-of-pocket expenses such as those for sick visits will apply to the deductible.

Health insurance policies can differ so dramatically that it's almost impossible to compare them item by item. Start by using a checklist, such as the one above, to identify several policies that meet your needs. Only then look at the differences in rates. Too often, consumers base their selections on rates and find out later they're stuck with a lemon.

Figure 12.1 provides definitions of some common terms used in the health insurance field.

Figure 12.1 Health Insurance Glossary

Coinsurance or **Copayment:** The percentage that you will still have to pay after the insurance kicks in, usually up to an out-of-pocket limit.

Deductible: The amount you pay out of pocket before the insurance company pays a cent. Make sure your deductible renews each calendar year rather than for each incident. For most, a higher deductible means a reduction in monthly premiums that will more than make up for the larger amount you'd initially have to pay if something drastic happened. *Tip:* Divert your premiums into a liquid investment vehicle, earmarked for health emergencies.

Exclusion: A condition not covered by the insurance policy. Read the full policy, not just the brochure, to be sure you understand the plan's exclusions.

Health Maintenance Organization (HMO): Provides a comprehensive benefits package with services coordinated by your primary care physician.

Lifetime Benefit Cap: Although about 70% of health insurance policies have a lifetime cap (typically about $1 million per insured person), in a real catastrophe you could use up your lifetime allotment in a matter of years and be left at the mercy of government programs such as Medicaid. Look for a policy that forgoes the lifetime cap and support legislative efforts being lobbied by Christopher Reeve, an actor who became paralyzed from the neck down in a 1995 accident, that would require a $10 million minimum for lifetime caps.

Point-of-Service (POS) Plan: Combines the advantages of both HMOs and PPOs, but is generally more expensive.

Preferred Provider Organization (PPO): Contracts with a variety of physicians and hospitals.

Stop-Loss Provision: Policy provision that sets a limit on your total out-of-pocket spending, after which the insurance pays 100% of covered costs. No matter what your deductible or coinsurance amount, *never* purchase a policy without a stop-loss provision.

Traditional Fee-for-Service Plan: Covers major medical expenses and office visits, but usually carries deductibles and copayments.

Disability Insurance

Most people worry about getting life insurance, when they're much more likely to become disabled than to die by accident when their children are young. Although health or life policies you may have through work might have a disability rider, you're probably not well enough protected. If you're between ages 30 and 50, you stand at least a 33% chance of becoming disabled for at least 90 days before you reach age 65—that's three to four times the likelihood of dying during the same period, according to the Paul Revere Insurance Group.

While it may sound unfeeling, the truth is that a disability is potentially more financially devastating to a family than a death, because a disabled person's expenses can continue for years, even decades.

Government Coverage

Social Security disability definitions are stringent, first looking at work credits and earnings before even considering your medical condition. Currently, maximum monthly benefits for a single 50-year-old stand at $1,342 and $2,013 for a family, although the benefits, like regular Social Security retirement payments, depend upon past earnings and credits.

Those whose work patterns have kept them from paying into the system (i.e., nonearners who play the support-person role at home) often don't qualify for coverage under Social Security disability. The rules state that you must have worked for 10 years minimum (unless you are too young to have worked that long) and have a "current connection" to the workforce. The latter means you must have been employed at least 5 out of the last 10 years.

State laws vary on workers' compensation, but usually, to be covered, your illness or injury must be job-related.

Private Coverage

Unless your employer provides substantial disability coverage (several states now require that employers provide minimal policies), you should consider private disability coverage.

Two key variables—the amount of coverage and the waiting period—determine the price of your policy. Experts generally recommend that you have enough disability insurance to provide 60% to 70% of your current after-tax income, but the truth is, this kind of coverage can be prohibitively expensive for many.

If you belong to a professional or trade organization, take advantage of coverage offered periodically. Even if you take only the minimum that's preapproved, you'll find that the premiums will be much lower than for a policy purchased on the open market. The reason: Insurance companies offer these policies as an inducement for group members to purchase larger, more costly policies.

Likewise, contrary to advice often given in financial articles, take a second look at lender-sponsored mortgage insurance. Conventional wisdom shows that mortgage disability insurance is not a good investment because the odds are you won't use it. However, it may be a good deal for the peace of mind. The benefit is paid monthly, and because you usually don't have to qualify, the actual dollar cost is low and the stakes are high.

The following variables will determine the price of your policy. Choose the ones that are most important to you.

Waiting Period

Just about all disability policies stipulate a waiting period—the time before payments begin. The longer the waiting period, the cheaper the insurance.

Betting on the duration of your illness versus the extra cost for early coverage is a crapshoot. If you skimp on premiums to obtain early coverage that kicks in after 90 days or longer, you may find that your insurance does very little good, since the average disability lasts 9 months, according to the Health Insurance Association. On the other hand, among disabilities that last more than 3 months, the average disability period extends to 19 months. And studies show that 30% of all disabilities are permanent.

To calculate how long you can carry yourself, add up all your potential sources of income: workers' compensation, Social

Security, savings, union disability coverage, state-mandated disability coverage, employer sick-leave benefits, accrued vacation time, and spouse's income. Factor in those expenses likely to decline, such as clothing, lunch, and commuting. If you can comfortably survive for several months, then select a disability policy that costs less but starts later.

OWN-OCCUPATION COVERAGE

With this provision, your policy will pay full benefits if you are unable to perform your regular occupation—even if you can perform other work. Others pay only if you can't do any work, or can't work in an occupation for which your education and experience qualify you.

AUTOMATIC BENEFIT INCREASES

Often available as a rider, this provision will pay off if you have a permanent or long-term disability by adjusting your benefits to cost-of-living increases.

LENGTH OF COVERAGE

Benefits typically run for one, two, or five years, to age 65 or for a lifetime. If you can afford it, purchase a policy that would cover you until age 65, when your Social Security benefits kick in. At the very least, purchase three years' worth of coverage to give you time to get back on your feet.

NONCANCELABLE VERSUS GUARANTEED RENEWABLE

Noncancelable policies cannot be altered in any fashion as long as the premiums are paid. Guaranteed renewable also is unalterable except for premiums that can be increased only for an entire class of policyholders (not just for you).

GROUP COVERAGE

If you can get three or more coworkers to buy as a group under the aegis of your employer (you pay but the employer provides some administrative chores), your premiums may be 40% to 50% less than if you buy individually. If you aren't a member of an existing group, try this option.

Nonearners

Shockingly, given the cost of replacing their services in the family, at-home support people cannot purchase private disability insurance. What's being insured is the lost wages—not measurable in the case of nonearners.

Life Insurance

There's been a long-running debate over whether term or whole life insurance is a better deal. But the best choice depends upon your circumstances.

Term insurance can be far cheaper for the same death benefit as whole life, but it does not build capital or equity for you. On the other hand, many experts contend that term is a better value overall because one could independently invest the savings in premiums and come out with a better return than the investment value of a whole life policy.

It's the difference between renting an apartment and buying a home. You get the same space (or amount of coverage), but while rent may be cheaper, you're throwing the money down the drain. Owning a home is probably more expensive, but your payoff is the amount of equity you build that you can either borrow against or cash in by selling.

Other insurance products, such as universal life, have evolved in an attempt to offer consumers the best of both worlds. Such policies allow greater flexibility than whole life or term by letting you vary throughout your life how long you want the death benefit to be in effect, how long you will pay premiums, and how much cash value you want to accumulate. You may also raise or lower premiums and raise or lower the death benefit. Although the policy's first-year premium is more than that for term insurance, your ability to vary premium and death benefit and to build cash makes the policy an attractive alternative. Universal life insurance can pay more aggressive returns and build up cash value more rapidly than whole life. Consumers who have known genetic health-risk factors may find universal life to be the best option, and the earlier in life they buy it, the better the value.

> ### ESTIMATING YOUR LIFE INSURANCE NEEDS
>
> 1. How many years do you want to provide income to your family? _____
> 2. How much will they need per year? _____
> 3. Multiply line 1 by line 2. _____
> 4. How much will you set aside for burial costs? _____
> 5. What are your projected probate or trust expenses? _____
> 6. Add line 3 plus line 4 plus line 5. _____
> 7. What are your total current assets, not counting your home, less your liabilities? _____
> 8. Subtract line 7 from line 6. _____
>
> The amount in line 8 is the face value of the life insurance policy you need now to provide for your dependents and keep your other assets intact. This chart assumes no inflation and that the insurance proceeds will be exhausted at the end of the term.

INSURE YOUR PROPERTY

Any coverage you can possibly think of is already out there waiting to be bought. But there are certain policies that most of us take for granted: automobile insurance, because it's mandated by law in most states, and home-owner's insurance, because it's usually tied up in our mortgage payments in an escrow account, so we practically forget about it.

AUTOMOBILE INSURANCE

Automobile insurance is more straightforward and the industry is competitive enough to offer good deals. Here, spending a lunch hour or afternoon making phone calls to comparison shop can often result in dramatic savings for the same coverage.

If you lease or if your car loan isn't paid off, you may be restricted about the type and amount of coverage you can opt for. However, in all cases you will consider some combination of liability (covers the damage you do to others) or collision (covers the damage you or somebody else does to your own car) as well as an amount for medical injuries.

Most states require a minimum amount of liability insurance. Don't try to save money by automatically buying just the minimum. If you're in an accident with a high-value vehicle, your minimal policy won't go very far. The same goes for medical liability. The state's minimum doesn't consider the high medical costs and potential for lawsuits.

You have more leeway with your collision coverage, and it's up to you to decide whether you'll gamble. Collision rates can be so high that some people actually base their car-buying decisions on the costs of the premiums, driving their agents crazy with numerous calls to look up certain makes and models.

HOME-OWNER'S POLICY

Renters have lost everything in a fire only to discover that their landlord's home-owner's policy didn't cover any of the contents of their home. This mistake could wipe you out at a time when you're already vulnerable. A simple version of a home-owner's policy, called *renter's insurance,* could help ease the transition. After taking inventory of your home, you determine an approximate value for your goods and purchase a policy. It's even possible to carry riders for natural disasters such as hurricanes, tornadoes, floods, or earthquakes on your renter's insurance. Depending on the area, you should look into the appropriate coverage.

A regular home-owner's policy covers the land, home, and contents, as well as medical liability for accidents on the property. With both renter's and home-owner's policies, be sure to buy the option that increases coverage to the replacement cost of the home and its contents rather than only the actual value. In other words, if your TV is stolen, you should get the amount of money it would take to purchase a new TV, not the amount that your old TV was worth. Depreciation is usually figured by the age of an item, so you could really lose money on electronics, appliances, and computer equipment unless you get replacement-cost insurance.

Make sure your renter's or home-owner's policy also contains a general liability *umbrella* clause to protect you in case of lawsuits that arise from accidents on your property.

MAKE THE MOST OF YOUR COVERAGE

You might have thought the hard part was over when you made your policy choices. But when calamity strikes and it's time to file a claim, your choice of agents and knowledge of the claim process can make the difference in whether you really get the value for which you paid.

AGENTS

A reliable insurance agent can save you trouble and often get you a better price if you carry several policies through the same agency. It's definitely less confusing in your time of need when you know exactly whom to turn to.

Once acquainted with your circumstances, your agent will better project your insurance needs. For instance, your home-owner's policy may require extra riders to cover expensive computer equipment. If you happen to mention your recent computer upgrade, the agent will be sure to remind you to upgrade your insurance as well.

When the time comes for a claim, having cultivated a relationship, you're more likely to receive the help you need. You can also call on this agent for special favors, such as issuing you a binder over the phone when you purchase a new vehicle.

While this person will become a valuable addition to your circle of professionals, and perhaps even a good friend, keep in mind that an insurance agent isn't a financial planner. Choose only objective third parties for your financial planning needs. Insurance agents are too close to the situation, with the promise of sales commissions possibly clouding their judgment. Beware especially of insurance salespersons posing as financial planners who offer to help you plan your estate.

Claims

The whole point of buying insurance policies is that, although you'd rather not, odds are you'll eventually need to file a claim.

Unfortunately, the insurance industry is there to make money. It hedges its bets by including loopholes and exclusions in policy language, by requiring tedious paper trails and filing protocols, by charging higher premiums for riskier types of coverage.

If you don't follow the rules you agreed to when you signed up (and who knows all the rules of all their policies?), you may lose some or all of your benefits. Your dealings with the company should be above reproof. If you follow all its protocols to a T, the company will have more reason to take you seriously. Be professional and assertive with company representatives with whom you come into contact. Create a paper trail of all your dealings, from saving receipts, policies, and company literature to taking the extra trouble to make copies of all the forms you send in or letters you write. While telephone negotiations can be useful, they're harder to document. Be sure to take accurate notes of the time and date, the name and title of your contact(s), and the results of your call.

If you're unhappy with the company's award, using internal channels to challenge a company's initial decision can provide a happy medium between slinking away with your tail between your legs and calling for a courtroom dogfight. If you complete the process successfully, you will have avoided the major expense and headaches that go hand in hand with seeking justice through arbitration or the courts.

Move up the chain of command to direct letters of complaint against supervisors. As with the original claims form, keep your facts straight and your delivery neat and precise. If you think the adjuster has been negligent in some way, such as by failing to treat your case promptly or follow proper procedures, point this out. Remember, you're hoping that each step you take will be the one that resolves the standoff, but you never know if it's just another step in the road toward court. Document every step you take, whether it's a meeting with the company executive or a simple phone call to check on your claim.

If you're dealing with a potentially large sum, you should bring an attorney to in-person meetings or at least consult one before you go, to both familiarize yourself with your legal rights and help determine if you have any holes in your argument. Afterward, send a letter of confirmation outlining your perspective of the meeting's results. A courteous and prompt follow-up will demonstrate that you've really got your act together.

If you must move to arbitration, realize that, although it will be more informal and less expensive than going to court, you're still looking at an expensive proposition. Typically, you and the company must each pay for your own arbitrator and must split the cost of a third one. You may even need your attorney to be present in complex cases. Arbitration guidelines may be specified in your policy and may vary by state. Check to see whether they're binding or nonbinding before you agree to the procedure. If you're turned down in a binding arbitration, you can still choose to appeal in court, though your chances of success will be greatly reduced.

TYPICAL CLAIM PROCESS

Familiarize yourself with claim procedures now—before you're under emotional strain from a crisis. Quick and precise action will be required when the time comes, so be prepared for the following typical claims process:

1. *Notify the insurance company* within the time limits set forth in the policy (e.g., 30 days from the initial incident), in the way required by the policy (by phone, in writing, etc.), and to the location specified in the policy (usually a specific phone number or address).
2. *File a claim form.* Keep copies of claim forms on hand so you'll know ahead of time what questions might be asked later on. That way, you're more likely to pay attention to important details while you're still on the scene. Always use the most up-to-date form available.

3. *Respond as necessary to the adjuster investigating your claim.* The adjuster will first look for legal ways to deny your claim. For instance, you will be automatically rejected if you were behind on your premiums or if your policy contained an exemption to the condition for which you're filing. Next, the adjuster will attempt to verify your assertions. You may be asked for receipts for stolen goods, death certificates for life insurance claims, or official documents such as police accident reports. Finally, the investigation will move to a more subtle playing field. The adjuster will determine whether you acted in such a way as to worsen the damages or reported the true value of the loss.
4. *Receive the company's decision in writing.* The company based its decision on the adjuster's recommendation, which could have been to honor your claim fully, to honor it partially, or to resist your claim. You may be asked for a signature on a proof-of-loss form prior to receiving the decision.
5. *Receive the award.* You may receive a direct payment or a payment through your defending agent in court.
6. *You agree or disagree with the award.* WARNING: If you sign an insurance award check, you have legally indicated that you accept the payment as payment in full, unless you can prove that you were forced or misled into signing it.

LEGAL LESSONS: LEGAL HEALTH INSURANCE PROTECTIONS

Despite the fanfare it received when it passed in 1996, the Kassebaum-Kennedy Health Insurance Act doesn't help people with individual policies or no policies. And it doesn't make insurance more affordable, only more available. It ensures that people with group medical coverage won't lose access to it. The key word is *access*.

Since it went into effect in July 1997, the law provides for:

Preexisting condition protections, which stop insurers from denying coverage for more than 12 months for a preexisting condition that was diagnosed or treated within the previous 6 months. Also, insurance companies can't impose preexisting condition exclusions on anyone who has maintained continuous coverage, meaning no gaps longer than 65 days.

Continued coverage for individuals and their dependents if they leave or lose their jobs. This provision applies only to those who have had continuous coverage for the preceding 18 months and who are not eligible for a COBRA plan (COBRA refers to the Congressional Omnibus Budget Reconciliation Act, a federal law that guarantees extensions of eligibility for group coverage in certain situations).

Premium stopgaps, which prohibit insurance companies from charging higher premiums or denying coverage to people who are in group plans and have health problems.

Extended coverage, which forces insurers to sell insurance plans to employers with between 2 and 50 workers.

Tax benefits that allow long-term medical care, such as home health care and nursing home costs, to be deducted like other medical expenses. It also permits certain premiums for long-term care to be tax-deductible. In addition, it incrementally raises the tax deduction on premiums for individual health insurance for the self-employed to 80% from the current 30% over a 10-year period. Finally, it creates 750,000 tax-exempt medical savings accounts for the self-employed, the uninsured, and those in firms with less than 50 people.

Criminal penalties for people who knowingly transfer assets to qualify for Medicare.

Beware: One puzzling inclusion in the law is a provision that nullifies previous disclosure laws that protected consumers by preventing insurance agents from selling duplicate coverage. Now agents may more easily sell unwary people two premiums for the coverage of one.

Figure 12.2 Special Advice on Insurance Trade-offs

TYPE OF FAMILY	ADVICE
Two-earner	• Review life insurance to see that it adequately covers the current and projected economic contribution of each earner. Disability is also important.
Single parent	• *All single parents:* Adequate disability, life, and health insurance are key for single parents. • *Divorced and separated:* If you are covered under your estranged spouse's employer benefits, be careful to avoid lapses in coverage. • *Widowed:* Check for policies you might have overlooked in your time of grief. Credit cards, bank accounts, and credit union accounts often hold small courtesy policies. If your health insurance coverage was through your spouse's, you are eligible to continue coverage under federal law.
Blended	• Review coverage for each member of the family to make sure everyone is covered. Determining who is covered under which policies can be confusing when previous divorce agreements required ex-spouses to cover the children.
Cohabiting (opposite sex)	• You can name your partner and children as your life insurance beneficiaries. • However, since you are not legally married, your partner and/or his or her biological children may not be eligible for family health insurance coverage under your group plan.
Cohabiting (same sex)	• Unless one of you works for a progressive company, you may have trouble getting family coverage for your partner and his/her biological children.

FIGURE 12.2 (CONTINUED)

TYPE OF FAMILY	ADVICE
Adoptive	• With children under your care, you may need to update your policies.
Foster	• Find out if the state covers health insurance for your foster child and what to do in medical emergencies.
Wife as breadwinner	• While life and disability insurance are important for the breadwinner, they are equally important to the stay-at-home spouse who is making an economic contribution through domestic activities.
Multicultural	• Investigate whether race-related genetic tendencies (such as sickle-cell anemia) are influencing the amount of your insurance premiums.
Older parents	• Review your own health insurance plans for long-term care benefits. Also ensure that you carry adequate life and disability insurance.
Adult children living at home	• If your young-adult children are still in college, they may be eligible for group health insurance coverage under your family plan. • Unless they have dependents of their own, there is no reason for your adult children to carry life insurance policies. However, you may want to carry a small burial benefit.
Grandchildren living with grandparents	• Although life insurance is key for providing for the children, if you are older, it may be too expensive. Check with Social Security to see what their survivor benefits would be and use that as a benchmark to supplement.

FIGURE 12.2 (CONTINUED)

TYPE OF FAMILY	ADVICE
Grandchildren living with grandparents *(continued)*	• In addition, if you are covered under Medicare for your health insurance, you may have to cover the children separately under individual policies, an option that can be costly. Look into well-child policies through their school as well as public health benefits such as low-cost immunizations.
May-December	• *December:* If your primary income comes from investments, you may not need to carry life insurance.

CHAPTER THIRTEEN

After You're Gone

Estate planning gives you a chance to be in the driver's seat even after you're gone. When family structures are complex, you are the best person to designate how your loved ones are to be provided for in your absence. With antiquated inheritance laws, thorough estate planning is crucial to ensure that your belongings and capital are passed on to those you love—when legal relationships may be fuzzier than you realize.

To plan successfully, familiarize yourself with the state intestacy and federal estate tax laws that can affect your decisions. Then, understand the various estate planning tools at your disposal. Finally, while you should certainly do your homework, don't attempt estate planning on your own. The appropriate advisors can make the difference between hope and despair for your loved ones.

STATE AND FEDERAL LAWS THAT AFFECT YOU

If you don't prepare a legally binding estate plan with a will and a trust, state intestacy laws will designate your heirs and the dispersal of your property. At the very least, dying intestate (without a legally binding estate plan) can be burdensome to your relatives and children. At worst, the consequences can be devastating.

State Intestacy Laws

Whether you fail to make a will or make one early on and don't update it, the state will step in to disburse your property, choose a guardian for your children, and select an administrator. Since laws vary by state, you would need to check your own state's intestacy laws to determine how you would be specifically affected. But why not use that same energy to begin your estate planning? If you don't, the following consequences may apply.

In general, spouses receive one-third to one-half of the estate, and *issue,* or your children (which may or may not include adopted children), receive the rest of the estate to be divided among them. This type of provision could be a problem for those whose divorces have not been finalized.

If you prepare a will but then remarry, your spouse will get the intestate share in community property states or what is known as a *forced* or *elective share,* which may be smaller than the intestate share, in common-law states. To provide for your new spouse and your children, you should revise your will or draft a new one when you remarry.

Likewise, *pretermitted heir statutes* in most states are predicated on the idea that failure to mention a child in a will was an oversight, so the omitted child should get a share of the estate.

State intestacy laws don't provide for charitable gifts, so if you wanted to leave a gift to your college or favorite charity, you're out of luck.

Federal Estate Taxes

Under current federal tax law, estates under $625,000 are exempt from federal estate taxes and don't require federal tax returns.

Estate tax rates start at 37% for taxable estates over $625,000 and top out at 55% for taxable estates over $3,000,000. For taxable estates of over $21 million, a flat 55% tax applies, with no graduated rate on the smaller amounts.

The Internal Revenue Code defines the *taxable estate* as the gross estate minus allowable deductions. The *gross estate* is "the value at the time of [your] death of all [your] property, real or personal, tangible or intangible, wherever situated" (IRC Sect. 2031).

To calculate the approximate value of your taxable estate, you need to add the value of

- Your home, less the mortgage on the property
- Life insurance owned by you or transferred within the last three years
- Your bank accounts
- Stocks, bonds, and certificates of deposit
- Interests in partnerships, ventures, money market funds, and mutual funds
- Your car, jewelry, clothes, furniture, and artwork
- Any other assets owned by you or held by the trustee of any revocable trusts you created

Then you can subtract the estimated allowable deductions, including funeral and administrative expenses, claims against the estate, unpaid mortgages and other indebtedness in respect of property included in the gross estate, and certain state and foreign death taxes (IRC Sect. 2053). A further deduction is allowed for public charitable and religious transfers. Uncompensated casualty or theft losses that arise during the settlement of the estate may also be deducted.

If you are married or plan to remarry, you should know that current law provides an unlimited deduction for qualified bequests to a surviving spouse.

YOUR ESTATE PLANNING TOOLBOX

Your selection of estate planning documents will depend on your state laws, assets, income, legal relationships, and the amount of control you wish to exercise after you're gone. Before you begin learning about your options, ask yourself a few questions:

- What are my assets?
- What is the estimated total value of my assets?

- To whom should I leave them?
- Whom would I consider as a guardian of finances for my minor children?
- Whom would I consider as a physical guardian for my minor children?
- Would my estate executor be different from the guardian? If so, whom?

If, like most people, your taxable estate is under $625,000, no special tax concerns govern your choice of documents. You may use a will, trust, or combination to ensure that your money passes hassle-free to your children, spouse, or partner. If a will is used in conjunction with a trust, the will would cover residual gifts (for property left outside of the trust) and guardianship appointments.

> **FEDERAL ESTATE TAX EXCLUSIONS**
>
> In 1998, the first $625,000 of your estate is excluded from federal estate taxes. The exclusion amount will be increased incrementally until it reaches $1 million in 2006 and thereafter. Estates held in qualified family-owned businesses enjoy a greater exclusion amount—up to $1.3 million in 1998 and thereafter.

THE BASIC WILL

The younger you are, the more likely a simple, less expensive will should suffice. A will avoids the hassles involved in transferring title each time assets change as the young adult progresses through life.

In its most basic form, a will states how your money or property will be dispersed among your heirs as well as designating who will take care of your minor children and/or dependent parents as well as oversee their financial decisions.

Be sure to discuss guardianship plans fully with any potential guardians as well as with your children. Don't appoint someone as a guardian unless the person expressly agrees. Then, to be sure your wishes are followed, include the details in your will or living trust document.

If you're divorced, you'll need to reach agreement on the choice of guardian with your former spouse, and both your individual wills should reflect this agreement. The physical guardian of your children—for example, your sister—needn't be the same as the legal or financial guardian—for example, your attorney. In fact, if necessary, you can individually stipulate all three. You might have a loving sister who would make a good parent, a family lawyer who would serve as the best overall custodian of legal questions that might arise, and a financially capable friend whom you would trust to protect your children's financial future by ensuring that your assets were kept intact for them.

Take time to sit with your children and discuss your plans. Express that, while you expect to be around for a long time, the reality is that no one knows exactly how long his or her life will be. If possible, empower your children by allowing them to assist in the arrangements you make, especially for physical custody.

If you have a former spouse who is the natural or adoptive parent of your children, the law generally assumes that the other parent will become the children's guardian. If you have concerns that the finances would not be properly handled, you can still separate the financial arrangements and appoint a trustee for the money in your estate, leaving your former spouse with only physical custody. In marriages where money was an issue, this plan will provide you peace of mind regarding your children's future welfare.

Failing to appoint a guardian can lead to protracted and costly litigation with various relatives and even friends laying claim to parenting your children. While possibly motivated by the best of intentions, the effect on the children can be devastating.

The same set of concerns holds true if you have aging parents who count on you for all or part of their support. In this instance, you might wish to leave the money in trust for them or arrange for a financial custodian to provide for them and preserve the funds.

If you have adopted children, be sure to specifically include them in the language of your will. Because of antiquated rules that trace bloodlines for the purpose of selecting kings and earls, our own laws sometimes omit adopted children.

In one case, a childless beneficiary of a trust adopted a child. Because of the trust language chosen ("issue of my body" rather than "natural and adopted children"), the remainder of the trust would not go to the adopted child but to a distant cousin. Be sure to protect your own adopted children. Nothing could be more devastating to these children than to learn that, after all, they are not full family members.

If you fear that the other parent will somehow disinherit your child, you should realize that sanctity of family is sufficiently strong that the law looks with disfavor on such practices. Between generations, the reasonable expectation exists that family money, property, and personal mementos will be passed from one generation to the next. The law assumes that children will inherit equally from their parents.

Disinheritance is more common for adult children who have disappointed their parents. There is also a growing trend toward the wealthy giving only modest inheritances to their children out of a belief that they should learn to make their own way.

If you are divorcing, your marital dissolution agreement should include a clause that prohibits your former spouse from neglecting your child in favor of a new family. If there was never a marriage but paternity was established and child support paid, you should ask your lawyer whether there are estate planning issues from the other parent's perspective and how much control you have over them.

Much of estate planning advice centers on married couples. Estate tax law provides huge breaks for married persons. No such similar provisions occur with single persons or people who have chosen to live together without marrying. But the new social reality is that many unmarried couples want to ensure that their relationships are preserved in their estate plans because no spousal exemption is available.

Putting property in both names or in a living trust can protect this commitment. Either joint tenancy or a living trust can protect the surviving partner. However, property passed through joint tenancy or placed in a revocable trust is still considered part of the gross estate for tax purposes, so estate taxes cannot be avoided through this arrangement if the estate of either partner exceeds $625,000.

Also, in the case of unmarried persons who have children together, these children are legally "illegitimate." In some states, their rights to their parents' property are, nevertheless, recognized (with the best protection in Louisiana). However, by preparing a will or trust that makes intentions clear, such children can be best protected.

With homosexual couples, additional problems of inheritance can occur if the couple suffers family disapproval. If one partner's inheritance comes from ancestors, the family may feel it has a stake in the disposition of "family" money.

Some states permit adult adoption between homosexual couples. After an official adoption, the couple can gain some of the estate planning protections offered other legally recognized family members, such as an intestate share if the deceased partner's will is found invalid.

Even though a will is normally the simplest estate planning tool to use and execute, in some states even the simplest of wills can be subjected to a lengthy run through the court systems. However, there's a growing movement toward states adopting *universal probate codes,* or simplified probate codes that will streamline the systems and make laws that now vary dramatically from state to state more unified. If your state has adopted such a code, you'll probably be able to draft your will by hand (legally called a *holographic will*), with or without a witness. While a hand-drafted will is better than nothing, it's always safest to draft a formal, witnessed, and lawyer-approved will.

TRUSTS: TAX SHELTER AND CONTROL

Within the past few years, trusts have gained popularity as a way to circumvent lengthy probate codes and save on estate taxes and legal fees. Do-it-yourself kits abound and many consumers are confused. Aren't trusts for wealthy people? Do they replace my will or complement it? Do I need a lawyer? Are trusts suitable for the estate planning needs of new families? Here's a primer on the types and uses of various trusts.

If provisions are not made to fund the trust, the legal document can become a moot point. In other words, somewhere there will be deeds, titles, or bank accounts designated to the trust. The document will name trustees (an individual or board of individuals) to control it and provisions on how to select replacements for them. While the variations and complexities of trusts are as individual as the desires and fears of the grantor, there are some basic types, each of which retains specific objectives and tax treatments.

Testamentary trusts, created by will at the death of the grantor, cannot be modified except by the express modification provisions, if any, contained in the will.

Inter vivos trusts, set up to take effect during the life of the trust grantor, include both revocable living trusts and irrevocable trusts.

Revocable living trusts can be modified or canceled so long as the grantor is alive. They are commonly used to avoid probate, for ease of administration, and for flexibility. They have no estate tax consequences. Single parents who don't have a trusted relative or close friend can set up a revocable living trust and name a bank as the trustee, allowing them to be in complete and total control of their finances during their lifetimes, but permitting the bank to step in as trustee should they become ill.

Once created, *irrevocable trusts* cannot be changed, except within some limited parameters that must be outlined in the original trust document. They can be used to shelter assets from estate taxes in a number of ways. For example, up to $1 million can pass to grandchildren (or to anyone two generations down from the grantor).

If you're married, consider that *marital deduction trusts* allow you to pass an unlimited amount tax-free to a spouse and up to $625,000 tax-free to later beneficiaries.

Creating a Living Trust

1. Ask your lawyer or accountant whether a living trust is appropriate for your estate planning needs.
2. Choose your trustees carefully. You may serve as the first trustee, with one or more others as alternative or cotrustees. *Caution:* Cotrustees retain the same rights as you and can revoke (end) the trust at any time. If you can't find someone in whom you have absolute faith, use a bank trustee.
3. Choose a name for the trust that matches its purpose. For example, "The Jones Family Trust" or "Brian Jones Educational Trust."
4. Ask your attorney to prepare the living trust document.
5. Include your primary assets in the trust. The deeds to your home and other real estate, for example, would be signed over to the trust. (*Note:* You or your attorney should double-check the possible property tax consequences of placing your assets in a living trust. Ask your mortgage lender if such a move would trigger an *acceleration clause*.)
6. Remember that being held in trust makes transactions lengthier since cotrustees' signatures must be obtained. Therefore, you would not put your day-to-day personal checking account or any other changeable assets in the trust.
7. Do not place your life insurance or retirement accounts in your trust. Any transfer of the IRA, Keogh, company pensions, or 401(k)s will trigger taxes plus a penalty if you're under 59½ years old.
8. Don't use a living trust for your children. To preserve tax-free advantages, children's trusts should be irrevocable.
9. Although you should include a general provision to cover all property not specifically listed in the trust, it may or may not fully cover all potential assets of the estate.
10. Your trust document should state clearly how much you wish the trust to cover expenses if you're ill, such as for life extension, medical care, nursing home, and in-home nurses.
11. You must still leave a will, although it then becomes a simpler document. In addition to naming a guardian for minor

(continued)

> ### Creating a Living Trust (Continued)
>
> children, the will disposes of any assets that don't fall under the trust. For example, if you were to die in an accident and your estate were able to sue the person responsible, the proceeds would be covered by your will.
>
> 12. Send your deeds and titles to the county recorder or clerk to have them signed over to the trust. When returned, they should be kept in a safe location such as a safety deposit box or at your attorney's office, along with one original of the living trust document.
>
> 13. Discuss the living trust provisions with your heirs and cotrustees.

Durable Powers of Attorney

The durable power of attorney allows your loved ones or attorney to carry on for you when you are not in a position to help yourself. Whereas the living will deals with preserving or letting go of your physical self, the durable power of attorney deals with the mental and physical capacity to cope with your financial and legal affairs.

Properly drawn, the durable power allows others to take over for you when you are temporarily or permanently incapacitated. Unlike *conservatorship*, which requires a court order for someone to step in and help you, the durable power of attorney has flexibility.

The durable power of attorney for health care (DPHC) enables you to delegate to anyone the power to make decisions about your medical treatment during your incapacity, including the decision to terminate life support. Because of the complexity of the legal, ethical, and medical issues involved in this area, it is important that your DPHC be made in strict accordance with your local laws. Medical professionals are usually willing to work with attorneys-in-fact, but want to protect against potential litigation in this highly charged area.

This power can be set up as either a separate document if your estate plan includes a will or as a part of your living trust document if you have a family trust, and it is governed by state law.

Living Wills

Some states allow a living will that directs your doctors regarding the extension of your life by extraordinary measures. This enables you to leave clear written information on your views about preserving your own life in the face of lingering illness. Like the DPHC, the living will must strictly comply with state law. Unlike the DPHC, the living will can be used only by your physicians in extremely limited circumstances.

Be sure to indicate your wishes about artificial life support for extended periods, organ donations, and autopsies. Be as explicit as you can. These decisions often involve hefty hospital fees, so your loved ones could find themselves facing a "my money for your life" choice. Under life-and-death pressure, few of us would say of a loved one, "don't spend the money." Your guidance, planned in advance, will help your significant others tremendously.

Burial Instructions and Arrangements

Because the funeral industry has come under serious criticism in recent years, the Federal Trade Commission (FTC) has promulgated regulations that attempt to protect unwary and vulnerable consumers. However, rather than rely on arms-length federal assistance, provide your heirs with clear instructions about your own preferences.

Know the burial costs and customs of your area, but don't assume that you'll die where you live now. Many funeral homes offer a preneed funeral arrangement linked to the services of their particular establishments. If a person dies in a different location from the funeral home, these policies are often not worth their price because the cost of flying the body back might exceed the cost of the burial.

In planning your own funeral, remember to specify the following items:

- The type of service you want
- The type of burial or cremation
- If burial, the type and general expense level of the casket

- The location where you wish to be buried
- Any other information that's important to you

Obviously, to think these issues through, you'll need to do some research. If getting caught up in plot purchasing turns you off, then talk with your extended family. If you're an urban resident in a major city, plots can be prohibitively expensive and, if bought under burial pressure, difficult to choose. A better alternative is to see if members of your family are buried in locations outside the city where a grave can be added. The cost of flying a body and casket runs about the same as a coach fare, so some people may prefer this solution to the cost of an urban plot.

Although it's easy to ignore issues such as whether you have burial insurance and where you would wish to be buried, you must make these decisions so the burden does not fall on others.

STEPS TO TAKE WHEN A LOVED ONE DIES

After a death, grief-stricken survivors must cope with practical matters at a time of extreme personal loss. Familiarize yourself with these critical steps to help plan a smooth transition for your heirs or for reference if a loved one passes away.

1. Determine preferences for burial or cremation and for funeral rites or the memorial service.
2. Establish whether there is burial insurance or a burial policy through a particular funeral home, and try to find out about this coverage before giving the mortuary final instructions.
3. If there are no burial benefits or insurance, someone from the family will have to pay the mortuary in cash or by credit card before the final ceremony. If paying cash is a problem, negotiate for installment payments or credit before moving your loved one's body to a mortuary.
4. Notify the newspapers and call close friends with details about the service, including whether the family prefers flowers or a donation to a favorite charity as a memorial expression.

5. If the deceased served in the military, determine whether the burial service should include military honors. For more information, call the Veterans Administration at 800-827-1000.
6. Social Security pays a one-time $255 allowance to the spouse or minor children of the deceased or to other beneficiaries who are living with the deceased at the time of death. Call the Social Security Administration at 800-772-1213 for more information and a claim form.
7. Take time to deal with your own grief and be sure to spend quiet moments with other family members, especially those who have traveled from distant locations, before addressing the details of the estate.
8. Locate the will or family trust document. Do not try to cope with all the provisions before the funeral. Explain to the likely heirs that the reviewing of the will is scheduled some days after the funeral. Mail copies of the will to all potential heirs or have your probate attorney handle this chore.
9. Insist that an inventory be taken before any personal effects are removed from the home of the deceased. A preexisting checklist can help family members avoid disputes; of course, many items will have been enumerated in the will.
10. Many aspects of closing the estate, including selling a car, deferring debt payments, obtaining Social Security benefits, and closing bank accounts will require a death certificate. Obtain a minimum of 10 certified death certificates from the funeral home, and file one copy in a secure location in case you need to order more later.
11. Identify the executor or executrix (i.e., personal representative of the deceased after death) named in the will and/or the trustee of any living trust, to assure that the deceased's wishes are carried out.
12. Be sure the executor or trustee handles all outstanding mortgages and other debts. Do not pay off credit cards and other debts from your own funds. Beneficiaries are not

responsible for such debts, and should the debts exceed the assets of the estate, the debts are extinguished. In addition, because estates are taxed on net assets, if you reduce debts using nonestate funds, you lose the benefit of the deduction and increase the taxes.

13. Don't expect the estate to be settled quickly and don't make specific financial commitments based on funds you haven't yet received. For example, don't sign a purchase contract on a home on the basis of an anticipated inheritance—you may not have the required money in hand by the closing deadline.

14. Go slow on both the personal and financial fronts, giving yourself ample time to adjust. In fact, wait a full year after a parent's or loved one's death before making major changes in your life. (In less than 12 months, one grieving heiress twice canceled her marriage plans and took over the management of her complex financial affairs after firing all her advisors; it would have been wiser for her to get used to her changed personal circumstances before altering them further and increasing her stress.)

For more information, consult *Managing Your Inheritance: Getting It, Keeping It, Growing It—Making the Most of Any Size Inheritance* by Emily W. Card and Adam L. Miller (Times Books/Random House, 1997).

THE IMPORTANCE OF ADVISORS

While it is pertinent to engage in a certain amount of self-help to build your knowledge, your self-help should not replace the service of a reputable lawyer or accountant. Even official-looking will forms, kits, and computer programs should be approached cautiously.

If you fail to consult an appropriate advisor, legal loopholes or ill-chosen wording in your document can create critical problems when it comes to carrying out your wishes. Self-help can be dangerous when so much is at stake. Instead, use your self-help kits or books to educate yourself, then seek counsel to ensure that your measures were appropriate.

Any but the simplest asset base and family structure will require both an attorney and an accountant. Your family structure is probably too complex to attempt estate planning on your own, especially if you have had multiple marriages or if the children in your custody have different biological parents from their siblings. In addition, if you have adopted, ancient rules regarding bloodlines that underlie some states' legal provisions could stand in the way of your child's rightful inheritance.

While insurance death benefits may be a large part of your estate planning if your assets are limited, you shouldn't trust insurance agents posing as financial planners to put together your estate plan. Those with larger estates must realize that handling the planning yourself may cost your heirs more in legal fees and taxes later on.

After your concerns about heirs and property are considered, federal tax laws will come into play to help you determine how to set up your actual estate. Your lawyer or accountant should inform you about how local estate, death, and inheritance taxes would affect your estate. Generally, the larger the estate, the more these state variances will matter. If you have assets located abroad, you will need to consult a specialist to deal with international tax issues that apply.

LEGAL LESSONS: WHERE TO KEEP ESTATE PLANNING DOCUMENTS

Your estate planning efforts will be wasted and the probate process more cumbersome for your loved ones if your documents can't be accessed at critical moments.

WILL

You should have only one original will, but keep copies of your will in at least three locations: with your attorney, in your safety deposit box, and with a close relative or at your home. If you don't want to leave an original outside the safekeeping of a bank or law office, be sure to have a photocopy available. Opening a safety deposit box involves legal steps that may consume valuable time if your executor and others are not aware of your wishes.

Living Trust

This document should be kept in the same locations as the will. You will also have deeds for property belonging to the trust that should be kept with the original trust document.

Living Will

Put this document on file at your family or primary care physician's office. Place another copy with other key documents and keep them together in a marked envelope in your home. Share a copy of this document with close family members as well. If you have verbally reinforced your wishes, it will help them to implement your wishes if the need arises. In addition, file an original with your family attorney.

Durable Power of Attorney

An original of this document should be on file with your family attorney as well as with a key family member or the person who would exercise the power. Of course, you must trust the person you have selected not to be overreaching in choosing when to activate the power. However, if you only place the document in a safety deposit box, a court order would probably be required to open the box, defeating the purpose of the durable power of attorney, which is to avoid going to court when and if you are incapacitated.

Burial Instructions

Leave your burial instructions somewhere that can be readily accessible to your survivors. Include information about the location of your will with these instructions. Remember, the funeral instructions will be needed first, so arrangements can be made immediately. It's best to locate a copy in your home and place backup copies with your minister or rabbi, a trusted friend, and even your doctor. A master copy should also be left with your attorney and in your safety deposit box. But remember, either a death certificate or a court order is ordinarily required to open the safety deposit box even if you have made an heir a signatory, because such boxes are frozen upon the death of the box renter.

FIGURE 13.1 SPECIAL ADVICE ON PLANNING FOR YOUR CHILDREN'S FUTURES

TYPE OF FAMILY	ADVICE
Two-earner	• Each of you should review your estate plan in light of your current assets and marital situation. • Be sure both of you know where the paperwork is kept, but tell a close relative or friend in case a tragedy hits both of you at the same time.
Single parent	• *All single parents:* Be sure your estate plans clearly designate both a physical and a financial guardian for your children. A close relative, friend, or adult children should know where you keep a copy of your will and burial instructions. • *Divorced:* Remind your ex-spouse to make provisions for your children in his or her will. If you are the custodial parent, be sure your own plans clearly designate both a physical and financial guardian for your children. • *Separated:* Before divorce papers are signed, be sure that you include a provision that your ex must have a will drawn up leaving a percentage of the estate (30% is customary) to children from your union.
Blended	• See "Two-earner" above. • Remind your ex-spouses to make provisions for your children in their wills.

FIGURE 13.1 (CONTINUED)

TYPE OF FAMILY	ADVICE
Cohabiting (opposite sex)	• Because your relationship is not legally recognized (i.e., in the case of your partner and your partner's biological children), your estate plans should be especially thorough. Have a lawyer review the language.
Cohabiting (same sex)	• See "Cohabiting (opposite sex)" above.
Adoptive	• An attorney should review your wills and trust documents to ensure that your adoptive children receive the same consideration as your biological children.
Foster	• See "Adoptive" above.
Wife as breadwinner	• See "Two-earner" on previous page.
Multicultural	• See "Two-earner" on previous page. • If you think extended family members (or in-laws) might have trouble with your burial wishes for cultural reasons, discuss them ahead of time and be sure to provide detailed written instructions.
Older parents	• See "Two-earner" on previous page.
Adult children living at home	• If your adult child is unable to deal with finances because of a medical condition, be sure that you designate a financial guardian or trustee for your child.
Grandchildren living with grandparents	• If you are your grandchildren's legal guardians, your estate plans should provide substitutes.
May-December	• *December:* Statistically, your estate planning needs are more urgent.

Conclusion

While some general advice is great for everyone, financial advice is not "one size fits all." Use the advice that applies to your family and, remember, the only constant in life is what we can do for ourselves. If your partner or family is agreeable about your new financial mission, all the better. If not, start setting an example. Take some important steps on your own.

CLEANING UP YOUR FINANCIAL ACT

Use the following checklist to help clean up your financial act:

- ✔ Establish credit and open bank accounts in each adult's own name.
- ✔ Review health, life, disability, and auto insurance to ensure that they are adequate. If marital or employment status has changed, avoid lapses in health insurance and seek new coverage.
- ✔ Use tax laws to advantage. Check into new tax deductions or credits that may apply to you, and so forth.
- ✔ Schedule an annual financial fitness checkup to monitor net worth and cash flow; revise your budget accordingly.
- ✔ Pay yourself first: Put a budgeted amount in savings before spending on other bills.

- ✔ Start a retirement plan.
- ✔ Make a will and name a guardian.
- ✔ Plan to buy a home or think about how to pay rent in retirement if you don't want to buy a home.
- ✔ Start a fund for your children's college education.
- ✔ Invest discretionary income.
- ✔ Review and revise wills after life changes such as acquiring new property, having another child, marrying, and so forth.

MAKING A DIFFERENCE FOR OTHER FAMILIES

In the feverish pace of family life, it can be hard to slow down and help ourselves learn new financial strategies and habits, much less take the time to instigate changes in the system. But if every family carves out a little time to make its wishes known, government policies will catch up with the realities of the variety of family structures that are now the norm.

CONTACTING GOVERNMENT OFFICIALS

You can use the following addresses to contact your government officials.

U.S. House of Representatives
Washington, DC 20515

U.S. Senate
Washington, DC 20510

Congressional Switchboard 202-224-3121

The President
1600 Pennsylvania Avenue, NW
Washington, DC 20500
White House Switchboard: 202-456-1414
White House Fax: 202-456-2461
White House Home Page: http://www.whitehouse.gov
E-mail: president@whitehouse.gov

APPENDIX A

Agencies Enforcing Credit Legislation

The appropriate agency to contact for information or to file a complaint depends on the type of creditor involved.

- *Retail store, department store, consumer finance company, gasoline credit card, travel and entertainment card, or state-chartered credit union:* Contact one of the Federal Trade Commission regional offices, or

    Federal Trade Commission
    (Name of the act you are concerned with)
    Washington, DC 20580

- *Nationally chartered bank:*

    Comptroller of the Currency
    Consumer Affairs Division
    Washington, DC 20219

- *State-chartered bank that's a member of the Federal Reserve System:*

    Board of Governors of the Federal Reserve System
    Division of Consumer Affairs
    Washington, DC 20551

- *State-chartered bank insured by the Federal Deposit Insurance Corporation (but not a member of the Federal Reserve System):*

    Federal Deposit Insurance Corporation
    Office of Bank Consumer Affairs
    Washington, DC 20429

- *Federally chartered or federally insured (FSLIC) savings and loan association:*

    Federal Home Loan Bank Board
    Washington, DC 20552

- *Federally chartered credit union:*

    National Credit Union Administration
    Division of Consumer Affairs
    Washington, DC 20456

- *Other state agencies that can help (check the government blue pages in your phone book):*

    State Attorney General's Office
    State Banking Department

Source: Emily Card, *Staying Solvent: A Comprehensive Guide to Equal Credit for Women* (New York: Holt, Rinehart & Winston, 1985). Used by permission of the author.

APPENDIX B

Venture Investment Organizations

The Angel Capital Electronic Network (Ace-Net)
U.S. Small Business Administration (SBA)
http://www.ace-net.unh.edu

The Capital Network
3925 W. Breaker Lane, Suite 406
Austin, TX 78759
Phone: 512-305-0826
Fax: 512-305-0836
http://www.utexas.edu/depts/ic2/c2e/tcn.html

Environmental Capital Network
416 Longshore Drive
Ann Arbor, MI 48105
Phone: 313-999-8387
Fax: 313-996-8732
E-mail: ecm@bizserve.com
http://www.bizserve.com/environmental.capital.network

Global Partners, LLC
P.O. Box 6108
Napa, CA 94581
Phone: 800-788-0154
Fax: 707-257-7923

National Association of Investment Companies (NAIC)
Provides referrals to venture capital firms specializing in minority business investments.
1111 14th Street, NW, Suite 700
Washington, DC 20005
Phone: 202-289-4336
Fax: 202-289-4329
http://www.naichq.org

Social Venture Briefings Company
3220 Sacramento Street
San Francisco, CA 94115
Phone: 415-929-4910
Fax: 415-929-4915
http://www.svbc.com

Technology Capital Network at MIT
290 Main Street
Cambridge, MA 02142
Phone: 617-253-7163
Fax: 617-258-7395

U.S. Hispanic Chamber of Commerce
1030 15th Street, NW, Suite 206
Washington, DC 20005
Phone: 202-842-1212
Fax: 202-842-3221
http://www.ushcc.com

The Women's Growth Capital Fund
3005 O Street, NW
Washington, DC 20007
Phone: 202-965-1640
Fax: 202-965-3834

APPENDIX C

Child Care Resources

GENERAL CHILD CARE RESOURCES

Child Care Action Campaign
330 Seventh Avenue, 17th Floor
New York, NY 10001
212-239-0138

Child Care Aware
2116 Campus Drive, SE
Rochester, MN 55904
800-424-2246

Child Care Law Center
22 Second Street, 5th Floor
San Francisco, CA 94105
415-495-5498

Lipton Corporate Childcare Centers, Inc.
1223 20th Street NW, Suite 701
Washington, DC 20036
(202) 416-6875

National Association of Child Care Resource
and Referral Agencies
1319 F Street, NW, Suite 608
Washington, DC 20004
202-393-5501
Call or write for information on referrals in your area.

National Association for the Education of Young Children
1509 Sixteenth Street, NW
Washington, DC 20036
202-424-2460

National Association for Family Day Care
725 Fifteenth Street, NW, Suite 505
Washington, DC 20005
800-359-3817

National Coalition to End Racism in America's Child Care System
22075 Koths
Taylor, MI 48180
313-295-0257

NANNY PLACEMENT SERVICES

American Council of Nanny Schools
Delta College
University Center, MI 48710
(517) 686-9417

American Nanny College
4650 Arrow Highway, A-10
Montclair, CA 91763
714-624-7711

Delta College
Nanny Training Program
University Center, MI 48710
517-686-9417

DeMarge College
Certified Professional Nanny Program
3608 Northwest 58th
Oklahoma City, OK 73112
405-947-1534

English Nanny and Governess School
30 South Franklin Street
Chagrin Falls, OH 44022
216-247-0600

Nannys and Grannys
6440 West Coley Avenue
Las Vegas, NV 89102
702-364-4700

Northwest Nannies Institute
11830 Southwest Kerr Parkway
Lake Oswego, OR 97035
503-245-5288

Sullivan College
Professional Nanny Program
P.O. Box 33-308
Louisville, KY 40232
502-456-6504

Vermont School for Nannies
207-232 Skitchewaung
Springfield, VT 05156
802-885-3556

Vincennes University
Professional Nanny Program
1002 North First Street
Vincennes, IN 47591
812-885-6820

Source: American Council of Nanny Schools.

U.S. AUTHORIZED AU PAIR AGENCIES

American Heritage Association
Flavia Hall
P.O. Box 147
Marylhurst, OR 97036
503-635-3702

American Institute for Foreign Study
102 Greenwich Avenue
Greenwich, CT 06830
203-869-9090

American Scandinavian Student Exchange
250 North Coast Highway
Laguna Beach, CA 92651
714-494-4100

Ayusa International
One Post Street, Suite 700
San Francisco, CA 94104
415-434-8788

Educational Foundation for Foreign Study
1 Memorial Drive
Cambridge, MA 02142
617-225-3838

Exploring Cultural and Educational Learning/
Au Pair Registry
2098 Oak Haven Place
Sandy, UT 84093
801-944-5900

Interexchange Au Pair
161 Sixth Avenue, #902
New York, NY 10013
212-924-0446

World Learning
1015 Fifteenth Street, NW, Suite 1100
Washington, DC 20005
202-408-5380

Source: United States Information Agency.
Caution: Recent high-profile cases have illustrated the importance of careful screening of child care workers. Don't rely solely on the referral agency for screening.

APPENDIX D

Helpful Organizations

The Alliance for Children's Rights
3600 Wilshire Boulevard, Suite 1904
Los Angeles, CA 90010
213-368-6010
Fax: 213-368-6016

The American Academy of Matrimonial Lawyers
150 North Michigan Avenue, Suite 2040
Chicago, IL 60601
312-263-6477

American Association of Retired Persons
Social Outreach and Support Section
1909 K Street, NW
Washington, DC 20049
202-434-2277

The Association for Children for Enforcement of Support
723 Phillips Avenue, Suite J
Toledo, OH 43612
800-537-7072

Big Brothers and Big Sisters of America
230 North 13th Street
Philadelphia, PA 19107
215-567-2748

Birthright
686 N. Broad Street
Woodbury, NJ 08096
609-848-1818 or 800-848-LOVE

Center for Battered Women's Legal Services
105 Chambers Street
New York, NY 10007
212-349-6009

Center for Parenting Studies
Wheelock College
200 The Riverway
Boston, MA 02215
617-734-5200

Child Custody Evaluation Services of Philadelphia
P.O. Box 202
Glenside, PA 19038
215-576-0177

Childhelp USA/IOF Foresters
National Child Abuse Hot Line
800-4-A-CHILD
800-422-4453

Children's Defense Fund
25 E Street, NW
Washington, DC 20001
800-233-1200

Children of Divorce and Separation
P.O. Box A
Glenside, PA 19038
800-366-8786

The Children's Foundation
725 15th Street, NW, Suite 505
Washington, DC 20005
202-347-3300

Children's Rights Council
220 I Street, NE
Washington, DC 20002
202-547-6227

Committee for Mother and Child Rights
210 Old Orchard Drive
Clearbrook, VA 22624
703 722-3652

Consumer Federation of America
P.O. Box 12099
Washington, DC 20005-0999
Send a self-addressed stamped business-size envelope to receive a free brochure, *Managing Your Debts: How to Regain Financial Health*
Access the brochure on-line at:
http://www/visa.com

Consumers Product Safety Commission
800-638-2666
800-492-2937

Crittenton Services
Child Welfare League of America
440 1st Street, NW
Washington, DC 20001
202-638-2952

Custody Action for Lesbian Mothers
P.O. Box 281
Narberth, PA 19072
215-667-7508

Equifax Credit Information
P.O. Box 105873
Atlanta, GA 30348
800-685-1111 or 770-612-2500

Experian (formerly TRW Credit Data)
P.O. Box 2104
Allen, TX 75013-2104
800-682-7654 or 800-392-1122

Ex-Partners of Servicemen for Equality
P.O. Box 11191
Alexandria, VA 22312
703-941-5844

Family Service Association of America
11700 West Lake Park Drive
Milwaukee, WI 53224
414-349-2111

Fatherhood Project
Bank Street College of Education
610 West 112th Street
New York, NY 10025
212-663-7200, ext. 246

Federal Trade Commission
Consumer Response Center
6th Street & Pennsylvania Avenue, NW
Washington, DC 20580
202-326-3128

Find Dad
800-729-6667
This private collection agency retains a percentage of any past-due child support that it collects on your behalf. If it fails to collect, nothing is owed.

Grandparents United for Children's Rights
137 Larkin Street
Madison, WI 53705
608-238-6751

Health Insurance Association of America
P.O. Box 41455
Washington, DC 20018
800-277-4486

Housing Discrimination Hot Line
800-424-8590

Institute of Certified Financial Planners
800-282-PLAN
http://www.icfp.org

International Association for Financial Planning
800-945-4237
http://www.iafp.org

International Child Resource Institute
1810 Hopkins Street
Berkeley, CA 94707
510-644-1000

Joint Custody Association
10606 Wilkins Avenue
Los Angeles, CA 90024
213-475-5352

Mothers Without Custody
P.O. Box 27418
Houston, TX 77227
800-457-6962

National Association for the Self-Employed (NASE)
P.O. Box 612067
Dallas, TX 75261-2067
1-800-232-NASE (6273)

National Association of Personal Financial Advisors (NAPFA)
888-FEE-ONLY (toll-free)
http://www.napfa.org

National Center for Missing and Exploited Children
2101 Wilson Boulevard, Suite 550
Arlington, VA 22201
703-235-3900
800-843-5678

National Center for Women and Retirement Research
Long Island University
Southampton Campus
Southampton, NY 11968
516-283-4809

National Center on Women and Family Law, Inc.
799 Broadway, Suite 402
New York, NY 10003
212-674-8200

National Congress for Men and Children
851 Minnesota Avenue
P.O. Box 171675
Kansas City, KS 66117
800-733-DADS
800-733-3237

National Council on Family Relations
1910 West County Road B, Suite 147
Roseville, MN 55113
612-633-6933

National Gay and Lesbian Task Force
1734 14th Street, NW
Washington, DC 20009
202-332-6483

National Runaway Switchboard
800-621-4000
800-972-6004

NOW Legal Defense and Education Fund
99 Hudson Street, 12th Floor
New York, NY 10013
212-925-6635

Parenting Effectiveness Training, Inc.
531 Stevens Avenue
Solana Beach, CA 92075
619-481-8121

Parents Without Partners
401 N. Michigan Avenue
Chicago, IL 60611-4267
800-637-7974

Pension Rights Center
918 16th Street, NW, Suite 704
Washington, DC 20006
202-296-3776

Security First Network Bank
3390 Peachtree Road, Suite 1700
Atlanta, GA 30326
800-736-2321
http://www.sfnb.com

Single Moms, Inc.
2223 West Wellington
Chicago, IL 60618
312-871-8422

Single Mothers by Choice
501 12th Street
Brooklyn, NY 11215
212-988-0993

The Single Parents Association
4727 Bell Road #45-209
Phoenix, AZ 85032
602-788-5511
800-704-2102
Fax: 602-788-7866
e-mail: ed@singleparents.org
http://www.singleparents.org

Single Parents Resource Center
1165 Broadway, Suite 504
New York, NY 10001
212-213-0047

Social Security Administration
(To order form SSA7004, Request for Statement of Earnings)
Commissioner of Social Security
6410 Security Blvd.
Baltimore, MD 21235
800-772-1213

Social Security Administration
(To order the report with proposals for Social Security)
Office of Public Inquiries
6401 Security Blvd.
Baltimore, MD 21235
410-965-7700
http://www.ssa.gov/policy/adcouncil/toc.html

Solo Center
6514 35th Street, NE
Seattle, WA 98105
206-522-7656

Stepfamily Association of America, Inc.
215 Centennial Mall S., Suite 212
Lincoln, NE 68508
402-477-STEP
402-477-7837

Stepfamily Foundation, Inc.
National Headquarters
333 West End Avenue
New York, NY 10023
212-877-3244
Fax: 212-362-7030
E-mail: stepfamily@aol.com
http://www.stepfamily.org

Trans Union Corporation
P.O. Box 390
Springfield, PA 19064
316-636-6100
770-396-0961

United Way, Community Services Division
701 North Fairfax Avenue
Alexandria, VA 22314-2088
703-836-7100

Bibliography

Atoma, Joyce D., Anjani Chandra, William D. Mosher, Linda S. Peterson, and Linda J. Piccinino. "Fertility, Family Planning and Women's Health: New Data From the 1995 Survey of Family Growth." Washington DC: U.S. Dept. of Health and Human Services, 1997.

Bamford, Janet, Jeff Blyskal, Emily Card, Aileen Jacobson, with Greg Daugherty. *The Consumer Reports Money Book: How to Get It, Save It, and Spend It Wisely.* 4th ed. Yonkers, New York: Consumer Reports Books, 1997.

Belli, Melvin M., Sr., Mel Krantzler, and Christopher S. Taylor. *Divorcing.* New York: St. Martin's Press, 1988.

Berenstain, Stan, and Jan Berenstain. *The Berenstain Bears' Trouble with Money.* New York: Random House, 1993.

Berkeley Publishing Group. *The Lesbian Almanac.* New York: Berkeley Publishing Group, 1996.

Briles, Judith. *The Dollars and Sense Guide to Divorce: The Financial Guide for Women.* New York: Ballantine, 1991.

Brothers, Joyce. *Widowed.* New York: Simon & Schuster, 1990.

Burke, Phyllis. *Family Values: Two Moms and Their Son.* New York: Random House, 1993.

Card, Emily, and Adam Miller. *Business Capital for Women: An Essential Handbook for Entrepreneurs.* New York: Macmillan, 1996.

Card, Emily. *Global Investing.* New York: Random House/Times Books, forthcoming in 1998.

Card, Emily, and Adam Miller. *Managing Your Inheritance: Getting It, Keeping It, Growing It—Making the Most of Any Size Inheritance.* New York: Times Books/Random House, 1997.

Card, Emily. *The Ms. Money Book: Strategies for Prospering in the Coming Decade.* New York: E.P. Dutton, 1990. Available for $15 (includes shipping and handling) from the Women's Credit and Finance Project, P.O. Box 3725, Santa Monica, CA 90403.

Card, Emily, with Christie Watts Kelly. *The Single Parent's Money Guide: A Blueprint for Managing Your Money When You're the Only One Your Family Can Count On.* New York: Macmillan, 1996.

Card, Emily. *Staying Solvent: The Comprehensive Guide to Equal Credit for Women.* New York: Holt, Rinehart & Winston, 1985. Available for $15 (includes shipping and handling) from the Women's Credit and Finance Project, P.O. Box 3725, Santa Monica, CA 90403.

Cassidy, Daniel. *Worldwide College Scholarship Directory.* 4th ed. Franklin Lakes, N.J.: Career Press, 1995.

CCH Incorporated. *1997 Tax Legislation: Law, Explanation and Analysis Taxpayer Relief Act of 1997.* Chicago: CCH Incorporated, 1997.

Conkling, Winifred. *Securing Your Child's Future: A Financial and Legal Guide for Parents.* New York: Random House, 1995.

Consumer Information Center. *Social Security: What Every Woman Should Know.* Write: Consumer Information Center, #526B, Pueblo, CO 81009.

Consumer's Resource Handbook. Write: "Handbook," Consumer Information Center, Pueblo, CO 81009.

Deits, Bob. *Life After Loss: A Personal Guide to Dealing with Death, Divorce, Job Change and Relocation.* Tucson, Ariz.: Fisher Books, 1992.

DiCanio, Margaret. *The Encyclopedia of Marriage, Divorce, and Family.* New York: Facts on File, 1989.

Domini, Amy. *Investing for Good.* New York: HarperCollins, 1993.

Elkind, David. *The Hurried Child.* New York: Random House, 1995.

Elrod, Linda D. *Child Custody Practice and Procedure.* Deerfield, Ill.: Clark Boardman Callaghan, 1993.

Emily Card's MoneyLetter for Women. Periodical newsletter published by The Card Group, Inc. Annual subscriptions $29 (12 issues). 1158 26th Street, Suite 450, Santa Monica, CA 90403. 310-285-8088.

Englander, Debra Wishik. *Money 101: Your Step-by-Step Guide to Enjoying a Secure Future.* Rocklin, Calif.: Prima Publishing, 1995.

Federal Student Aid Information Center. *The Student Guide: Financial Aid from the U.S. Department of Education.* (Washington, D.C.: Annual). Call 800-4-FED-AID, 800-433-3243, or write to Federal Student Aid Information Center, P.O. Box 84, Washington, DC 20044-0084. TDD line for hearing-impaired people: 800-730-8913.

Fisher, Roger, William Ury, and Bruce Patton. *Getting to Yes: Negotiating Agreement without Giving In.* New York: Houghton Mifflin, 1992.

Gilles, Tom, and Joe Kroll. *Barriers to Same Race Placement.* North American Council on Adoptable Children, 1991.

Godfrey, Joline. *No More Frogs to Kiss: 99 Ways to Give Economic Power to Girls.* New York: HarperCollins, 1995.

Godfrey, Joline. *Our Wildest Dreams: Women Entrepreneurs Making Money, Doing Good, Having Fun.* New York: HarperCollins, 1993.

Godfrey, Neale S., and Carolina Edwards. *Money Doesn't Grow on Trees.* New York: Simon & Schuster, 1995.

Harrington, John. *Investing With Your Conscience.* New York: John Wiley & Sons, 1993.

Hoffman, Carl J. *Dead Beat Dads: How to Find Them and Make Them Pay.* New York: Simon & Schuster, 1996.

Hogan, Patricia Turner, and Sau-Fong Siu. "Minority Children and the Child Welfare System: An Historical Perspective." Silver Springs, MD: National Association of Social Workers, 1988.

Leobardo, E. "Hispanics," in *Encyclopedia of Social Work.* Silver Springs, MD: National Association of Social Workers, 1987.

Leonard, Robin, and Stephen Elias. *Nolo's Pocket Guide to Family Law,* 4th ed. Berkeley, Calif.: Nolo Press, 1994.

Mayer, Robert D. *Power Plays: How to Negotiate, Persuade, and Finesse Your Way to Success in Any Situation.* New York: Times Books, 1996.

Miller, Timothy. *How to Want What You Have: Discovering the Magic and Grandeur of Ordinary Existence.* New York: Henry Holt, 1995.

Million Dollar Directory: America's Leading Public and Private Companies: Top 50,000, 1991. Bethlehem, Pa.: Duns Marketing Strategies, 1991.

Nader, Ralph, and Wesley J. Smith. *Winning the Insurance Game: The Complete Consumer's Guide to Saving Money.* New York: Doubleday, 1993.

National Center for Women and Retirement Research. *Women and Divorce: Turning Your Life Around.* New York: Southampton, 1993.

National Organization for Women. *Child Support Legal Resource Kit, Divorce and Separation Legal Resource Kit.* Available from NOW Legal Defense and Education Fund, 99 Hudson Street, New York, NY 10013.

Neal, Leora. "Don't Ignore Race Factor." *USA Today,* 1994.

Otfinoski, Steve. *The Kid's Guide to Money: Earning It, Saving It, Spending It, Growing It, Sharing It.* New York: Scholastic, 1996.

Peck, Scott M. *The Road Less Traveled.* New York: Simon & Schuster, 1978.

Pension Rights Center. *Your Pension Rights at Divorce.* 195 pages, $23.95. Pension Rights Center, 918 16 St., NW, Suite 704, Washington, DC 20006-2902.

Stepfamily Association of America. "Facts Sheet." Stepfamily Association of America, 215 Centennial Mall South, Suite 212, Lincoln, NE 68508. Call 402-477-STEP.

Tobias, Andrew. *The Only Investment Guide You'll Ever Need.* San Diego: Harcourt Brace, 1996.

Ward's Business Directory of U.S. Private and Public Companies 1998. New York: Gale Research, Inc., 1997.

Wiegold, Frederic C., ed. *The Wall Street Journal Lifetime Guide to Money: Everything You Need to Know About Managing Your Finances—For Every Stage of Life.* New York: Hyperion, 1997.

Wilkinson, Elizabeth. *Making Cents: Every Kid's Guide to Money.* New York: Little, Brown, 1993.

Wymard, Ellie. *Men on Divorce: Conversations with Ex-Husbands.* Carson, CA: Hay House, 1994.

Order Emily Card's books at http://www.womenmoney.com. Any of the books listed here may be ordered through http://www.amazon.com.

Index

Acceleration clause, of living trust, 243
Adjusted gross income (AGI), 71
Adoption:
　cross-ethnic, xv
　transracial, rise in, 18–19
Adoptive families, 13, 18–19
　special advice (figures) for:
　　budgeting, 66
　　financial emergencies, 108
　　goal setting, 35
　　insurance trade-offs, 233
　　investments for changing times, 170
　　planning for your children's futures, 252
　　rescuing your retirement, 213
　　selecting and paying for education, 195
　　tax strategies, 91–92
　　teaching children about money, 145
　　yours-mine-ours boundaries, 134
Adult children living at home, 13, 20
　special advice (figures) for:
　　budgeting, 66
　　financial emergencies, 109
　　goal setting, 35
　　insurance trade-offs, 233
　　investments for changing times, 171

　　planning for your children's futures, 252
　　rescuing your retirement, 214
　　selecting and paying for education, 195
　　tax strategies, 92
　　teaching children about money, 146
　　yours-mine-ours boundaries, 134
Alternative minimum tax (AMT), 78
American Camping Association, 175
American Family, The (Quayle), 14
Angel network, 167
Annuities, as investment vehicle, 209–210
Asset allocation, 149
　4M investment, 154, 155 (figure)
　major/mega portfolio, 153–154
　medium/major portfolio, 152–153
　modest portfolio, 151–152
Au pair(s):
　agencies, list of, 261–262
　government regulations for, 176
Auto leasing, 61–62

Baby boomers, xiv, 163
Bankruptcy:
　avoiding, 102–103
　Chapter 7, 101
　Chapter 11, 101
　Chapter 12, 101

Bankruptcy *(continued)*:
  Chapter 13, 101
  number of filings for, 100–101
Basis points, 161
Blended families, xv, 13, 16–17
  special advice (figures) for:
    budgeting, 65
    financial emergencies, 108
    goal setting, 34
    insurance trade-offs, 232
    investments for changing times, 170
    planning for your children's futures, 252
    rescuing your retirement, 213
    selecting and paying for education, 194
    tax strategies, 91
    teaching children about money, 145
    yours-mine-ours boundaries, 133
Bond market:
  inflation-indexed treasury bonds, 164
  interest rates and performance on, 163–164
  and stock market, 162–163
Budget/Budgeting:
  for automobile, 60–64
  and being active consumer, 50–52
  Budget Worksheet, 42–46
  buying vs. renting decisions, 55–60
  changes for success, 40, 47
  compared to dieting, 39–40
  methods of, 47–50
  and savings, 47
  special advice for, 64–67 (figure)
  using federal credit laws, 64, 105–106

Capital gains, and tax law, 199
Child care:
  au pair agencies, 261–262
  general, 259–260
  nanny placement services, 260–261
Children:
  adult, living at home, 13, 20–21
  Census Bureau definition of, 3, 16
  planning futures of, 251–252 (figure)
Children and money, 138–142
  4M pointers for, 142 (figure)
  4Ps checklist approach to, 144
  instilling healthy attitudes, 137–138
  special advice chart, 144–146
Closed-end funds, 160
COBRA Act, 231
Cohabitation, as defined by Census Bureau, 17
Cohabiting (opposite sex) family type, 13, 17
  special advice (figures) for:
    budgeting, 65
    financial emergencies, 108
    goal setting, 34
    insurance trade-offs, 232
    investments for changing times, 170
    planning for your children's futures, 252
    rescuing your retirement, 213
    selecting and paying for education, 194
    tax strategies, 91
    teaching children about money, 145
    yours-mine-ours boundaries, 133
Cohabiting (same sex) family type, 13, 17
  special advice (figures) for:
    budgeting, 65
    financial emergencies, 108
    goal setting, 34
    insurance trade-offs, 232
    investments for changing times, 170
    planning for your children's futures, 252
    rescuing your retirement, 213
    selecting and paying for education, 195
    tax strategies, 91

INDEX

teaching children about money, 145
yours-mine-ours boundaries, 133
Coinsurance, 220
College Savings Worksheet, 181–184
CollegeSure CD, 185–186
Community property, 132
Conservatorship, 244
Consumer Credit Counseling Service, 102
Contract marriage, 15
Copayment (health insurance), 220
Credit legislation, federal:
   agencies enforcing, 255–256
   Equal Credit Opportunity Act, 106
   Fair Credit Billing Act, 64, 106
   Fair Credit Reporting Act, 64, 106
   Fair Debt Collection Practices Act, 107
   Truth in Lending Act, 105–106

Deductible (health insurance), 220
Deductions:
   as basic tax strategy, 70
   depreciation, 74–75
   Schedules A and C, 74
   standard, 73
Defined-benefit retirement plan, 203
   Keogh-type, 206
Defined-contribution retirement plan, 204
Depreciation, 74–75
Disabled persons, rights of, xv
Disinheritance, 240
Divorce, increase of, 15
   See also Single-parent families
Domini 400 Social Index[SM], 162, 166
Downsizing:
   corporate, 40
   of junk, 41
Durable power of attorney, 244, 250
   for health care (DPHC), 244
   and living will, 245

Earned income tax credit (EITC), 253

Education:
   and child care, 173–178
   College Savings Worksheet, 181–184
   government grants for, 188
   HOPE credit, 180
   lifetime learning credit, 180
   private scholarships for, 187
   savings options for, 185–187, 191–192
   selecting/paying for, 194–195 (figure)
   selection of, 179–184
   student loans for, 189, 190 (figure)
   university scholarships for, 188
Effective tax rate, 75
Elective share, *see* Forced share
Electronic funds transfer (EFT), 48–49
Equal Credit Opportunity Act, 106
Equity mutual funds:
   classification of, 159 (figure)
   investment objectives/performance, 158, 159 (figure)
   main types of, 161
   questions to ask about, 158
   research sources for, 162
   structure of, 160
Equivalent taxable yields, 78, 79 (figure)
Estate planning, 235
   checklist, 237–238
   and children's futures, 251–252 (figure)
   and durable power of attorney, 244
   and establishing a will, 238–241
   and federal estate taxes, 236–237
   importance of advisors in, 235, 248–249
   and state intestacy, 236
   and types of trusts, 241–244
Estate planning documents:
   burial instructions, 250–251
   durable powers of attorney, 250
   living trust, 250
   living will, 250
   will, 249–250
Excel™ (software program), 151
Exclusion (health insurance), 220

Fair Credit Billing Act, 64, 106
Fair Credit Reporting Act, 64, 106
Fair Debt Collection Practices Act, 107
Family:
  Census Bureau's definition of, 3
  income, levels of, 5
  new structures for, 11–13 (figures)
Family finances:
  balance in, 119–122
  boundaries of, 111–116
  checklist for, 253–254
  domestic/marital property rights in, 128–130
  family money checklist rules for, 9
  financial fitness quiz, 8–9
  and financial habits, 6–7
  goals/strategies for, 27–36
  legal checklist for couples, 131–132
  and rights in successful management of, 126–128
  techniques in, 117–119
  variables affecting, 4–5
Family financial emergencies, 107–109 (figure)
Federal estate taxes, 236–237
  exclusions, 238
Federal Trade Commission, 53, 245
Fee-for-service plan, traditional, 220
Financial change, essence of, 8
Financial emergencies:
  avoidance of, 105 (figure)
  correcting credit reports, 103–105
  credit crisis, 97–103
  and federal credit protection, 64, 105–107
  preparation for, 95–97
  restoring credit, 103
Financial fitness quiz, 8–9
Financial goals/strategies:
  achievement of, 31–34
  checklist for, 253–254
  4M (modest/medium/major/mega), 32 (figure)
  importance of, 27
  samples of, 31
  setting of, 28, 29
  special advice figure for, 34–36
  written commitments, 30–31
Financial habits, 6–7
Financial income, levels of, 5 (figure)
Fixed-rate mortgage, 199
Forced share, 236
Foster families, 13, 18–19
  special advice (figures) for:
    budgeting, 66
    financial emergencies, 108
    goal setting, 35
    insurance trade-offs, 233
    investments for changing times, 170
    planning for your children's futures, 252
    rescuing your retirement, 213
    selecting and paying for education, 195
    tax strategies, 92
    teaching children about money, 146
    yours-mine-ours boundaries, 134
401(k) plans:
  borrowing from, 212
  as defined-contribution plan, 203–205
  portability of, 204
  taxation on, 212
4Ms (modest/medium/major/mega):
  as designation of family income, 5
  financial goals, 32 (figure)
  investment guidelines, 154, 155 (figure)

Generation Xers, 167, 200
Get-rich-quick schemes, 9
Goals, financial, 27, 31, 32 (figure)
Goal setting:
  "creating the future" exercise in, 29
  "Make-It-Happen" worksheet in, 33
  special advice figure for, 34–36
  techniques for, 31–34
  time horizon for, 28
  written commitments in, 30–31

Grandchildren living with grandparents, 13, 21
  increase in numbers of, 21
  special advice (figures) for:
    budgeting, 66
    financial emergencies, 109
    goal setting, 35
    insurance trade-offs, 233–234
    investments for changing times, 171
    planning for your children's futures, 252
    rescuing your retirement, 214
    selecting and paying for education, 195
    tax strategies, 92
    teaching children about money, 146
    yours-mine-ours boundaries, 135
Grandparents, 21
Grief, stages of, 133
Gross estate, 236–237, 241
Gross income, 71
Guardian:
  appointment of, 238–239
  failure to appoint, 239–240

Health insurance, 217
  "Getting the Most for Your Health Insurance Dollar" worksheet, 218–219
  glossary of terms, 220
  legal protection, 230–231
Health maintenance organization (HMO), 220
Helpful organizations, 263–270
Holographic will, 241
Home ownership:
  programs for, 58–59
  steps to, 57–58
Homosexual couples, adoption by, 18
HOPE credit (education tax credit), 180, 185
Household, Census Bureau definition of, 3
Household Employers tax guide, 176
Hurried Child, The (Elkind), 175

Income:
  adjusted gross (AGI), 71
  defined, 71
  discretionary, investment of, 254
  gross, 71
  securing, 202–210
  taxable, 71
Index funds, 158
Individual retirement accounts (IRAs), 203
  deductible IRA, 207–208
  nondeductible IRA, 209
  Roth IRA, 208–209
Informal workout, in avoiding bankruptcy, 102–103
Insurance:
  automobile, 225–226
  claims process, 229–230
  coverage, 215–217, 227–229
  disability, coverage of, 221–224
  health, *see* Health insurance
  homeowner's/renter's, 226–227
  life, *see* Life insurance
  property, 225–226
  Review Worksheet, 216
  trade-offs, 232–234 (figure)
Internal Revenue Code (IRC), and estate taxation, 236–237
Internet banking, 48
Inter vivos trust, 242
Intestacy, 235–236
Investing for Good (Domini), 166
Investing With Your Conscience (Harrington), 166
Investment portfolio:
  asset allocation in, 149–150
  and bonds, 162–164
  and cash flow, 150–151
  and direct venture capital investments, 167
  and diversification, 150
  and equity mutual funds, 157–162
  and global investments, 165–166
  and growth, 150
  guidelines for, 154, 155 (figure)
  and liquidity, 150
  major/mega portfolios, 153–154

Investment portfolio *(continued)*:
  medium/major portfolios, 152–153
  modest portfolios, 151–152
  and risk, 150
  and socially responsible investments (SRIs), 166
  and stock market, 155–157
  and tax consequences, 150
  use of professional advisor in, 167–169
Investments, for changing times, 169–171 (figure)
Investor's Guide to Low-Load Mutual Funds, The, 162
Irrevocable trust, 242
IRS code 501(c)(3), *see* Nonprofit organization

Joint tenancy, 132, 240–241
Junk bonds, 163

Kassebaum-Kennedy Health Insurance Act, 230–231
Keogh plans, 203–206
Keynes, John Maynard, 157

Life insurance, 224–225
Lifetime benefit cap, 220
Lifetime learning credit (education tax credit), 180, 185
Living will, 245, 250

"Make-It-Happen" worksheet, in goal setting, 33
Managing Your Inheritance: Getting It, Keeping It, Growing It (Card and Miller), 248
Marginal tax rate, 76
Marital deduction trust, 242
Marital property:
  community-property states, 130
  rights, 128–129
  separate-property states, 129
  titles, 132
  types of, 129

May-December marriages, family type, 13
  special advice (figures) for:
    budgeting, 67
    financial emergencies, 109
    goal setting, 36
    insurance trade-offs, 234
    investments for changing times, 171
    planning for your children's futures, 252
    rescuing your retirement, 214
    selecting and paying for education, 195
    tax strategies, 93
    teaching children about money, 146
    yours-mine-ours boundaries, 135
Money™ (software program), 48
Money, teaching children about:
  4M pointers for, 142 (figure)
  4Ps checklist approach to, 144
  infants and toddlers, 138–139
  preschool children, 139
  school-age children, 139–140
  special advice on, 144–146 (figure)
  teenagers, 140–141
  young adults, 141–142
Morningstar, Inc., rating guide, 162
Multicultural families, 13, 19
  special advice (figures) for:
    budgeting, 66
    financial emergencies, 109
    goal setting, 35
    insurance trade-offs, 233
    investments for changing times, 170
    planning for your children's futures, 252
    rescuing your retirement, 213
    selecting and paying for education, 195
    tax strategies, 92
    teaching children about money, 146
    yours-mine-ours boundaries, 134

Multiculturalism:
  census recognition of, 4
  and cross-ethnic adoption, xv, 4
  and multicultural families, 19
Murphy Brown, 14
Mutual Fund Council Directory, 162
Mutual Fund Education Alliance, 162
Mutual funds, *see* Equity mutual funds

Nanny placement services, list of, 260–261
National Association of Black Social Workers, 18
National Association of Personal Financial Advisors, 168, 267
National Center for Health Statistics, 16, 17
National Survey of Family Growth, 16
Net asset value (NAV), 160
No-load funds, 160, 161
Nonfamily household, Census Bureau definition of, 3
Nonprofit organization, 204–205
Nontraditional families:
  financial planning for, xiii–xvii
  "new family tree" of, 12 (figure)
  new structures/types of, 13
    adoptive families, 18–19
    adult children living at home, 20
    blended families, 16–17
    cohabiting (opposite sex) situations, 17
    cohabiting (same sex) situations, 17
    foster families, 18–19
    grandchildren living with grandparents, 21
    May-December marriages, 21
    multicultural families, 19
    older-parent families, 20
    single-parent families, 14–15
    two-earner families, 12–14
    wife as breadwinner, 19
  rise of, xv, 11–21
  statistical comparison of, 23–25 (figure)
  universal issues for, 6–8

Older-parent families, 13, 20
  special advice (figures) for:
    budgeting, 66
    financial emergencies, 109
    goal setting, 35
    insurance trade-offs, 233
    investments for changing times, 170
    planning for your children's futures, 252
    rescuing your retirement, 214
    selecting and paying for education, 195
    tax strategies, 89
    teaching children about money, 146
    yours-mine-ours boundaries, 134
Open-end funds, 160
Own children:
  as defined by Census Bureau, 3, 16
  stepchildren considered as, 16

Personal security account, 201
Point-of-service (POS) plan, 220
Preferred provider organization (PPO), 220
Pretermitted heir statutes, 236
Producer Price Index, 163
Property titles, 132

Qualified Domestic Relations Order (QDRO), 204
Quayle, Dan, 14
Quickbooks™ (software program), 48
Quicken™ (software program), 48, 151

Real estate:
  buying vs. renting, 199–200
  residential, benefits of, 199
  superiority of, as investment, 199

Retirement:
  and annuities, 209–210
  assumptions about, 197
  checklist for, 197–198
  and employer-sponsored plans, 203–204
  and individual retirement accounts (IRAs), 207
  and living expenses, 198
  and place to live, 198
  and self-employed, 205–207
  and Social Security benefits, 198
  special advice on, 212–214 (figure)
  and tax-deferred vehicles, 202–203
Retirement Planning Worksheet, 210–211
Revocable living trust, 240–241, 242
  creation of, 243–244
  document, where to keep, 250
Roth IRA, 208–209

Savings:
  4M goals for, 47 (figure)
  three-pronged approach to, 33–34
  two unbreakable rules of, 47
Security First Network Bank, 48
Self-employed, retirement plans for, 205–207
Series EE savings bonds, 185
Simplified employee pension (SEP-IRA), 203, 206–207
Single-parent families, 13–15
  special advice (figures) for:
    budgeting, 65
    financial emergencies, 108
    goal setting, 34
    insurance trade-offs, 232
    investments for changing times, 169–170
    planning for your children's futures, 251
    rescuing your retirement, 212–213
    selecting and paying for education, 194
    tax strategies, 89–90

  teaching children about money, 145
  yours-mine-ours boundaries, 133
Socially responsible investments (SRIs), 166
Social Security:
  and baby boomers, 163
  benefiting from, 200–202
  benefits, xv–xvi
  checking statement of earnings report, 201
  disability insurance through, 221
  rules, impacting families, 202
  shrinking reserves of, 197
Social Security Advisory Council, 200
Special advice figures:
  Budgeting, 64–67
  Family Financial Emergencies, 107–109
  Goal Setting, 34–36
  Insurance Trade-offs, 232–234
  Investments for Changing Times, 169–171
  It's Never Too Early (Teaching Children about Money), 144–146
  Planning for Your Children's Futures, 251–252
  Rescuing Your Retirement, 212–214
  Selecting and Paying for Education, 194–195
  Tax Strategies for New Families, 89–93
  Yours, Mine, and Ours, 133–135
Stepfamilies vs. nuclear families, 16
Stepfamily Association of America, 15, 16
Stock market, investing in, 156–157
Stop-loss provision, in health insurance, 220
Student loans, 189

Taxable estate, 236
  calculation of value of, 237
Taxable income, 71
Taxpayer Relief Act (1997), 69
Tax stairs, 75–76

Tax strategies:
  annual financial checkup, 85–86
  comparison of deductions/
    exclusions/credits, 79 (figure)
  five tax basics:
    credits, 70, 78–79
    deductions, 70, 73–75
    deferrals, 70, 80
    exclusions, 70, 72–73
    rates, 70, 75–78
  4M, 85 (figure)
  for new families, 89–93 (figure)
  and tax comparisons, 80–82
  and tax policy, 86–89
  tax terms, 83–84
Tenancy by the entirety, 132
Tenancy in common, 132
Testamentary trust, 242
Traditional family vs. nontraditional, 11–25
  statistical comparison of configurations of, 22–25 (figure)
Transracial adoption, 18–19
Treasury Direct program, 164
Truth in Lending Act, 105–106
Two-earner families, 12–14
  special advice (figures) for:
    budgeting, 64
    financial emergencies, 107
    goal setting, 34
    insurance trade-offs, 232
    investments for changing times, 169
    planning for your children's futures, 251
    rescuing your retirement, 212
    selecting and paying for education, 194
    tax strategies, 89
    teaching children about money, 144
    yours-mine-ours boundaries, 133

Uniform Marital Property Act, 129
Universal probate codes, 241
U.S. Bureau of the Census, 11, 14
  definition of cohabitation by, 17
  definition of family advocated by, 3
  figures on multicultural families, 19
  projections for stepfamilies, 16
U.S. Department of Health and Human Services, 16
U.S. government debt:
  bills, 164
  bonds, 164
  notes, 164

Venture investment organizations, list of, 257–258
Vesting, 203–204

Wife as breadwinner, family type, 13, 19
  special advice (figures) for:
    budgeting, 66
    financial emergencies, 109
    goal setting, 35
    insurance trade-offs, 233
    investments for changing times, 170
    planning for your children's futures, 252
    rescuing your retirement, 213
    selecting and paying for education, 195
    tax strategies, 92
    teaching children about money, 146
    yours-mine-ours boundaries, 134
Will(s):
  basic, 238–241
  importance of, 254
  living, 245
  revision of, 254
  where to keep, 249–250
Women's movement, xiv, 12
  effect of, on family, 7–8
Worldwide College Scholarship Directory, 187

Yours-mine-ours boundaries, 133–135 (figure)

ABOUT THE AUTHORS

EMILY CARD, editor in chief and publisher of *Emily Card's Money-Letter for Women,* is an attorney and nationally recognized financial expert. Her breakthrough work as a Senate Fellow in 1974 resulted in the passage of the Equal Opportunity Act, opening the door for women's access to consumer credit, and set the tone for a lifetime devoted to educating consumers about money. She resides in Santa Monica, California, with her 13-year-old son.

CHRISTIE WATTS KELLY is a writer specializing in personal finance and family issues. She resides in Memphis, Tennessee, with her husband and two children.

We welcome your stories, comments, and suggestions for future revisions of the book. Please write to us at Families, P.O. Box 3725, Santa Monica, CA 90403.

Visit our Web site at http://www.womenmoney.com, or e-mail us at ewcard@aol.com or ewcard@womenmoney.com or cwkelly@womenmoney.com.

Note: We have attempted to write in a genderless language. Examples are composites based on interviews with clients, friends, and family members.